Auditory Processing
Disorder (APD)

Auditory Processing Disorder (APD)

Identification, Diagnosis and Strategies for Parents and Professionals

Alyson Mountjoy

Jessica Kingsley Publishers
London and Philadelphia

First published in Great Britain in 2021 by Jessica Kingsley Publishers
An Hachette Company

1

Copyright © Alyson Mountjoy 2021

The cover image is for illustrative purposes only, and any person featuring is a model.

The information contained in this book is not intended to replace the services of trained medical professionals or to be a substitute for medical advice. You are advised to consult a doctor on any matters relating to your health, and in particular on any matters that may require diagnosis or medical attention.

A CIP catalogue record for this title is available from the British Library and the Library of Congress

ISBN 978 1 78775 282 5
eISBN 978 1 78775 283 2

Printed and bound by CPI Group (UK) Ltd, Croydon CR0 4YY

Jessica Kingsley Publishers' policy is to use papers that are natural, renewable and recyclable products and made from wood grown in sustainable forests. The logging and manufacturing processes are expected to conform to the environmental regulations of the country of origin.

Jessica Kingsley Publishers
Carmelite House
50 Victoria Embankment
London EC4Y 0DZ

www.jkp.com

Contents

Acknowledgements

This book is dedicated to all the children and adults who live with Auditory Processing Disorder (APD) and those who support them (whether as parents and partners, friends or family). I also dedicate the book to the parents and adults with APD who provided me with invaluable information over the years, and those who contributed via case studies. I am also grateful to the professionals who are working tirelessly to spread APD awareness and improve testing, in the UK and globally.

I want to thank my family too, for their continued support and patience; also, my friends. They have all kept me going so many times, even when they didn't know that I needed it, just by being themselves and silently walking beside me.

Introduction

Behind the book

This book is the culmination of everything I have learned since my journey started almost 20 years ago, when looking for answers for my child. I wrote it because there is currently a lack of accessible, objective information about what it is like to live with APD, but also to dispel any myths and misinformation surrounding APD. There are books by professionals and books by parents about their children. This book discusses everyone with APD from birth to late adulthood. I have tried to explain APD in plain English, to provide answers to the recurring questions that I am often asked with as little jargon as possible (and explaining terms where necessary).

The contents of this book might be dismissed as anecdotal, or the ramblings of someone who is 'just a parent'. On my journey, I have learned two important things. First, there is still no cure for APD, or any APD therapies or treatments that have been reliably, or scientifically, proven to work in any great or lasting way, which is why they are not included in this book.

Second, yes, I *am* a parent, but I have also worked in administration for the NHS and local government and as a special needs Learning Support Assistant with children with severe Dyslexia, those with emotional and behavioural problems, and a variety of other conditions and learning difficulties. Among other things, I have published resources for children with difficulties in literacy, comprehension and other key skills, and I am also an author of an ongoing series of supernatural fiction novels for adults. I home educated my own gifted child with auditory processing difficulties,[1] visual processing/perceptual difficulties and Hyperacusis from the age of eight, and I suffer from several chronic, disabling health conditions myself.

I have been supporting families affected with APD since 2002, initially as co-founder of the APD voluntary organization APDUK, which disbanded in 2014. I am chair of the unincorporated association APD Support UK, which I founded in 2014, currently the only UK support organization for APD. I also manage five APD-related support groups. I am an invited parent/patient member of both UK and international research projects on APD, and I have co-authored papers on the subject. The point of including all this is that I might 'just' be a parent (and a very proud one), but no one is 'just' one thing. We are all multifaceted and there is so much more to each one of us than any disability or label.

What the book covers

I have heard and read the same comments over and over from hundreds (if not thousands) of parents and adults with APD who have contacted me over the years, via my groups, helpline calls and hosted research chats. Amongst that wealth of first-hand information, I began to see patterns and realized that there are similarities in the difficulties and in the way that APD affects real people, in real-life situations. There are differences due to the unique nature of APD and the effects of other coexisting difficulties, but there are also many similarities that I now know to have already helped to improve the lives of those living with APD and their loved ones.

This book is a guide to their collective knowledge, coping strategies and self-advocacy skills. It explains the value of acceptance and how to support people with APD of all ages, in a variety of situations, plus strategies and observations taken from my own research.

The case studies[2] contain replies to a questionnaire about how APD

---

1   A diagnosis of auditory processing difficulties means that the severity and/or quantity of difficulties don't meet the criteria for a full diagnosis of APD, but just one difficulty can still have a huge impact on processing and understanding speech, affecting communication in all aspects of life.

2   Short, selected extracts have been included in the book, but the case studies can be accessed in full from https://library.jkp.com/redeem using the voucher code ZYASEZE. I strongly recommend that you read them all, to get the full impact of APD on all ages.

affects individuals in everyday terms. Parents responded on behalf of their children and teenagers. As much as possible, I have included their replies and those of the adult participants, in their own words (ages are listed at the time of responding). This is because they all explain their experiences far better than I ever could. The case studies reflect the difficulties that affect families and individuals with APD every day, the support they need and how they cope. I am grateful that the participants trusted me with their honest and heartfelt accounts.

The many people I have spoken to have given me hope for a better future for people with APD. The one common factor over the years is their resilience. There *is* light at the end of the tunnel if you have a map to follow on your journey. I hope that this book will provide that map, that blueprint for success.

Who this book is for

This book was written for the parents who want to understand and support their children, as well as for the adults who have struggled all their lives to understand themselves and get the help they need. It is also for the education professionals who teach children and adults with Auditory Processing Disorder (APD), in the hope that *they*, too, might grow in knowledge, acceptance and support. Also, it is for home educators striving to provide the best education for their children when the system cannot, and those who have chosen this path for other reasons. I've been where you are.

It is for the medical professionals too, for those who may not know much about APD, and for those who may have that specialist knowledge, but who want to know more about how it affects their patients in everyday settings; they are the ones who know that living with APD needs far more than just a diagnosis.

I hope that this book will serve as a guide for others as well: the disability advisers, employers, work colleagues, those who work in the benefits system, in fact to anyone who has been drawn to read this book, whether to help yourself or someone else, then this book is for you, and I hope it is helpful.

The 'A' Plan

The book is set out in what I have found to be a logical order, chronicling the journey from baby to adult. I have set it out in stages, with steps to follow, problems faced and strategies with which to cope and get around them, plus the types of support that people with APD will also need from others along the way. It is a guide on how to live better with APD, and I hope it helps you in some way to do that, or will help others to do so.

When I started on this voyage, it was uncharted, with no accurate testing or diagnosis available in the UK. APD awareness has come a long way since then, but there is more work to be done. I hope this book will help you all to navigate the confusing, distressing world of APD. This book is not my family's journey with APD; it is the knowledge that I have accumulated with the help of so many lovely people, for you to read, learn and share. Although I am based in the UK, the content is just as applicable worldwide.

This 'A' Plan is a list of stages that are needed for the identification, diagnosis, management and support of APD. Each of the chapters in this book describes a vital stage in this process. The 'A' Plan also includes information on how to support APD in various situations. I recommend following all the stages, preferably in the order given below:

1. Awareness: Identification. It all begins with the information-gathering stage – how to identify a child who might have APD, the prevalence, causes, unique presentation of APD in a young child, plus common symptoms and effects.

2. Answers: Seeking diagnosis. Each child and adult with suspected APD must be able to access full testing and diagnosis by trained specialists, not just basic screening.

3. Acceptance: The process. Focusing on the importance of acceptance by a child or adult with APD (and other difficulties), their family, friends, education and medical professionals and others they meet.

4. Additions: Coexisting conditions. Discussing the additional difficulties and coexisting conditions (comorbidities) it is likely that a child with APD will have. These will interact reciprocally with their APD, making them all the harder to deal with. These, too, will need to be identified, diagnosed and fully supported.

5. Action: Coping strategies and support at home. How each child with APD must develop individual coping strategies so that they can learn to manage the effects of APD and work around it (plus all other coexisting conditions and difficulties affecting communication and other aspects of life). Support and understanding at home are vital.

6. Advocacy: Finding a voice. Parents will have to advocate for their child with APD in order to get the support that they need, at least until the child is old enough to do so; this may need to be learned. Children will also need to learn (or be taught) how to explain APD and to ask for the help that they will need.

7. Adjustments: Education support. Individually tailored, reasonable adjustments must be provided at school for every child with APD plus any/all other comorbid conditions and difficulties. These must be both appropriate and adequate so that each child can meet their personal potential. This includes gifted children who also have additional needs (2E),[1] who will need full support for both aspects.

8. Alternatives: Flexible education. Alternative types of education are available in addition to mainstream education. Some learners with APD and other difficulties might benefit from education at home, especially where their needs are not being met in a school setting.

9. Adolescence: Teenage years and life skills. Teenagers with APD and other difficulties will have a totally new range of challenges to face and overcome while coping with adolescence. Ongoing support will be necessary. Career options should be based on gifts, skills, interests

---

1   Individuals who are bright/gifted with additional needs are known as twice exceptional or 2E or referred to as having dual exceptionalities.

and maximizing their strengths. Life skills should also be taught, to prepare them for independent living.

10. Adulthood: Problems and possibilities. Like adolescence, adulthood brings difficulties of its own. Adults diagnosed early in life, those with late-onset APD and those only diagnosed as adults will also need support. Suitable strategies and environments can make a huge difference to work or education and relationships, helping them to maximize their employment potential and enjoy other types of success on their own terms.

11. Anxiety: Stress and mental health. People with APD of any age can find it hard to cope with their APD and comorbid issues. For many, this can cause a great deal of stress and anxiety, so additional strategies and support will be needed, especially if they also have additional mental health problems.

CONTACT ME

As mentioned, APD affects everyone differently, throughout life and in all aspects. If I have missed something out that affects you, your child or someone you know, or you might have found additional coping strategies that have helped, please let me know. You are welcome to join the appropriate APD-related Facebook group/s that I run, and join our community of support, or email me[2] with your suggestions and comments so that I can pass them on.

FINALLY...

I don't claim to have all the answers, or presume to tell anyone how to live their life. I have tried my best to give an objective view, and this book is not just based on my experiences; it is largely acquired knowledge and written with the bigger picture in mind, to help and support everyone with APD. But before you read on, whether you are an adult with APD, a parent or professional struggling to understand APD, indeed anyone wanting to find information or ways to help, I want you to know that you are not alone. Ironically, the best way to support someone with APD is to listen to what they need and provide it. I hope that this book proves that I was listening.

---

2   apd.support.uk@aol.co.uk

1

Awareness

IDENTIFICATION

About Auditory Processing Disorder

Auditory Processing Disorder (APD) is a medical condition believed to be of neurological origin and it affects the way that the brain processes sound, including speech. Children with APD will become adults with APD because APD is a lifelong disability that has no cure. They will therefore need ongoing, individually tailored support from family, friends, teachers and employers. This support is also vital for all other coexisting conditions and will vary from person to person. Someone with APD can have multiple auditory processing difficulties, each of which can vary in severity, and no two individuals who have APD are affected in the same way. This depends on a variety of factors such as type, severity, the person's unique coping strategies and strengths. APD is not in itself a learning difficulty, but it can lead to great problems in learning, communication and social skills. APD does not, however, affect intelligence.

Even from an early age, symptoms will be visible. Adults who may have lived with APD all their lives (before their parents knew about APD or before a diagnosis was available) may have come to take their problems as personal quirks without looking for a cause. Or they may have been searching their whole lives to find out why they struggle. Learning about APD can provide an 'Aha!' moment, finally providing answers to many unanswered questions. The same is true for parents seeking answers for their child.

As mentioned, APD affects processing what we hear, but what does that mean in real terms? Well, for a person with APD, the brain doesn't correctly interpret what is heard. Remember that the brain is, of course, a vital part of the hearing process, and it has long been debated whether APD should be included with hearing disorders. I agree with this view, because without the brain's ability to interpret sound or language efficiently, it's all just unintelligible noise. For someone with APD whose brain doesn't work efficiently in the processing of sound, what they hear may make little sense (with varying degrees of severity). Processing what you hear is different to not being able to hear it, and APD can exist in those with or without hearing loss, making it even harder to identify. However, a person with hearing loss can hear with hearing aids, but a person with APD will still not be able to process (or therefore understand) some, most, or all of what they hear.

Prevalence: how common is APD?

According to international research from various sources, it is estimated that between 7 and 10 per cent of the worldwide child population has some degree of APD. (To put that into perspective, 1.1 per cent of children in the UK and 1 in 160 of children worldwide are thought to have Autism.) This means that each teacher could have at least one pupil with APD in their class. It is also thought that up to 20 per cent of adults might have this condition worldwide, and many of them could still be undiagnosed because testing was unavailable when they were children.

It may not be until an adult with a child who is diagnosed with APD recognizes that they have similar difficulties that the penny drops and they seek testing for themselves. But because of the development of natural coping strategies, and other conditions that can mask the condition (or never hearing of APD or suspecting what caused their difficulties), many adults with APD may remain undiagnosed. Therefore, greater awareness of APD is needed, for the adults as well as for the children.

APD as a disability

APD is recognized by the World Health Organization (WHO) and has a classification in the currently implemented 2018 International Classification of Diseases (ICD-10) (which also lists conditions), and is set for inclusion in ICD-11, due to be implemented on 1 January 2022.

Depending on its severity and its impact on daily life, APD can meet the criteria of a disability for many sufferers, being a physical impairment that substantially and negatively affects a person's ability to perform normal daily tasks. The ability to effectively communicate is one of the most important of these. People with this condition are entitled to all the support that this definition entails. This includes the fact that people with APD of all ages might qualify for certain disability benefits and are entitled to apply. These applications are assessed on a case-by-case basis, and awards depend on the severity and effects of APD and other difficulties, disabilities and health problems on daily living. Different countries vary in their legislation and provision, so it is best to check in your own country for support.

Suspected causes

The current view (from the UK and accepted by other countries) is that APD is believed to be either developmental, acquired or secondary.

- *Developmental* APD presents in childhood, with no hearing loss or other medical causes apart from a family history of APD. It might therefore be present from birth.

- *Acquired* APD means that it can occur at any age from a known event such as illness, injury or ageing.

- *Secondary* APD occurs as a result of processing in the presence of hearing impairment, either permanent or temporary. (Secondary does not mean it is of secondary importance or less severe or less worthy of full support than developmental APD, acquired APD or any other condition.)

The effects of APD are thought to remain into late childhood, teenage years and adulthood too. The difficulties can improve a little until the maturation of the auditory processing system, estimated at around the age of 12/13, but no improvement is thought to occur after that. People with APD will need lifelong support.

Various acquired causes are suspected. Some people can have more than one cause, which can worsen its severity.

Developmental causes

- Hereditary link: it is known that APD can run in families, although a genetic pattern has not yet been established (it can skip generations, and not all siblings may be affected; even with twins, one might have APD and the other might not).

- Pre-, peri- and post-natal damage (this might be due to damage in utero/foetal alcohol damage or damage to the foetus by maternal drug use, or lack of oxygen at birth etc.).

Acquired causes

The list of suspected causes below is not exhaustive, with more coming to light all the time:

- Head injury/traumatic brain injury.

- Epilepsy causing damage to one or more area/s of the brain that deal with auditory processing.

- Global processing difficulty, as in Autism or Autism Spectrum Condition (it is now speculated that all children with Autism will have a measure of APD).

- Effects from other conditions such as Multiple Sclerosis and Down's Syndrome.

- Alcohol or substance abuse.

- Certain medications.

- Certain illnesses.

- Late onset due to illness or injury, stroke, dementia, and so on.

Secondary causes

- Permanent hearing loss: APD can exist in children with hearing loss too.

- Transient hearing loss, for example recurring ear infections in childhood can lead to middle ear effusion or glue ear, which causes intermittent hearing loss. One explanation raised is that the brain struggles to accommodate this transient hearing loss, and when hearing returns to normal, the brain struggles to process using the new pathways that it has developed to cope, and has difficulty returning to the ones that it used before, resulting in APD. (Glue ear should always be diagnosed and treated as it can lead on to the development of APD in some children.)

So APD can be present at birth or develop at any age – there are many adults with late-onset APD. However, the cause doesn't matter; the results are the same and it doesn't affect the ways in which it needs to be managed or fully supported. The way forward for anyone with APD who is diagnosed at any age is to accept it, learn to live with it, develop coping strategies and self-advocacy skills, find alternative ways around it, and put appropriate support in place in education and at work.

Early signs

It is possible to see the effects of APD in a very young child; even a toddler can display symptoms. The most obvious early symptom of APD is usually that a child may appear not to hear you when you speak to them, especially when it is noisy or you don't get their attention first. I remember standing right behind my son when he was four, talking to him loudly while he was watching TV, and he didn't even notice I was there. When I called him by name, or turned the TV off, he turned around. You might consider this as an attention issue, and it might be in some children, but it is also a strong indicator of APD. Another red flag was that he was unable to follow more than one instruction at a time. Schools or playgroups may pick up on these indicators, and suspect hearing loss, like our school. However, parents might be the ones to first notice the signs.

> I suspected something wasn't quite right with her from when she was about three. (Parent of a child aged 10 with APD)

A problem with hearing in the traditional sense should be ruled out as early as possible via a simple hearing test. In many children with APD, a hearing test will often show no problem with hearing (although APD can also exist in children with hearing loss). People with APD usually have normal structure and function of the hearing system (known as peripheral hearing). If, after a standard hearing test, the child's hearing is found to be normal, parents seeking answers tend to be reassured and sent away. The child with APD and hearing loss will receive appropriate support for the hearing loss, usually hearing aids, which, as stated earlier, only help with hearing, but that child might still have problems in processing. They, like the child with perfect hearing will receive no help at all. The processing difficulties in both will persist and APD should be pursued further.

> [Hearing] results were always inconclusive. (Parent of a child aged 10 with APD)

> ...at one point we were told she was going deaf. (Parent of a child aged 11 with auditory processing difficulties)

Some indicators of APD

> Never hearing/understanding what we said first time...isolated in his own world...not taking part in conversation. Always asking 'What?' even with short, simple sentences. (Parent of a child aged 9 with Spatial Processing Disorder)

> [She] would always get instructions wrong... (Parent of a teenager aged 15 with APD)

Some of the more common APD symptoms are listed below (with their technical name in brackets). They will be discussed in further detail in later chapters, in relation to support at home and in education (see Chapters 5 and 7):

- Not understanding speech (auditory processing of speech): this affects gaining meaning from what is heard and manifests as requests for repetition or clarification of what was said, looking blankly at the speaker, appearing confused or showing in some way that what you are saying makes no sense to them.

- Forgetting what is said to them or asked of them (auditory memory difficulty). They might not remember what was *just* said to them (auditory short-term memory difficulty). This affects processing, retaining and recalling what they heard. Having a poor auditory working memory means that they might not respond appropriately straightaway to a question that they were just asked, or do what was requested, or they might complete one or more of a set of directions, but not all. This is because they are unable to hold spoken information in their head for long enough to act on it (see Chapter 5).

- Not remembering the correct order of multiple spoken instructions (auditory sequencing difficulty) means not being able to carry out a sequence of verbal instructions in the right order or missing out steps in the sequence.

- Not being able to process speech or understand it when there is even low-level background noise (auditory figure-ground difficulty) or their comprehension of speech may be worse or incomplete when there is competing noise. This is because the speech gets mixed up with the noise. It means that they will be unable to process what a teacher says in class when it is noisy, or follow a conversation with more than one person speaking at once.

- Not being able to selectively process speech coming from a particular direction or suppress background noise in order to do so (spatial processing difficulty): this can lead to difficulty knowing which voice to listen to when there is more than one person speaking, for example in a classroom setting, or locate the teacher's voice (the voice they should be listening to). This is different from auditory figure-ground difficulty and merits a stand-alone diagnosis of Spatial Processing Disorder where it is the only difficulty of qualifying severity, or it can count as one of the two needed for a full diagnosis.

> [She] cannot understand you talking next to her in a room with background noise. (Parent of a child aged 12 with APD)

> Muddling up words... She struggled to understand what was being said in the car.... We realized that she was lipreading everything. (Parent of a child aged 10 with APD)

> ...she couldn't learn the lyrics to simple baby songs. (Parent of a child aged 12 with APD)

- Having difficulty processing the difference between words or sounds that sound similar (auditory discrimination difficulty), for example cook/book, goat/coat, or ch/sh, f/v. With this difficulty, a child with APD can also have problems separating sounds and blending them, which can affect speech acquisition, reading and spelling.

- Not processing the gaps between words efficiently (gap detection difficulty), making it hard to separate the words that they hear from one another; to varying degrees and depending on severity, this means that words can blend together, speech can just sound like one long noise, and it may not make any sense.

- Having a problem processing when undertaking higher-level listening tasks (auditory cohesion difficulty) leads to problems drawing inferences from conversations, understanding riddles or comprehending verbal maths problems.

You might say that anyone might have these difficulties occasionally, but the difference is that in people with APD they are there for life, even though they will have good days and bad days.

Most children with APD will not have *all* the known difficulties, despite misinformation to the contrary. You only need two difficulties of qualifying severity to receive a diagnosis of APD, but even one of the difficulties can be disabling depending on its severity, as can a collection of even low-severity APD problems.

> [Primary school] accused her of being lazy and not interested in learning, although she LOVED school; poor grades, daydreaming... not following instructions. (Parent of a child aged 12 with APD)

It is also often incorrectly assumed by schools that the symptoms of APD must be the same as another child with APD they have come across, or it is not APD. This confusion wastes valuable time in parents seeking a diagnosis. It can also be mistaken for other conditions.

> [His school had noticed a problem] but thought it was associated with his ADHD [Attention Deficit Hyperactivity Disorder]. (Parent of a teenager aged 16 diagnosed with Spatial Processing Disorder)

Other common effects of APD

As a result of these and other difficulties, APD can affect a child's development of both receptive and expressive language, which can cause problems with communication and reading. APD can also have an impact on creative writing. A person with APD may have difficulties in word retrieval: finding the right word when speaking or writing. APD can also lead to safety concerns (see Chapter 5).

An inability to effectively process language has many far-reaching problems – children with APD may be lacking in social skills and are often socially vulnerable, which might make them easily led or manipulated, or fall prey to bullying.

> At her first primary she was seen in a very negative light. Other children were quick to see that she struggled and would blame things on her. She would then take the blame. (Parent of a teenager aged 15 diagnosed with APD)

The effects can be intermittent and random in their severity and frequency, something that seems to be difficult for some people to accept. These and other APD-related issues are discussed later in the book, with reference to both home and education support (see Chapters 5 and 7).

What it's like to have APD

You might have come across videos on the internet mimicking the effects of APD. Although they can give a rough idea of what it's like, the experience of each person with APD could be better or worse than depicted, or just different. There are many such recordings, but they are all subjective to the person who made them, as is much of what is written about APD. Unlike most other medical conditions, there is no such thing as 'just' having APD. The truth is that every child and adult with APD will be uniquely affected by their APD, in addition to having any combination of other difficulties and conditions as well. APD does not fall into neat parameters, and this means that one person's experience is not the same as another, even though there may be commonalities. It can be crippling and devastating for some people, totally isolating them from the outside world. In others it can be mild and more manageable. But those effects will still need to be identified and addressed.

A person with APD might process the start, middle or end of a word, phrase or sentence, or none of it. To explain further, let's compare the brain of someone with APD to the workings of a faulty car radio that is having problems in maintaining a consistent signal from a radio station. Imagine that you are a passenger on a car journey with your family or friends, trying to listen to a discussion on the radio. Due to the intermittent radio signal, you may be able to follow what is said for a while, then perhaps only the start of a sentence will make sense, or just the end. You can *hear* all of the words, but they are obscured by periods of static. At times, it is just a blur of noise. Then add to that the sounds of passing traffic, dogs barking and other people in the car chatting amongst themselves, distracting you or trying to get your attention. Trying to make sense of that talk show, especially if the announcer's voice is unfamiliar to you and with no clues as to the topic, can be a nightmare. This is what the world can sound like to someone with APD: their brain has faulty wiring, the radio announcer represents someone speaking to them (perhaps a parent, teacher, partner or work colleague) who they have to listen to and understand, and all the other sounds (like the people and the dogs etc.) are the background noise that they have to cope with whilst trying to make sense of what is being said to them. What would it be like having to answer questions about that talk show, or making notes on it as you listened? Imagine that happening all day, every day: how would you feel? How would you cope? That is a snapshot of everyday life for many people with APD. Some may be less affected, some differently, and for some it is worse.

I recently needed to have an MRI and my experience made me think of a child with APD in the classroom. The sounds that the machine made plus the music that was played to me through headphones was very distorted (which reminded me of the background noise in a classroom, with chairs scraping and other children holding separate conversations etc.). It all made the speech of the technician very difficult to hear or understand when she spoke to me, despite the music volume being reduced. I understood one word in every three or four, and the meaning of each sentence was lost. For a child with APD trying to make sense of what the class teacher said, even without children talking out loud, there are still whispers and scuffling noises, paper rustling and other ambient noises. Children without APD can make sense of what they hear in noise like this, but a child with APD can mis-process speech even in a silent room. The noise just makes it harder still.

Another aspect is the random nature of APD; there will be good days and bad days. APD can also vary in its effects at different times of the day, day to day, even minute to minute. It may be easier to process in a quiet room, one to one, with no background noise, but auditory processing can still be affected in this situation too, especially in conversation with a person with a strong accent, or a new person whose voice pattern will be unfamiliar (and even with someone with whom the person with APD *is* familiar). The effects of APD are also worse when a person is ill, tired or stressed, because coping strategies may fail due to the brain diverting energy to cope with those situations.

> ...he was very inconsistent day to day in his abilities. (Parent of a child aged 9 with Spatial Processing Disorder)

Other coexisting conditions can also make things worse, having reciprocal effects on the APD, and APD can, and does, coexist with pretty much any other condition or disability.

In short, APD is a complex and far-reaching disability. Any one of the APD difficulties, however mild, can cause problems in a wide variety of scenarios. APD affects all aspects of a person's life throughout life, not only in education, but also in communicating at school, in workplace relationships, with partners, family and friends, choice of suitable careers, enjoyment of hobbies, and so on. It can affect them anywhere, at any time, and with anyone. The world can be a scary place for a child with APD, and it never goes away.

What to do

Once the symptoms of APD are noticed in a child, it is wise to keep a record of them and wait until the child is old enough for testing. This is the time to gather evidence. A parent is often the closest to the child and will notice more. Input from school is also invaluable when they have reported problems. But education and even medical professionals don't always notice, know what to look for, or believe parents. When people tell you often enough that you are imagining it, you can come to believe it, but you would not ignore the symptoms of any other medical condition or let anyone dissuade you. Trust your instincts, even if your partner or other family members or professionals disagree or just don't see it, which can happen.

Although APD is still not as well known as it needs to be among medical and education professionals, suspected APD should always be investigated. The only way to know for sure whether a child has APD is to seek full diagnosis, and the next chapter will guide you through that process.

2

Answers

SEEKING DIAGNOSIS

Once there is a suspicion of APD in a young child, seeking a diagnosis should be the next step.

Why full testing is needed

Accurate diagnosis is *vital* if parents (and schools) are to find out exactly how a child is uniquely affected by APD. There is no such thing as just having APD. It is almost impossible to get support without diagnosis, and without identifying their unique APD profile, any support will be generalized. A child with APD needs, and deserves, full accurate testing and then individually tailored support.

Who can diagnose?

APD is a medical condition of neurological origin that can be a barrier to learning and communication. Considering the unique nature of APD in each child, it needs full, accurate testing by the appropriate medical (not education) professional, in order to identify all APD difficulties. Only a fully trained consultant in audiology/audiovestibular paediatric medicine is qualified to diagnose APD as it is a highly specialized area of audiology, and as such, needs specialist testing.

In addition to the need for full testing, the test results also need to be accurately interpreted by a consultant who is experienced in APD. You may have read that there is no such thing as a 'gold star testing' method available for APD, that is, no preferred or reliable method.

It is true that no national APD testing guidelines have so far been agreed in the UK (or anywhere else), but the specific APD tests developed in the UK and available since 2004 will provide an accurate and full diagnosis. UK and international research is being undertaken all the time to further improve on these tests, to develop reliable, scientifically proven treatment options.

Full testing for children in the UK is currently only available in a handful of APD testing centres, and there are only a couple of testing centres providing reliable testing for adults. These are listed in the document of recommended full testing centres, available on my website, for children and adults, which will be updated as more become available.[1]

At some centres, testing is available free on the NHS, and some provide private testing (where parents and adults need to pay). If you have private insurance, prior to referral it is advisable to ask your insurance provider if your policy will cover APD testing (and then check with the testing centre you choose whether they will accept your insurance cover).

Some testing centres provide a multidiscipline service (where funding is available), which is preferable. My advice would be to try to get a referral to one of the full testing centres, if your child meets the criteria and you are able to travel there. It is hoped to ultimately have a full NHS APD testing service available to everyone in the UK who needs it, but at the moment a great many centres are still needed.

Screening versus full testing

A growing number of clinics, NHS hospitals and private centres claim to offer 'testing' but they often just use basic screening or assessment computer programs that may not lead to a valid diagnosis, especially in the hands of inexperienced users. This basic screening can result in limited and, in some cases, unreliable and incomplete testing and generic recommendations, where not all the available tests are even used. I have heard worrying stories from parents about children who have been turned away as having no difficulties, later to be found on full testing to not only have APD but also to be severely affected. In

---

1 See https://apdsupportuk.yolasite.com

some cases, parents have been interviewed and testing refused without ever meeting the child. The only benefit to screening is that it can be provided locally for some people (and might be beneficial for children who don't meet the criteria for full testing, for whom any answers are better than none). Some centres are not qualified to diagnose or may not have a consultant. Full testing is always preferable where possible. (I refer to it as *full* testing because some screening centres do not even use a complete set of screening tests, just one or two, and each child needs to have all the tests applicable to their symptoms, which again relies on the experience of the specialist.)

> He had a screening...which highlighted an issue with auditory processing, but they refused to diagnose... (Parent of a child aged 10 with APD)

Screening and generic recommendations are virtually useless when children are affected uniquely and have various other conditions impacting on the APD and vice versa. It is for parents to decide whether locality is preferred over quality of testing and the expertise of the audiologists involved to accurately interpret the results. Personally, I would not advise that you go anywhere else until standardized full testing is available UK-wide (unless your child does not meet the current criteria).

It isn't that there are more people with APD now; it's that parents, adults who suspect APD and some professionals are becoming more adept at recognizing the signs. That is a good thing, although the number of referrals is becoming greater than the capacity of the centres that are available. This then results in increasingly long waiting lists, which means that more testing centres are needed. If you are unhappy with this situation of limited full testing provision, contact your local health board or clinical commissioning group and MP to request that standardized testing is provided locally. They will then be made aware that there is a growing demand for this service as awareness increases. It is your right as a parent or adult with APD to do so (supportive professionals can do the same).

Gathering evidence, testing criteria and the referral process

Once suspicion of APD has been raised and the symptoms identified, the child's parents or adults who suspect APD are the ones who must seek diagnosis. Keep a diary of observations as soon as any difficulties are suspected. Any reports from school are also helpful evidence, and teachers' comments from school about difficulties should be requested in writing.

In the UK, testing criteria for children can differ between testing centres (factors such as age, which professionals can refer, location restrictions, method of referral, type of professionals providing reports, excluded conditions, etc.). Find or request the criteria for the testing centre that you choose and study them before asking for a referral. Accompanying reports including evidence of suspicion of APD from relevant professionals is usually needed with a referral, as well as all reports concerning any comorbid conditions that have already been diagnosed, plus observations by teachers and parents.

Most testing centres will not test a child for APD under six years old, because it is thought that most children under six are not capable of responding appropriately to testing, and also because there might be a maturational delay in the auditory processing system, which could right itself, or improve, making testing unnecessary or inaccurate.

A child with glue ear causing effusion or discharge and/or its accompanying intermittent hearing loss may not be able to undergo APD testing until the fluid has cleared or they are able to hear accurately. A hearing test is therefore required within the three months before the referral is sent (and that report should also be sent). A child with hearing loss will normally not be able to be tested on the NHS in the UK because additional tests are needed, time slots are limited and waiting lists are growing, but it can be done privately, depending on the consultant and if other criteria are met.

Ideally, testing for any other suspected conditions should be carried out prior to a referral APD testing, if possible. This is because children with certain conditions might be excluded from APD testing where those conditions can cause the child to be unable to respond appropriately to testing (which, on average, takes about an hour-and-a-half plus consultation time before and after), and maintain attention throughout. Failure to complete the testing, or to pay attention appropriately, would skew the results, or make testing incomplete or impossible, thus wasting an appointment and possibly distressing the child, with no definitive diagnosis possible at the end of it. In some cases, other conditions might cause the type of difficulties suspected as APD (such as attention problems), and testing might also be refused. But each referral is considered on its own merits.

Once you have gathered all the necessary reports and evidence (and are confident that your child meets the criteria for your preferred testing centre), you can seek a referral from your GP, audiologist, paediatrician, and so on (as listed in their criteria).

So if any child (or adult) exhibits the symptoms of APD, they should be referred for testing for APD. It is the only way to be sure.

Parents in the UK often find difficulties in obtaining an NHS referral.

We kept being told that someone else needed to make the referral – school, GP, SALT [Speech and Language Therapist] etc. [They ended up paying privately.] (Parent of a child aged 9 with Spatial Processing Disorder)

...I insisted something wasn't right... The consultant...suggested... because I myself worked with the deaf, that I wanted my own child to be deaf. I asked to be transferred to [another] hospital... (Parent of a child aged 12 with APD)

NHS referral...was refused partly due to funding and the GP not knowing how to refer out of area... [The GP] hadn't even heard of APD. (Parent of a child aged 10 with APD)

Every time I mentioned...APD, they ignored me or acted as though it was the first time they'd heard it... It was so frustrating to believe she had APD but being told by medical professionals who weren't qualified to diagnose APD that she didn't have it, but still needing them to refer us so we could get the diagnosis!! (Parent of a child aged 10 with APD)

There is normally a long waiting list for an appointment due to increasing demand to be seen. Prepare travel arrangements and possibly even staying over if the testing centre is far from your home. Some centres will reimburse you for travel expenses if you keep the receipts, so check with them beforehand.

APD testing in the UK

At the appointment the testing process is in three stages; allow several hours and take along drinks and snacks for your child plus books, toys or other ways to help them pass the time.

This is an example of the standard of testing and the process you should expect to receive at any of the recommended testing centres. Private and NHS testing should follow a similar process, although privately the testing might be carried out over two or three days. They may all vary slightly, and the choice and number of tests will depend on the presentation of the patient on the day:

- First, the consultant will take a detailed and comprehensive history (this part takes at least an hour), looking at problems that the child has, parents' concerns, teachers' concerns, speech and language issues, cognitive issues, reading, written work, memory issues, other diagnoses, such as Autism Spectrum Disorder (ASD), Attention Deficit Hyperactivity Disorder (ADHD) and learning difficulties. Visual problems, current educational environment, and support, pre-, peri- and post-natal problems, developmental milestones, history of middle ear, neurological and other medical problems, ear problems, and so on plus family history might all be discussed.

- Then there is an examination of the ears, a general examination, and an observation of speech quality. The child is then taken to a soundproof booth where APD testing takes place using headphones. A parent can ask to accompany them, and breaks can be taken, if needed. The testing alone should take around an hour-and-a-half, or longer. The consultant will choose the type and number of tests needed as a result of the evidence provided and the consultation.

- Tests are selected based on suspicions raised in the above two stages. They should test from this list, as applicable:

  - Tests of peripheral auditory function.

- Cochlear feedback pathway.

- Ability to hear degraded speech.

- Ability to hear speech in noise.

- Spatial processing.

- Binaural resolution.

- Temporal processing.

- Auditory pattern sequencing.

Further tests may be requested if seen to be relevant, for example electrophysiology (ABR, cortical auditory evoked potentials) and an MRI, if applicable. These will not usually be done on the day and might not be at the same hospital, but you can ask the consultant to explain why they are recommended.

The audiologist you see must have sufficient knowledge to interpret each of the tests, understand the losses or conditions that may affect the outcome of each test, and if there are other issues, for example language, how that might affect the test results and interpretation. They also need to have a very broad understanding of available interventions, if any, and find the most suitable to help the child.

If you have any questions about the testing, ask at the initial consultation or when you receive the results. The whole process is normally undertaken on the same day, if it is possible to complete all of the relevant tests, and the consultant is available to give the results. A follow-up appointment is normally only given if further testing is needed, or if the consultant is unavailable to discuss the results on the day. Occasionally a review may be needed a year or more later, possibly if the results were borderline or an improvement due to maturation might be expected where the child is very young, for instance. There is no cause for concern about why this is needed, but you can ask the consultant for the reason when the results are given.

The results

After testing, the consultant will explain the results. It is currently generally accepted that you need two or more difficulties of qualifying severity to receive a diagnosis of APD. One difficulty of qualifying severity, or any number of difficulties of lesser severity, will get a diagnosis of auditory processing difficulties. However, a child or adult with even one auditory processing difficulty needs that one difficulty fully supported in the same way as a child with a diagnosis of APD will need support for all of them: each one can have a huge impact on communication, education and work. The consultant might suggest a referral to a professional of a different speciality, and you can ask them why if they don't explain. Whatever the outcome, a report containing the results, implications and support recommendations will be sent out, usually a few weeks later, although the length of time for this to happen will vary.

APD testing outside the UK

Other countries have different processes for accessing APD testing for children and adults. For example, in the US, parents should seek diagnosis privately from a qualified APD specialist in audiology/ audiovestibular medicine where provision is available. Funding for this testing can be obtained via certain insurance providers. The individual seeking testing should make their own enquiries in their country of residence.

What comes next

Even if, after testing, neither APD nor auditory processing difficulties is present, testing will not have been a wasted exercise. For a child with complex needs like those with APD, ruling anything out is one step closer to finding out what is left to investigate. (The importance of diagnosing coexisting conditions will be discussed later, in Chapter 4.)

However, for a child who *is* found to have APD or auditory processing difficulties, diagnosis is just the first step on a very long journey. In order to continue this journey, there needs to be acceptance of the diagnosis of this lifelong condition and all that it entails.

3

Acceptance

THE PROCESS

Those with APD fight a daily battle for acceptance by others; it is the most vital of commodities and often one of the hardest things to find. It is also essential to their wellbeing, education and happiness.

The same principles of acceptance can also be applied:

- To any further diagnoses that the child receives.

- To any parent who has a child with any health condition, mental health condition, chronic illness or disability, in fact, any child with additional needs.

- To adults with any additional needs.

However, full acceptance has three aspects, and I believe that all of them need to be met to support the wellbeing of any child with APD. They are all equally important:

- First is the acceptance of the parent(s) that their child has APD, plus all that it will entail for their child's future.

- Second is acceptance by the child that they have APD.

- Third is the acceptance of others: close and extended family, friends, peers, education and medical professionals, and anyone else they might meet.

With diagnosis, validation is provided for both the child (as the patient) and the parent/s seeking the diagnosis. What is important now is not only that the child accepts it, but also that everyone around them accepts it fully, and is willing and prepared to support them. Acceptance, like the need for it, will not happen overnight and it is not just needed temporarily. Acceptance and support are vital within the family, but more than that, it all needs to carry on at school too, and at work, for the rest of their life. Even when there is full acceptance there must also be support. Also, a parent providing support without fully accepting or understanding the diagnosis (or the child) will not help.

Acceptance by parents

Obtaining a diagnosis of APD for a child can be a pivotal moment for a parent. The same applies to any other condition, difficulty or disability (medical or otherwise).

After a diagnosis of APD, or anything else, all sorts or feelings may come bubbling to the surface, even if the diagnosis is expected. The new reality, for some, is often met with mixed feelings. There can be feelings of joy and validation, that their suspicions (so often dismissed by those who are usually uneducated about APD) have been verified. But it can also raise negative emotions.

It is true that things may not seem the same. There is no way to sugar-coat that. The parent may feel that they have lost something they once had, either for themselves or their child: the future that they had imagined or even planned for them. But they are the same child they held as a baby, the same child they were yesterday or last week. A successful, happy future is still possible, albeit with maybe a few changes along the way, a few compromises.

A parent might feel relief that what they had observed in their child was not imagined. On the long journey to get there, they might have doubted themselves a few times; I certainly did. The diagnosis should be viewed as a positive thing. But it can still cause unexpected shock, panic or any other emotion that you can name. These are all normal. The important thing is that, despite these feelings (or maybe because of them), they must work through the stages of grief listed below, seeking help if needed, and inform the child of the diagnosis as soon as possible.

Sometimes one parent will want to pursue a diagnosis and the other won't; one parent will join the dots and come up with APD and the other won't see what is happening, or maybe they prefer not to know.

Or maybe they prefer not to know. Lack of acceptance by some parents to accept the APD might be because they don't wish to accept that their child is less than perfect in their eyes or to others. Sometimes this is from shame or embarrassment.

They might see the same difficulties in themselves and don't want to be blamed for passing it on, or maybe they don't want the child to be stigmatized or 'labelled'. In short, they might feel responsible. Or it might be fear that the child will be ridiculed by their peers, possibly bullied or ostracized. This is an understandable fear, and it can happen. But the difficulties are already there and they will show; now they can give a reason for it and it is far better to explain it than to hide it.

To some people, what other people think is everything, even more important than helping their child. Some parents might not want to have to go to the trouble of getting help organized in school. Others might have even gone along with the school's suggestion that there was something that their child needed help with, but might not have believed it, or seen it as their responsibility to do anything about it. Worse still is the parent who blames the child for not being able to understand or who sees it as a 'behaviour problem', or the parent who ignores it and pretends it isn't there. Sadly, there are also parents who just don't care. It isn't the child's fault or theirs, but in denying its existence, they also deny their child the help that they need. The same can apply to other family members too.

Parents will have learned details of the individual APD difficulties and severity from what the consultant may have said and later in the diagnosis report that will need to be passed on to the school. But it is just as essential for the child with APD to know these details too.

There are usually other coexisting difficulties to deal with, and APD can make coping with them more difficult and vice versa (more on this later in Chapter 4). Every diagnosis means that more acceptance is needed, for everyone. But at some point, the parent and child with APD will need to face the APD and deal with it, and the sooner the better. The future emotional wellbeing of the child will depend on whether the parent accepts, rejects or denies the APD, and them. Without it, they are alone.

The diagnosis opened our eyes to be able to understand how our child feels and sees the world, and it is only with this information that we can help and make life a little bit easier. (Parent of a teenager aged 14 with APD)

Acceptance by the child

It is vital that APD is accepted by the child who has just received the diagnosis. Everything that follows in their life will be affected by it. Once the APD diagnosis is made, even if one or both parents never fully accept it, the child has a right to know. A child cannot accept what they don't know about or understand, and their parents need to explain it to them.

When parents don't tell their child that they have APD, they go for years not knowing why they struggle, feel stupid and can't understand what is going on around them. A child who struggles alone suffers far more; children know when there is something wrong, and they deserve answers. APD itself does not affect intelligence, although they will notice that they might be falling behind their peers, that they miss a lot of what people say, that they misunderstand things or that they stand out (and they will wonder why). Children who are self-aware will know that they are somehow different. Acknowledgement and other people's acceptance of APD, ongoing family support and understanding are therefore as important as the diagnosis, in fact, even more so. If the people around them accept it (and them), they are much more likely to accept it themselves.

It can be very hard to grow up without knowing that you have APD, yet feeling that there is something about you that causes isolation through simply misunderstanding what is said, that maybe even causes others to shun you, something that makes you appear less than perfect or sets you apart from others. To find out that someone you love and trust knew about it all along and failed to tell you, or even help you, is far worse than denial by strangers, and can cause lifelong damage to the child, and within families.

How to help a child with APD come to terms with it

The best way to help a child with APD to come to terms with their diagnosis is by information, reassurance and patience. Parents should raise the topic as early as possible. Some choose to discuss the possibility of having APD even before testing, to prepare the child, but this will depend on the individual child. It can help to just tell them that they are going to see someone who will help them find out why they are having difficulties. A parent knows their child best, and that some children may be more distressed by knowing beforehand and become apprehensive and anxious about the testing, so this should be avoided. But after diagnosis, they need and deserve to know the truth.

It is their condition and their life that is affected. They will need to be given answers and validation. The importance of giving them this knowledge cannot be over-emphasized. It can be life-changing. In my research with adults with APD, I once took a poll about how many of them believed that knowing about their APD early in life would have helped them, and 70 per cent said yes.

A child with APD needs coping strategies, and they can't learn to cope with what they don't know they have. Parents should tell their child, and armed with that knowledge, they can begin their battle for acceptance and the long road to dealing with the condition, day after day, year after year.

It is harder for adults who acquire APD later in life because they are so used to living without difficulty in processing or communication. But, like a child who is born with vision or hearing loss, the child who is born with APD or acquires it early in life often adapts a lot better and quicker, because it is all they have ever known. Even before diagnosis they might already have developed coping strategies.

Some children will take the news in their stride, viewing the diagnosis with relief; to learn that they are not to blame, that there is a medical reason for their difficulties can be so liberating. They need to know that they are not stupid or lazy (as sadly some children are often called and may come to believe).

Other children might be frightened by the news, worried about what might happen. Children with APD can be reticent about change of any kind. How will this revelation affect their lives? Will they need to leave their school and their friends, or be made to go into a 'special class'? What will people think? Will their friends still like them? Parents must reassure them whenever needed, and be patient while they deal with this potentially earth-shattering news. They may have many questions, and parents should be ready to answer them openly and honestly, perhaps like this:

No, APD is not an illness. Yes, it is a medical condition, but you won't have to take medicine for it. It can get better if you find ways around it and get the help you need. It isn't your fault. Of course, I still love you. I will help you.

Just as people with APD are different, so are their reactions. But no matter how they take it, crucial to every sufferer is knowing at this stage that they aren't alone in having this condition or in dealing with it. Please tell them that. They might even have a sibling or a cousin with APD too, even if nobody knows it yet (although they will be affected differently).

Parents should make sure that their child becomes used to discussing their diagnosis as part of them, without blame or shame. The same applies to any previous conditions and those that may be identified later. Their difficulties are just a small part of who they are; our very complex children are so much more than that. Learning all about how their difficulties affect them in everyday terms should be the first task for the parent, the teacher and the child. This knowledge then leads to learning how they can help themselves.

Managing the news: the stages of grief

Before we discuss acceptance by others, it is important, I think, to discuss the process of acceptance. For a parent, child or adult with APD, diagnosis can come as a shock, even if it is expected and long-awaited. Acceptance (of the diagnosis and the condition) is a big part of learning to live with APD, for the sufferer and their family. It struck me a long time ago that for the individual and close family at least, this process is like going through the five stages of grief, and many people will experience this.

A parent might grieve for the life that they wanted their child to have, a life without the inevitable challenges that will arise. Children, I find, are more pragmatic and resilient, but teenagers with a recent diagnosis often find it harder to deal with: this is another reason why early diagnosis is vital, and explaining that diagnosis as soon as possible. An adult with recently acquired APD might grieve for the way of life they had before their illness, accident or injury (or if it is a late diagnosis of existing APD, for the life that they thought they had, had planned, or for the person they thought they were) (see Chapter 10).

Some people might skip some of the following stages, or maybe they will need to revisit them, but the outcome is usually the same once they have worked through them. As with the loss of a loved one, most people will reach acceptance, although sadly some never do. But whatever form their grief takes, it is important that they first give themselves permission and allow time to grieve. A parent should tell their child that grieving is normal, acceptable, and even essential, and they need to understand that themselves.

Any type of grief can stir up a variety of emotions. The best way to deal with this is to accept them, work through them and let them pass, rather than fight them.

DENIAL

After diagnosis, fears have become reality, and faced with the reality, it is natural to pretend it isn't happening and to carry on as normal. The child may hide from it and from telling others about it, but it will eat away at them. Parents might feel ashamed and guilty about their child's APD or think that it's caused by something they did, or didn't, do. They may search frantically for possible causes, something or someone to blame. But no one is to blame, and the cause doesn't matter, only what happens from now on. APD is a medical condition which no one is responsible for. It can't be caught and the genetic link is currently unknown and seems to be quite random. We can't predict accidents, other illnesses or injuries either, and 'beating ourselves up' over it doesn't help anyone.

Accepting APD, accepting that their child has a disability, doesn't mean that they are setting their child limitations; it is just acknowledging that the challenges already exist, learning to deal with them and helping their child to do so. Everyone at some time in their lives will have difficulty with something: we are not all born with infinite knowledge and we all have things to learn; some things will be harder for some people and other things harder for others. Even the most 'gifted and talented' have limitations.

For a parent, denying that their child has APD might be because suddenly it is real and final; it is there and it must be dealt with.

It can be especially difficult for teenagers too, at a time when it is so important to them to fit in, to be 'normal' and not to 'stand out'. They might wish the results had been different, but then they would not have been able to access help, if they choose to accept it (and refusing help is another act of denial). Therefore, early diagnosis can be accepted more readily.

The child with APD, like everyone else, has things that they struggle with, but at least everyone will know why and what they are, and that knowledge is powerful. Many people go through their whole life not knowing why they struggle; those who find out are often glad that they know why, because it is that knowledge that empowers them to improve their life.

It was a relief to her to know there was a reason for her difficulties. (Parent of a teenager aged 14 with APD)

Denial of APD can have many causes:

- Reluctance to see themselves or their child perceived as 'different' from others: everyone is different from each other anyway; even those who appear to be what is deemed 'normal' or 'neurotypical' have their own quirks or idiosyncrasies. No two people are totally identical, not even twins.

- Not wanting to appear stupid, incapable or unattractive: people with APD can be very capable in different areas and often have compensatory gifts that others find very attractive, like empathy, kindness, musical or artistic ability, or even something as simple as the ability to make people laugh (everyone is good at something, and a person's true worth does not come from their academic ability, intellect, career status or money).

- Not knowing how others will react: some might react negatively, but others might be glad of an explanation of what is making the child miserable, and may be only too happy to help, if they are permitted. A person with APD should never be too proud to accept help when it is offered, so long as it is the type of help that they need. It is not a sign of weakness or accepting defeat.

She's still not accepted it. She wants a pill that will stop it. (Parent of a child aged 12 with APD)

But the person who denies their APD is denying who they are, because it is a part of them and can give them the compensatory gifts that others lack. They should learn to accept them too and to use them.

ANGER

A parent might think or say, 'Why my child?' For the child or adult with APD, it's 'Why me?' But why not? APD doesn't discriminate. It also doesn't make anyone less of a person. It just provides additional challenges. It is common to rage against the perceived injustice of it all, but the anger can cause you to lash out at those closest to you, and this should be avoided.

A child with APD might start to behave differently with their friends and family. They can withdraw or exhibit outbursts or defiance, often out of the blue, for no apparent reason. Anger can come from anxiety, too, and it needs to be expressed – far better than bottling it up. Strategies can be taught, such as counting to 10, going to their room to punch a pillow or practising relaxation and breathing exercises, and so on. But an apology should be expected after an outburst, learning that actions have consequences and anger hurts people's feelings.

> She can be very aggressive to her siblings. (Parent of a child aged 12 with APD)

Coupled with the frustration of coping with APD itself, this new-found discovered condition might be perceived as the enemy, something unwanted to fight against. But the problem is that the enemy is within them. How can you fight yourself? It can lead to feelings of self-loathing, loss of self-esteem and confidence, if the APD itself hasn't already started them on that slippery slope. They will need patience and support, someone to tell them it will all be okay, and reassurance that their parents and other family members don't view them any differently, even if in some ways they might (which is also a natural reaction). A child with APD might be perceived as being different to a neurotypical child, but they are certainly no less capable. They simply process sound and verbal information differently, react differently, express themselves differently and will have problems understanding people. It will all take adjustment, for everyone. Knowing why is the key to finding a way forward, and there can be improvement.

> ...in the last year [she] is showing a more mature acceptance of APD and starting to help herself more in dealing with day-to-day difficulties. (Parent of a teenager aged 14 with APD)

BARGAINING

Parents might search for therapies, or seek ways of curing the APD, maybe losing themselves in research. They might look desperately for the cause, in the belief that it might somehow help. But it won't make any difference – their child will still have APD. They might chase miracles and fall prey to unscrupulous people who will take their money and sell them false hope. I have seen this too often. Children might even ask their parents to take the APD away, to find a cure. But there is no cure, and finding that out can take a long time for some people. For some parents it can mean a longer road to acceptance; with luck, they will eventually realize that their child doesn't need fixing because they aren't broken. Some parents may never reach that stage. Instead, they waste valuable time that could have been spent helping their child learn coping strategies earlier, supporting them in coming to terms with having APD.

DEPRESSION

The realization there is no cure can drag you down, leading to anxiety and depression in many people; coping with life in a different way is hard. Family life can change considerably, but it doesn't have to be in a bad way. The challenges might seem insurmountable, and it is harder if everyone concerned tries to pretend that nothing has changed. The parent or the child or adult with APD might revert to denial at any point, or bargaining. The parent should take time to be kind to themselves, work through the depression and help their child through it. They should also not feel guilty for engaging the help of professionals where necessary; this is not a sign of weakness either. It is also important not to lose sight if what is important – helping themselves and their child to cope with life from now on. They should take whatever measures are necessary to prepare themselves for that (see Chapter 5).

ACCEPTANCE

Hopefully acceptance will follow, for each child, teenager or adult, either accepting their APD as part of their life and part of who they are, or acceptance of APD by a parent or family member as part of who their child is. There may be a sudden realization that this is the same child as they were before their diagnosis, or that you are the same person as you once were. There is so much more to a person with any disability than the disability itself; it does not define them. Accepting this, whether as a child or parent, ultimately allows that person to be ready to move on.

And then they deal with it, get around it, live with it. Life goes on, maybe a different life, but it doesn't have to be a worse life. APD isn't all that a person is or will ever be; there is more to any individual than their various difficulties, conditions or disabilities. They do not (and should not) define anyone.

> I've always accepted it. In college I remember seeing something that referred to disabilities as different abilities and that has really stuck with me. It's not that I can't do things; I just have to work a little harder than others, and that's okay. (Adult aged 24 with APD)

Through acceptance comes self-awareness and self-knowledge, the ability to find and build on one's strengths, using what they are good at to help them to develop unique coping strategies that work for them. For a person with APD, finding out what they are good at and using it to create their own unique way of coping with life can be a real breakthrough. With acceptance, knowing how APD affects them and how to tell others about it, they can then learn how to ask for the accommodations that they need and are entitled to, so it becomes easier to manage it. They become who they were meant to be, and with that can come the acceptance of others, which is just as important, increasing their self-esteem and confidence. No one can expect others to accept them until they can accept themselves. The longer people fight against it and mourn what they might have had, or that they or others feel they should have had, the longer that management of APD takes to happen.

If you are a parent, be proud of your child. Manage your expectations and theirs in a positive way, and help them and others to do so too. Life with APD is just about doing things differently, and it is only through acceptance that progress can be made. This is where the support and acceptance of others can make a great difference; by accepting your child has APD you find that you are the best person to help them, especially if you have APD yourself and can pass on strategies that you have found useful. Acceptance can be liberating for everyone concerned.

> What makes us proud is: she keeps going. She's a fighter... APD is not all she is about. There's so much more to her. (Parent of a child aged 12 with APD)

Acceptance by adults with APD

Some adults who find out that they have had APD all their lives might expect it, and are also relieved to know that what has caused them to struggle all their lives is not their fault.

> ...I expected and I wanted [it]... (Adult aged 54 with auditory processing difficulties)

> It all makes sense and I've started to forgive myself. (Adult aged 49 with APD)

It can be a cathartic moment, a validation for some. But it can also come as a great shock for others. Any of them might go through the same grieving process, even when it is what they suspected and finally have answers. Acceptance of this diagnosis can allow them to open many new doors. With a diagnosis, they also have access to the benefit of disability law and support at work and in adult education, when they choose to apply for it. However, I know many adults with APD who never fully accept or declare it. (Declaring APD as an adult is a big decision and is discussed further in Chapter 10.)

Acceptance of adults with APD

APD is part of a person's make-up, their identity, whether they are born with it or acquire it from whatever cause. Validation of one's identity as being acceptable to others is vital to every individual. No one is without difficulty in something. We all need to feel that we belong and have the approval of our families, friends, peers, teachers, superiors and mentors. The smallest child will aim to please, thrive on attention and loves to earn praise and approval. Someone with an invisible disability needs it even more, although sadly, it is not always given.

Acceptance at home

Most families accept their children with APD and try their best to help them, advocate for them and push to help them get the support they need. They do whatever they need to do. But children need and deserve the same support and validation from other family members, teachers and other caregivers, who they often spend as much time with as their close family, maybe more. It can be hard to deal with the fact that someone you love has a disability, but it is far worse for the person who has it. Simple adjustments can make so much difference to a person's life and cost very little. But what means more is that you accept them and love them as they are.

Both parents, if both are at home or in their child's life, will need to accept their child's APD and support them. This can be hard when one of them might not believe that APD is as severe a problem as it can be, or has other strong feelings against diagnosis and support. They, too, might need to go through the grieving process to reach acceptance, or this might never happen. A difference of opinion such as this can add to tensions in the family, it can cause friction and resentment between parents, and it can even cause the parents to split up. A child in this situation will need even more support, especially if they feel that they are the cause of the break-up of their family.

Other children also need to be told, depending on their age and maturity, and this role usually falls to the parent/s. Their support will be vital, whatever the age. They will need to accept that their brother or sister with APD does things a little differently to other siblings or their friends. They, too, will need to know, in simple terms, the difficulties and ways to help. The child with APD might already have other diagnoses, in which case telling their sibling/s about APD should be easier. Or, if other diagnoses are added later, it can make them easier to understand. They will need to be patient as well, which is not always easy for children. As with any other medical condition or disability, it can be difficult having a sibling with APD, and this can cause its own set of problems that need to be addressed. There could be jealousy if the child with APD receives more attention and reassurance (which they will often need). Just like adults, children can feel frustration when the child with APD cannot understand them or converse with them, or they respond less quickly than expected. But these are things that they will get used to, and will often just accept as part of their brother or sister. Children can be more accepting of new situations than adults, but they can also be cruel and hurtful. The child with APD can often exhibit frustration and anger too, and arguments, sibling rivalry and even bullying can arise. Yet again, information, patience and reassurance are the three important factors in gaining acceptance, and siblings can help a lot.

> Our younger daughter now understands the need to speak slowly, face her when talking, repeat instructions...and explain some words... She also helps her with her memory. (Parent of a child aged 10 with APD)

Acceptance beyond close family

Next comes the decision whether to tell people outside the nuclear family or try to hide the APD by denying its existence. This decision is usually made for young children by their parents. Keeping it a secret is never advisable.

If a child has APD, some parents might want to hide it and hope that people will never find out and that they can just go along with life as though nothing has changed. But their child might be under-achieving at school, struggling and in distress. Their education is at stake, and, more importantly, their happiness.

Parents must inform their child's school of the diagnosis in order to get their child adequate and appropriate tailored support. But declaring APD to friends and family may be a major decision for some families that can depend on many factors: the parents' relationship with their family and their partner's family, their personality (whether they are outgoing or not), what effects they perceive this revelation will have on their lives or that of their child, for better or worse, or simply on how they feel this information will be received by others. Whoever reveals it, the result is out of their hands. The cat is out of the bag, and the truth cannot be taken back. Parents then need to help them understand and accept their child, as will family friends. In fact, I would recommend telling anyone who might have contact with your child, even if it is infrequent, to avoid any misunderstandings that might occur.

HELPING OTHERS TO ACCEPT A DIAGNOSIS OF APD

It can be hard for people who don't know about APD to understand or accept it. To look at someone with APD (or any other invisible disability) you might never realize anything is wrong. There is no wheelchair, guide dog or white stick, nothing to outwardly indicate that they are any different to the next person. If you are not told, you would never know. There is no indication that they need your help or acceptance, but that doesn't deny them the right to ask or receive it.

It is easy for people to understand that a child who has breathing difficulties needs to use an inhaler (because they have asthma), or a child with problems managing their sugar levels needs insulin (because they have diabetes). How, then, is it hard to grasp that a child with a problem in processing speech can have problems in understanding verbal communication?

> Not many of our family and friends know about it yet, and those I have mentioned it to really don't understand it or the impact it has. They don't really ask about it either! (Parent of a child aged 9 with Spatial Processing Disorder)

Once again, information is key, as well as patience. Explain what APD is and how it affects your child (or you, if you are an adult with APD). This form of explanation and information-sharing is part of advocacy (see Chapter 6).

'My child has a neurological condition which means they have difficulty with understanding verbal communication', is a simple way to start. Once your child has developed coping strategies, you can tell people how your child likes to receive information and what will make communication easier for them. Chapter 5 on coping strategies and family support can help with this, as can full support at school (see Chapter 7).

It is never unreasonable to ask for support or to expect that it be given. It is, however, unreasonable, inhuman and discriminatory to refuse.

Everyone around the child (or adult) with APD must accept their diagnosis as valid, that APD is lifelong and incurable, and that it isn't the sufferer's fault. Acceptance by others can lead to a vital network of support. But people can't be expected to help if they aren't told about it. Fear of rejection and isolation can determine whether to tell others about the APD at all. But would you hide any other medical condition that might affect your child's safety or interaction with others? Would you, for example, hide the fact that your child had a peanut allergy and might need to be injected with an EpiPen? A dramatic example, you might say (and life-threatening), but a need-to-know scenario. Yet APD can affect a child's ability to hear cars approaching, not process the sound of a fire alarm, and misunderstand directions that might lead to health and safety risks at school, at after-school clubs, or anywhere.

> We advise other adults who will be working with him (like Cubs leaders) that he will miss some of what they say and it's not that he is ignoring you. (Parent of a child aged 9 with Spatial Processing Disorder)

If the people around them don't realize this, it may potentially be life-threatening. If your child cannot follow what is said in a classroom and isn't learning, the same applies. APD affects communication daily, in all aspects of life.

The news might be met with lack of acceptance and support, even ridicule or a lack of willingness to understand or learn about it. In my experience, rather than not divulge it, making your child hide it, denying who they really are, and causing them to feel ashamed from having to hide it, it is wise to consider whether these are the sorts of people your child should come into contact with. A friend who doesn't support you when you need it most isn't a true friend, and family are those who are supposed to love you unconditionally. You can't choose your family, but you can choose to avoid those whose words and actions might damage your vulnerable child (or cause you pain).

The priority, in my experience, is to protect and support the child rather than subject them to the resulting negativity. I have seen many examples over the years of the lasting damage that this negativity can cause, leading to depletion of self-esteem and confidence, stress, anxiety and trust issues, and social avoidance (even school avoidance and disaffection). This damage can remain into adulthood, and is discussed later, in Chapter 10.

A person with APD is no less worthy of approval, acceptance or success than the person next to them. Anyone we meet may have an invisible disability, difficulty or condition that we know nothing about: people don't wear badges stating their problems or weaknesses. Yet the most disabling conditions I have come across are ignorance and bigotry, because the people who have them don't want to change or get around them.

Acceptance by professionals

Acceptance by medical and education professionals is just as important as acceptance by the individual, their family or friends. The many and varied APD difficulties can have an enormous effect on learning for a child or adult with APD, as well as the effects of comorbid conditions. Failure to accept a valid medical diagnosis or to support anyone with any additional needs by any member of school or local authority staff is disability discrimination. You might think that you can't avoid sending your child to school if they fail to support them, but you can look for another school, or seek alternative education arrangements (as discussed in Chapter 8). No matter how bad the situation seems, you always have options.

> [One parent voiced what was needed] Better educational and medical professionals' understanding. (Parent of a teenager aged 15 with APD)

The process of acceptance described in this chapter is just as applicable to any of the other unrelated conditions and difficulties that can coexist with APD, as described next, in Chapter 4.

> ...he could understand that it wasn't his fault. After each new condition, it became a lightbulb moment for him. (Parent of a child aged 10 with APD)

4

Additions

COEXISTING CONDITIONS

What is comorbidity?

Comorbidity means that a person with one condition, difficulty or disability can also have others (which may or may not be related). In my experience, APD never exists alone in children. There are usually other comorbid conditions or difficulties and most of them are unrelated. Children with APD are complicated and have multiple complex needs. Even if APD seems to exist alone when diagnosed, other conditions can come to light once it is realized that APD is present. When those difficulties caused by APD are isolated and accounted for, other difficulties might then stand out as not being part of it.

I have yet to find a child with congenital or early onset APD who had no other difficulties or conditions. Even if parents believed that APD was the only one, it was simply that they hadn't been identified yet, or they hadn't realized that they weren't part of APD and were caused by unrelated conditions. In those who acquire it (at any age), the cause of the APD might also leave them with new and unrelated neurological, medical, communication or education-based problems, depending on the cause (that is, by any sort of damage that affects the functioning of the brain). This does not mean that the APD has caused them.

Here are some other important points to consider:

- APD can coexist with pretty much any other disability, medical condition or learning difficulty, and any quantity of them.

- Symptoms that are *not* related to auditory processing should indicate other conditions to look at. However, it can be difficult to separate them when similar symptoms can present in a few different conditions. APD in its purest definition affects the processing of sound and speech. But as we have already learned in Chapter 1, it can also have indirect effects and lead to other problems. Therefore, parents and teachers need to learn which difficulties are and are not be caused by APD, so that they can identify what is unrelated and seek the correct cause.

- One of the types of misinformation occurring around APD is the mistaken belief that a child can either have APD *or* some other condition; they are not mutually exclusive. For example, Autism, Attention Deficit Hyperactivity Disorder (ADHD) and Sensory Processing Disorder can all be confused with APD. As well as APD, they are all examples of ways in which the brain acts differently to that of the neurotypical person: this is called neuro-divergence. Misdiagnosis can occur between them. It can also be assumed that only one condition is present and parents and professionals stop looking after one diagnosis. A child might have any or all of them, or others and each will need identification, testing and support. This is why teachers, parents, Special Educational Needs Coordinators (SENCos), Educational Psychologists, Speech and Language Therapists (SALTs) and other education professionals need to know about the possible symptoms of all learning difficulties and other conditions so that none are missed, or misdiagnosed, tell the parents to seek diagnoses for all of them, and make sure that misinformation is put to rest.

- APD is not a learning difficulty, but it can cause them in many children (although not all). The effects may depend on the type of APD-related difficulties experienced, their severity and the child's own strengths, learning styles and coping strategies.

- APD is not responsible for *all* the education problems that your child might experience. Other coexisting conditions can cause learning difficulties too, and these can be mistakenly attributed to the APD. This can happen where parents and relevant education professionals don't know about other conditions, or understand which condition causes which problem.

The failure of schools to support all these conditions and the difficulties that they cause can lead to increasing distress. They must all be identified, diagnosed and supported.

Noticing other problems

Obtaining a diagnosis for APD might have seemed like a marathon, but until all the other difficulties are ticked off the list, parents may feel like they are still stumbling about in the dark trying to complete a very difficult puzzle with several pieces missing, often without a picture to follow.

School staff might not pick up the signs of various conditions and are not trained to do so, but this doesn't mean that they shouldn't learn. Some are more knowledgeable and should help parents to seek referral and access support. But, as with APD, they are not qualified to diagnose any of the conditions.

If the school tells the parents that their child has had tests and they say that they have (or are suspected to have) APD, Visual Processing Disorder (VPD) or Dyslexia, this is not a diagnosis. The basic screening tests that they use were just intended to indicate the possibility of these conditions existing. It is evidence that the child needs full testing by the relevant specialist professional for the condition/s indicated, and a different specialist might be needed for each one. Similarly, if a child has been screened and parents are told that there is nothing wrong, they might look no further and the child is left struggling with a condition that no one ever knows about. They should still seek proper testing, because screening for any condition is not 100 per cent reliable and can miss some people.

Parents are well placed to see the difficulties that their child experiences and their observations are invaluable (although teachers spend as much time with children during the week as their parents and sometimes, they can be missed). They should alert their child's teacher/s of their concerns as soon as possible, but they should not leave it to the school to pursue it. Matters like this may not be followed up by busy schools, especially if they feel that the parent is making a fuss over nothing – 'Other children are worse off' is a common reply. But whatever the school says, parents should continue to gather evidence, list their own observations, update the school, and not let anyone dissuade them from seeking diagnosis and support. It is their legal right and that of their child, and their child will continue to struggle until all their difficulties are identified and managed.

Even with no direct effect on education, coping with any additional conditions can have a detrimental effect on a child who is struggling to learn, and stress can affect their coping strategies. Only by identifying all the difficulties that a child experiences can parents know all the things that are holding their child back from meeting their full potential (and see to it that they get there).

'Collecting labels'

Some people view diagnosis as a bad thing – it is sometimes seen as giving a child a 'label'. In my experience, it is true that *mis*diagnosis can be harmful in this way if it is the 'wrong label', but full, accurate testing and diagnosis is the only way to find that out whether a child has APD, or anything else. It can help, if only to rule things out.

Parents are often accused of 'collecting' diagnoses or 'labels' for their child that some schools and professionals seem to find unhelpful when it could actually make their lives easier if a child is failing and no one knows why. No one wants their child labelled, especially parents, but these are children with complex needs: this is a fact and not an opinion. Treatment may not be available for APD or for some of the variety of conditions that may exist alongside APD, but children will still need help in coping with all of them.

It is wise not to get overly concerned by the diagnosis itself, which is simply a means to an end. It is what the diagnosis represents that matters: access to support, information and validation. As with APD, the child is the same child they were the day before diagnosis, and the same applies to adults. But without full specialist testing, there is no way to access tailored support, and even with testing, it can be a battle. The lack of specialist testing stops so many children from meeting their potential.

> ...I really don't know where the one condition starts and another one ends. (Parent of a teenager aged 15 with APD)

Some common comorbid conditions[1]

These are some of the possible conditions that might also be found in someone with APD. There are many more, but the ones I have listed here seem to be the most common. They are known as invisible difficulties, as is APD, because there are no outward signs of disability to look at in the child. This also makes them harder to identify and for other people to accept.

Below are some basic descriptions of symptoms and effects. As this is not a comprehensive list and it does not include full details, please research further online, visit support websites for more extensive information and diagnostic criteria, then seek diagnosis from the appropriate professional.

Although these conditions might be common in children and adults with APD, they do not affect all of them. The conditions that coexist with APD can occur in any combination, with varying symptoms and severity. Many are neurological in origin. I have also listed some symptoms which they might have in common with APD, where they exist which can lead to misdiagnosis.

Hyperacusis

Hyperacusis is a hearing condition, diagnosed by an audiologist, and involves having increased sensitivity to certain frequencies and volume ranges of sound. The first aspect means that the sufferer will be able to hear sounds beyond the normal parameters, often high-pitched sounds. The second aspect involves hypersensitive hearing, meaning that the sufferer is particularly sensitive to sound, which can be perceived as louder than normal and can even cause pain. This can make the condition debilitating, particularly when you consider that they hear a greater range of sounds than normal. Loud, sudden or high-pitched sound seems to cause much distress (such as the sound of a vacuum cleaner, washing machine spin cycle or fireworks). It is therefore beneficial if the sufferer is warned beforehand that these will occur so that they can prepare, wear ear defenders or remove themselves,

---

1   Please read the full case studies, available online, for details of their many varied coexisting conditions, both diagnosed and awaiting diagnosis. The case studies can be accessed in full from https://library.jkp.com/redeem using the voucher code ZYASEZE.

although this is not always possible. Thunder, for example, is also distressing, but comes without warning, and open-plan classrooms can be a problem as well as rooms with poor acoustic control.

Either of these aspects means that auditory figure-ground/speech in noise difficulty in APD is harder to deal with, as the individual hears or perceives background noises as louder or more obvious, making speech even harder to distinguish from the noise. If someone has Spatial Processing Disorder, background noise can make it more difficult to locate the source of speech or speaker in order to pick out the speech. Hyperacusis can also make it harder for them to do so.

There is no cure, but an audiologist can provide therapy and suggest coping strategies.

> His Tinnitus and Hyperacusis impact greatly on his APD as the additional noise makes it harder to understand, process and hold long enough to action what is required. (Parent of a child aged 10 with APD)

There is a more extreme form of this condition called misophonia, which causes a strong aversion to certain sounds that can cause agitation and disgust. Certain 'trigger' sounds (often background noises) can provoke angry responses, one common trigger being the sound of family members eating; others are sniffing, breathing or humming (and there can also be environmental triggers). Those closest to the sufferer are believed to evoke the strongest responses, making relationships problematic. Misophonia can therefore be a source of tension between family members and friends. Triggers (known as the 'trigger set') and symptoms are thought to be unique to the individual. A 'fight or flight' response is also common. Tolerance therapies and Cognitive Behavioural Therapy (CBT) are thought to help.

Tinnitus

Tinnitus is itself a symptom with a variety of possible causes, and for that reason it needs medical investigation. A visit to a GP or primary health provider is the first step for a referral to investigate. Sufferers report hearing sounds for which there is no obvious external cause. These can include ringing, clicking, hissing or roaring noises. Some sufferers can hear their own blood pumping or the sounds occur in time with their heartbeat. Avoiding loud noises is thought to help, as well as strategies to treat the cause, if discovered. It is thought to affect about 10 to 15 per cent of the population.

As well as being common in people with APD, tinnitus often occurs in someone who also has Hyperacusis (and the combination of all three can cause even further problems with processing and comprehension of speech, particularly in noisy environments).

Scotopic Sensitivity Syndrome

Scotopic Sensitivity Syndrome (SSS), or Visual Stress, is also known as Irlen® Syndrome. This causes difficulties in processing visual information and in certain cases, it can affect reading. It can also exist with, and indicate the possibility of, additional visual processing or perceptual difficulties that make up VPD, discussed later.

Just as APD does not show up on standard heating tests, SSS will not be picked up by standard vision tests. It needs specific testing by an SSS specialist and cannot be diagnosed by an optician or orthoptist. Symptoms can include light sensitivity, headaches and tired or watery eyes, but also problems with reading or written work, which may include some of the following:

- Difficulty reading black text on white paper due to glare.

- Letters, numbers or words appearing distorted or blurred, or that may seem to move around on the page.

- Unable to track which line they are reading, often losing their place.

- Misreading words.

- Missing or confusing short words (for example, on, in, up, to).

- May prefer to read in dim light.

- May tilt the book or page that they are reading or writing on at an angle.

- Slow reading speed.

- Reading avoidance.

- Problems with copying.

- Poor depth perception.

- Poor placement of writing on the page.

- Difficulty filling in tables or drawing diagrams.

- Slow working.

SSS is thought to cause a processing deficit due to a fault in one of the visual pathways to the brain. As a visual perceptual difficulty, it is thought to be one of the causes of what is known as Visual Dyslexia, as well as those described below.

There have been reported improvements with coloured lenses or overlays. There are many different shades of colour, and it is necessary to find the specific shade that suits the sufferer (despite reports that children with this difficulty just need either blue or yellow). But, like glasses for standard vision problems, these are not a treatment or a cure; they just improve the wearer's ability to read or work when wearing them or using the same shade of coloured overlay. SSS centres provide testing, lenses and overlays.

Other types of visual processing difficulties

SSS it is just one type of visual processing or perceptual difficulty and there are several more. These can contribute to a diagnosis of VPD. Just as APD can occur in people with perfect hearing, VPD can occur in people with perfect eyesight or those with prescription glasses. A behavioural optometrist is the type of specialist you need to see for these difficulties, and they often provide SSS testing as part of the package (SSS centres may only test for SSS, so it is best to ask when booking). People with SSS can also have other VPD difficulties that should be ruled out if they exhibit symptoms. With VPD, as with APD, you can have any combination and severity of these difficulties (and you may also have SSS).

Difficulties can include:

- Visual discrimination issues: difficulty recognizing the difference between two similar letters, shapes or objects; can mix up letters, confusing *d* and *b*, or *p* and *q* when written down.

- Visual figure-ground discrimination issues: may not be able to pull out a shape or character from its background, have trouble finding a specific piece of information on a page or finding objects, especially on a busy background (for example, socks lying on a patterned quilt cover).

- Visual sequencing issues: difficulty telling the order of symbols, words or images; problems writing answers on a separate sheet; skipping lines when reading; reversing or misreading letters, numbers and words.

- Visual-motor processing issues: difficulty using visual information to coordinate the movement of other parts of the body, for example, writing within the lines or margins can be tough, or there is difficulty completing tables within the boxes; they might bump into things, or have difficulty copying from a book.

- Long- or short-term visual memory issues: difficulty remembering what they've seen or read; reading and spelling problems; difficulty using a calculator or keyboard.

- Visual-spatial issues: difficulty in recognizing where objects are in space (judging the distance of objects from them and from each other) – this includes objects and characters described on paper or in a verbal narrative; problems with reading maps and judging time.

- Visual closure issues: identifying an object when only parts are visible (for example, a car with missing wheels might not be recognized as a car, or a drawing of a person's face missing a facial feature might not register as being a face); great difficulty with spelling due to an inability to recognize a word with a letter missing.

- Letter and symbol reversal issues: switching letters or numbers when writing or making letter substitutions when reading after the age of seven; a problem with letter formation, which can affect reading, writing and maths.

Behavioural optometrists also offer testing for problems such as tracking issues (which are not part of a normal eye test) and provide vision therapy. If your child appears to have vision problems and passes a standard eye test, seek behavioural optometry testing.

APD, SSS AND VPD

There is obviously no overlap of symptoms with APD because SSS and VPD affect processing of visual information and APD affects processing of auditory information. However, they both seem to coexist often in people with APD, and they are all neurological in origin.

Sensory Processing Disorder

It is also common for people with APD to have Sensory Processing Disorder, also known as Sensory Processing Dysfunction. It is also thought to have a neurological cause.

At one time this was thought to only exist in children with Autism, but Sensory Processing Disorder can exist separately too. No formal, stand-alone diagnosis is recognized in the UK, although it is in the US. Because of the term 'Sensory Processing Disorder', it is assumed by some that APD is part of this and the two conditions are sometimes confused. But it is a separate condition that can affect *all* the senses, and the symptoms can vary in severity and combination. The full range of senses is visual, auditory, tactile, smell, taste, vestibular, proprioception and interoception.

There are three suspected subtypes of this disorder:

- Sensory modulation problems: problems with stimuli affecting movement, touch and body position. Difficulties can fall into one, two or all of these three categories. Anecdotal evidence shows that a child can even fluctuate between them.

  1. Over-responsive – avoids sensory stimulation (dislikes touch, the feel of water, moves stiffly, is a fussy eater because they dislike certain textures of food).

  2. Under-responsive – seems unaware of sensory stimulation (unaware of dirty hands and touch, feels things less strongly, grips pencil too tightly).

3. Sensory craver – seeks constant sensory stimulation (such as movement, fidgets a lot, very active, likes firm hugs and touching things).

- Sensory discrimination problems: difficulty with understanding the meaning if it is a sensation, or difficulty telling one sensation from another.

- Sensory-based motor problems: includes either problems with movement, balance or coordination of both sides of the body, or the symptoms of Dyspraxia, causing problems with fine/gross motor planning and performing coordinated and voluntary actions.

There seems to be a lack of consensus over these subtypes – some references mention them and others do not. However, people with this disorder seem to have trouble receiving sensory stimuli and regulating responses to sensory stimuli, which can trigger (sometimes inappropriate) motor, attentional, emotional and behavioural responses. Sensory Processing Disorder can also affect the way that the senses integrate or inter-relate. Assessment takes the form of judgement-based questionnaires by an Occupational Therapist who specializes in this area.

APD AND SENSORY PROCESSING DISORDER
The difference with APD is that it is a condition that only affects the way that auditory information, that is, sound and speech, is processed and understood by the brain. In APD, the areas of the brain that control auditory processing are simply not functioning properly. They are randomly and intermittently failing, and it has nothing to do with auditory sensitivity or seeking auditory stimuli.

However, the auditory discrimination element of Sensory Processing Disorder is like some difficulties experienced by those with APD in that it can cause misinterpretation of what is heard, so that may be what prompts people to believe that they are connected.

Autism
Autism or Autistic Spectrum Disorder (ASD) is also now called Autism Spectrum Condition (ASC) by those who don't like the connotation of a disorder. Asperger's is now considered part of the main classification and no longer has a separate diagnosis.

It now seems to be widely accepted that everyone with Autism has a measure of APD. It is also believed that many people with ASD will also have Sensory Processing Disorder. Autism is a wide-ranging condition with many possible causes and various symptoms that affect sufferers differently, hence why it is known as a spectrum disorder. APD has also been called a spectrum disorder because it has a wide range of difficulties, not because it is caused by Autism, so a person with APD is not necessarily 'on the spectrum'.

Some people also think that having Sensory Processing Disorder or APD means that you have Autism, which is incorrect: someone with APD or Sensory Processing Disorder does not automatically have Autism, and it should not be assumed that they do. Each can stand alone, or occur together in any combination.

APD AND AUTISM

Autism is a vast topic, so I will stick to the apparent overlapping symptoms with APD that can make identification of either condition difficult. I have come across many individuals who have symptoms that are thought to be autistic in nature, but these people have been found not to have Autism. Because of these similarities, the two conditions can be confused and misdiagnosis can happen.

Some of what are considered as autistic traits are present in many children with APD and might have developed as coping strategies. I have seen many examples of this behaviour, which backs up this theory. These include:

- Avoidance of noisy places and crowds: for a person with APD this is because background noise makes processing of speech more difficult (and they may also have Hyperacusis). This can cause lack of social interaction and avoidance if their friends all want to go to noisy places or meet up in large groups. Social avoidance is also common in people with Autism, and this may be because they also have APD.

- Need for routine or a dislike of change: so much of what happens in the life of someone with APD is outside their control that they may try to keep as much as possible regulated and familiar; they rely on routine, and any variation can cause distress and outbursts for reasons they may not be able to verbalize due to the APD. People with Autism, ADHD and other conditions also find routine reassuring and reject change.

- Repeating or speaking words and phrases or echolalia: this could be either due to repeating what was heard to try to process or make sense of it, rehearsing responses or practising something that they intend to ask or say. Palilalia is a whispered version of this. It can all be related to stress, too, as can vocal tics that are only stress-related and not caused by Tourette's Syndrome.

- Stimming (self-stimulation, usually by movement) also includes repetition of words, but also hand-flapping, rocking and spinning: this is not just an autistic trait; children with APD and other difficulties such as Sensory Processing Disorder might do this too. It may also be linked to the need for repetitive kinaesthetic input to aid auditory processing and memory, such as swinging on a chair, twirling a pen or pacing. They are necessary, should be encouraged and fidgets provided, as for children with Autism.

- Avoidance of eye contact: this may be because the person with APD is either lipreading or finds looking at someone visually distracting when trying to focus on processing what they say (with APD, other senses, particularly vision, can be heightened and detract from processing).

- Abnormal tone of voice or speaking too loudly or quietly: some people with APD cannot process their own tone (and some may speak in a monotone); they can also be unable to regulate their speech volume, unaware that they may be shouting or speaking very quietly.

- Unresponsiveness or being incommunicative: some people with APD can be so severely affected that they may be effectively deaf, and as this is not due to hearing loss, hearing aids will not help. They may also not develop speech as early or as well as neurotypical children, and in some rare cases might be non-verbal or speech delayed, if they are unable to process speech sounds well enough to learn them and reproduce them at the appropriate age. The absence of expressive and receptive communication can also be seen in Autism, possibly due to APD among other causes.

- Receptive and expressive communication issues can also be a source of frustration and anger for both those with Autism and APD; due to a lack of social skills and being unfamiliar with what is socially acceptable, they can also appear immature.

- As seen in Autism, difficulty with social cues or other people's tone of voice, idioms or sarcasm can affect a lot of children with APD who miss out on so much socially due to their inability to follow conversations, misunderstanding, misinterpretation and miscommunication; they can become socially withdrawn or isolated and prone to bullying; like other children, some may not be able to read facial cues or body language (although some do it well and rely on it).

Socially, she struggles in large group situations, mishears or misinterprets what people say, finds making friends difficult, has had problems with bullying both in primary and now in secondary. (Parent of a child aged 11 with auditory processing difficulties)

- Hyper-focus/preoccupation with specific topics: some children with APD also seem to be able to block out all sound as a coping strategy when concentrating; this allows them to focus extremely intently on what they are doing, which can be mistaken for the hyper-focus seen in Autism. Conversation can be very difficult for someone with APD, so they may only want to talk about what they know, sticking to their hobbies and interests (which they can do well due to familiar vocabulary and understanding the topic), whereas 'small talk' or general conversation on unknown topics may be beyond them and/or require a huge effort.

- Limited interests with vast, detailed knowledge: some people with APD are also gifted (more on this later in this chapter), which gives them unique talents that they transfer to their hobbies and interests, devoting a lot of time and energy to maybe one or two. The same applies to children with Autism.

Rather than a child with APD being suspected of being autistic because of their mannerisms, they could have both, and it is quite possible that the child with Autism adopts these mannerisms because of their APD-related difficulties. Or they might simply exist because of the APD alone.

> I have now been diagnosed with Autism, so it's difficult for me to identify which is APD and which is Autism. (Teenager aged 15 with APD)

I was recently asked how you could trust an Autism diagnosis when APD is thought to exist in Autism and there are several similar traits. There are other factors to consider in a child with Autism apart from processing and communication. If the person assessing the child is experienced, especially if they are familiar with APD, it shouldn't be a problem. My concern is more for children who are diagnosed with Autism who are now accepted as having APD and then unable to get APD testing because of that. They remain not knowing how they are affected by APD and are unable to get the tailored support they need.

Specific Learning Difficulties

The terms Dyslexia and Specific Learning Difficulties (SpLD) have often been interchangeable and used to mean the same thing. *They are not.* This umbrella term has grown to include a wide variety of difficulties totally unrelated to Dyslexia (reading or spelling), but they are individual conditions, the only common link being that they happen to be difficulties that exist together (comorbid conditions) and that they affect learning. As well as Dyslexia, these include ADHD, Dyspraxia, Dysgraphia and Dyscalculia. I have seen APD listed as one of them, but APD is a medical condition not a learning difficulty and it does not affect learning in all sufferers. These conditions all have different effects on specific areas of learning. These are now discussed below.

Dyslexia

The definition of Dyslexia, in its original, more accurate form ('dys-lexia'), is a problem with reading, although it can also affect spelling. Having Dyslexia does not mean that a child is totally unable to read, just that their ability to do so is impaired.

For many years, Dyslexia was thought to have been caused by Dyslexia itself. This view has never made sense to me. Based on my experience of working with children with severe Dyslexia and more recent research by a growing number of professionals worldwide, there are other, clear, neurological causes. This realization is what led me to find out about APD (and VPD) 20 years ago while working with learners with extremely severe Dyslexia, as all the severe dyslexics I supported had difficulties with auditory or visual processing, or both. Therefore, I believe that the main causes of Dyslexia by its purest definition, are APD, VPD, or a mixture of both. If a diagnosis of 'Dyslexia' is given without looking into the cause, the learner's APD and VPD are therefore being missed.

When you consider that reading and spelling are not the only difficulties that can be affected by APD and VPD, dyslexic children remain undiagnosed with anything but 'Dyslexia' (which is incorrectly accepted as the cause of everything). They will have these undiagnosed and therefore unmanaged difficulties that affect them for life, and may never have the answers or support for them. Because of this mistaken belief, parents who receive a diagnosis of Dyslexia often accept it as the final answer to their child's problems, because they believe what the professionals tell them. Education professionals and Dyslexia specialists need to know about APD (and/or VPD), and be aware that parents should seek diagnosis for these conditions as potential causes of the Dyslexia, and how they can access testing.

> They were Dyslexia-trained, not APD experts, but felt they could tell a parent categorically that our child did not have APD after one session! (Parent of a child aged 9 with Spatial Processing Disorder)

I have come across many parents who only found out about APD after the recommended approach to their child's reading and spelling difficulties had failed, simply because the professionals they worked with had not looked for the cause and used a one-size-fits-all approach, phonics.

At one time, phonics was thought to be the cure-all for every child with reading and spelling problems and was used to remediate every 'dyslexic' child. However, if a child has a neurological processing deficit whereby they cannot understand or use phonics, repeated use of phonics is not likely to work. Children with APD who have a problem learning phonics aren't wired to learn to read/spell that way; they need more visual-kinaesthetic teaching, namely 'whole word' and multisensory teaching. The same applies to a child with VPD who cannot process language efficiently visually; they are the ones who need phonics. The ones who have difficulties with both APD and VPD will also need multisensory teaching, each child needs a tailored approach. Parents are often told that knowing the cause of the Dyslexia will make no difference to how it is remediated. This is incorrect, as it makes a great deal of difference to the child. The ability to read is essential. So much in life relies on it, especially as having information in writing is one of the biggest coping strategies for APD. They must be taught in the way that they need.

Researchers have cited the brain scans of 'dyslexics' as being different from others as proof of the existence of 'Dyslexia' as a condition in its own right, simply because they use other parts of their brain to read than are normally used, but scans of right-brained visual-spatial learners can show the same thing. These learners do this naturally, maybe having learned to do so as a compensatory skill, because many visual-spatial learners are thought to have APD. The brains of children with Dyslexia might not be neurotypical, but it might not be the Dyslexia that causes that: Dyslexia is the effect, because the causes are either APD or VPD. If a child has a cough, it is not caused by the cough itself. To manage the Dyslexia appropriately, you *must* know the cause in order to help the child with their reading or spelling difficulties, and fully support the dyslexic child with their APD or VPD. As with a cough, the wrong 'treatment' will not work and might be harmful. To ignore a deficit in a child's brain and enforce just the method that causes them constant failure and distress is cruel, discriminatory and damaging. Similarly, If a child has a broken leg, walking on that leg won't make it better.

As mentioned earlier, with APD as the cause, this is what is referred to as auditory or phonological Dyslexia, and if the cause is VPD, this is what is known as visual Dyslexia. Umbrella terms like 'Dyslexia' and 'SpLD' only serve to cloud the issue.

Attention Deficit Hyperactivity Disorder

Attention Deficit Hyperactivity Disorder (ADHD) is a medical condition in which people have differences in brain development affecting attention and self-control and they may (or may not) exhibit hyperactive behaviour.

You will find varying lists of symptoms, but the main ones seem to include:

- Lack of focus of attention: seen as difficulty with attending to prolonged tasks, making mistakes with work, losing equipment, not completing tasks and poor attention to detail.

- Self-focused behaviour: interrupting others, blurting out answers or problems with waiting their turn.

- Daydreaming, staring into space or ignoring what is going on around them.

- Excessive talking.

- Getting up from their seat when they should remain seated (in class).

- Fidgeting and inability to sit still (especially for extended periods), which can cause them to be unable to play quietly or get on with schoolwork (but might also be necessary to aid processing).

- Forgetfulness.

- Organizational difficulties: keeping track of work or prioritizing tasks.

- Inability to complete tasks due to being easily distracted.

- Inappropriate or risky behaviour.

- Difficulty controlling their emotions.

- Impulsivity.

There are three subtypes of ADHD:

- Predominantly inattentive.

- Predominantly hyperactive-impulsive.

- Combined hyperactive-impulsive and inattentive.

Inattention, hyperactivity and impulsivity are vital symptoms for an ADHD diagnosis. Any child can have some of the difficulties at some time or in some settings, but the difference is that in a child with ADHD, these difficulties are seen regularly and in multiple settings. Therefore, a child or adult must also meet other criteria to gain a diagnosis, namely that:

- Several symptoms are obvious before they reach the age of 12.

- Symptoms are seen in more than one setting, such as school, at home, with friends or elsewhere.

- Clear evidence is shown of symptoms interfering with functioning at school or work, or socially.

- Their symptoms cannot be explained by other conditions, such as anxiety or mood disorders.

The type of ADHD will determine how it is treated or managed. The type can also change over time, so its management may need to change too. There is currently no cure for ADHD, but it can be improved by behavioural intervention and proprietary medication. Various medications are available, and these can be effective, but it can be a difficult decision for parents whether to medicate a child, and one that is not taken lightly. Children may still have ADHD as adults, although perhaps to a lesser degree. It is also believed that in some cases, ADHD can be outgrown as the brain matures. Again, the unique nature of the individual and their difficulties will play a part. Those who seek testing as adults will usually have had the disorder since childhood, just without a diagnosis. In adults, the symptoms may be different because of maturity of the brain. As with APD, the symptoms can range from severe to mild, and will be made worse by the effects of other conditions or disabilities, and the development of anxiety or depression that may arise from trying to cope with it all. (If your child has APD and ADHD, and ADHD medication helps with symptoms, this is because it is helping the ADHD, as no current medication can help with APD itself.)

APD can be mistaken for ADHD because of the distractibility of the child due to their other senses being enhanced as compensation. This is the only similarity apart from the seeming inattentiveness or apparent daydreaming when the child with APD is in sensory overload. There are similarities with APD which can lead to APD being mistaken for ADHD, but with different causes. In a child with APD, these might include the distractibility of the child due to their senses being enhanced (as compensation for the APD), forgetfulness (due to auditory-based memory issues) and seeming inattentiveness or apparent daydreaming (when the child with APD is in sensory overload). I have also seen children with APD exhibit hyperactive behaviour in noisy places (also due to sensory overload). Lack of focus and incomplete tasks can also be due to the inability to understand what they need to do and fidgeting can be a necessary aid to processing. Interrupting others can be due to wanting to speak before they forget what they want to say, also, excess talking can be a strategy to stop others talking, thus reducing the need to process speech (see Chapter 5). Any child with additional needs can find it hard to control their emotions due to frustration/stress (see Chapter 11). This is why appropriate testing needs to be sought.

Dyscalculia and Dysgraphia

These often accompany Dyslexia, and for many years were known as being under the so-called 'umbrella' of Dyslexia symptoms. But they are not caused by Dyslexia and are individual, unrelated conditions that may exist alone, together or alongside Dyslexia. APD can coexist with either or both, and is unrelated.

DYSCALCULIA

There are a couple of different definitions, but Dyscalculia is basically a deficit in learning arithmetic facts, number manipulation and recognition, and numerical calculations to an agreed age-appropriate level. It is not caused by poor ability in education or daily activities or intelligence level. It is thought to be neurological in origin. APD can cause difficulty with 'mental maths' if a child cannot understand what is said, but this does not affect their ability to do the calculation itself once understood, or when written down. 'Mental maths' therefore puts children with APD at a disadvantage. Similarly, with Dyslexia, causing an inability to read efficiently can affect the grasp of mathematical problems by not understanding what is asked in writing, but not the actual numerical processes involved. A child with Dyslexia caused by APD might have problems with both aspects, but these issues are not part of Dyscalculia.

DYSGRAPHIA

There are differing definitions for this condition described as a learning disability. One view is that it is a difficulty in expressing ideas and thoughts in writing. The other is that it is a motor impairment affecting handwriting, as well as a problem in learning to spell words in writing and a slow writing speed. This second definition states that the person with this condition can either have difficulty in handwriting, or a problem with spelling when writing, or they may have both.

This lack of a clear definition is unhelpful to say the least, and a consensus would greatly improve the level of support provided. There are similarities in that APD can also cause problems in some children with spelling and putting thoughts onto paper (if that definition is used), but they have different causes and different support is needed.

Developmental Coordination Disorder

Developmental Coordination Disorder (DCD), also known as Dyspraxia, is a disorder that is thought to affect motor skills. It is believed to be caused by a delay in the development of fine or gross motor skills (or both), or difficulty coordinating movements, and affects the ability of a child to unable to perform everyday tasks. No medical or neurological condition has yet been identified as the cause, although it has been described as a 'developmental disorder', previously known as 'Clumsy Child Syndrome', then Dyspraxia and other names.

There may be difficulty with:

- Fine motor skills (doing and undoing buttons or tying shoelaces) and other age-appropriate academic and self-care tasks.

- Gross motor skills, such as kicking, jumping, catching a ball or hopping.

- Scribbled writing, under-developed drawing skills and difficulty using scissors.

- Avoidance of these activities can occur.

- They might move their arms and legs while standing still.

Unusual postures, difficulty playing with toys that need good coordination and difficulty using cutlery in their first year can be early indicators of DCD. Children with DCD usually have normal or above-average intelligence. However, their motor coordination difficulties can affect their emotional development and socialization as well as progress in education. Other conditions (as above) can also coexist, as well as speech and language delays or emotional and behavioural problems.

DCD is life long. Children with DCD find new motor tasks problematic, and secondary difficulties can develop as a result. DCD cannot be cured, but treatment and support can help. There is no similarity to APD.

Executive function difficulties
These wide-ranging difficulties are thought to affect the person's planning, problem-solving, organization, prioritization, goal-setting and time management skills, which can affect any aspects of the brain's way of managing what we do, and all manner of daily tasks. Although not diagnosed as a condition in the UK, this can accompany any (or all) of the conditions and difficulties already described. Some strategies for supporting these difficulties are included in Chapter 5. This is a common comorbid difficulty with a lot of conditions. Although this condition is unrelated to APD, inability to process what they hear might affect a person's ability to organize their thoughts and plan what they want to do, say or write, but for different reasons.

Dual exceptionalities
This term refers to the gifted learner with additional needs, also known as twice exceptional, or 2E. Any type or number of conditions or difficulties can coexist alongside a child who is gifted or able and talented. It can be hard to identify these children when one aspect masks the other. These children have twice the challenges to overcome. It can be especially hard when no one believes that a child who is gifted can struggle as much as they do (and school or parental expectations of

them are set too high). Equally distressing is the child whose additional needs are recognized and their intellect is missed, so expectations of them are lowered. But these children are capable of great things, and no one knows about their intelligence or gifts because they stop looking. Those children who are doubly gifted need double the support. The gifted visual-spatial learner is one such child, and this type of learner often has APD (see Chapters 5 and 7).

In summary

These are just some examples of the comorbid conditions that can accompany APD. Please remember that any of these conditions alone can have an educational and emotional impact and affect life skills. It is so much harder coping with more than one. In addition to the difficulties listed, there can be many more – please don't stop looking until they have all been identified, diagnosed and support put in place.

Therefore, for a child with any additional needs:

- Prompt referral and accurate diagnosis is essential for each of their conditions.

- Just like APD, any of these additional conditions can be debilitating, affecting all areas of life, each impacting on the effects of the others (and there is usually more than one).

- School screening tests do not provide a diagnosis, even if the results indicate that they have what is being screened for, it is merely suspected. School testing cannot effectively rule anything out either; only full testing by an appropriate professional can do that.

- Children suspected of having any additional needs must be tested by the appropriate fully trained professional for that condition, whatever school screening tells you.

- Fully tailored school support should always be provided for all conditions; parents should also encourage the child to develop coping strategies and help them to develop them at home too.

5

Action

COPING STRATEGIES AND SUPPORT AT HOME

Once the child has an APD diagnosis, the dust has settled and everyone has come to terms with it, it is time for parents to act. After assisting their child to find acceptance, learning about how the difficulties affect them in everyday terms should be the next task, then helping their child to develop new strategies with which to cope and get around them. Parents need to learn and acknowledge the limitations imposed by APD (and anything else that affects their child) before they can attempt to learn strategies. They also need to understand the strategies that their child might already have in place, ones that they were either born with or have developed automatically out of need (maybe without parents' knowledge). These actions might be misinterpreted as bad behaviour instead of their necessary coping strategies; some are described later in this chapter, with regard to controlling behaviour.

Although this chapter is about families and difficulties at home, it is just as applicable to adults and to teachers and other professionals, because understanding these difficulties and strategies is relevant to all. As well as discussing APD-related problems, suggested strategies may also be of use to support other difficulties caused by other conditions.

Most barriers are not insurmountable, depending on the severity of their symptoms and the amount and quality of the strategies that the child can develop or learn. These are tried and tested and can improve as the child becomes accustomed to using them, and they can always develop new ones to allow them to adapt to new situations. A child who has APD and those around them all need to learn and understand these coping strategies as much as they possibly can, to support the child wherever they go. APD has an impact on whole families, extended families and their social network, not just the child or adult who has it.

The child needs to know what works for them as an individual, which might not be what others perceive as the right way to help. A person they know with APD might have totally different preferences to another. If there is more than one person in a family with APD, there can be common strategies, but they may each need different ones as well, either to support APD or additional difficulties and conditions, and they will usually have different difficulties of different severity (and different comorbidities) to address.

Learning to cope

There are many ways in which people with APD can find alternative ways of dealing with the restrictions of not being able to process accurately, or reliably, what they hear. They do this by using their own strengths and compensatory gifts to overcome their weaknesses, developing useful workarounds.

> She has asked to start an online sign language course...a visual language that she's very interested in. (Parent of a child aged 12 with APD)

Sign language is a very useful visual aid to communication, and using Makaton can also help with younger learners.

It is very important that the child knows and understands their preferred learning style, which affects their alternative types of communication and information presentation. It is also vital that others are prepared to accept and support it. Schools teach in an auditory-sequential way, which is not normally how a child with APD needs to learn. Vision is the primary sense and often the main compensatory sense for someone with APD. A problem with auditory sequencing is one of the most common found in children with APD, which means that this method of teaching puts so many children with APD at a distinct disadvantage. They are in a position of failure before they start school, and can always be a few steps behind those children who can learn in that way – even though they may be just as intelligent, or more so, they can fall behind through no fault of their own.

Multisensory reinforcement and even multisensory teaching are starting to become more popular again in some schools, but this may still not be prevalent enough to help all the children who might need it, even those without APD who may learn in a different way. Teaching according to preferred leaning styles is seen as expensive, but the cost to our children is greater. What is needed is a system whereby children are taught from the beginning using visual, auditory and kinaesthetic cues to reinforce the information that we want them to remember, using all their senses to learn, and their strengths to remediate their weaknesses.

> A visual routine on the kitchen door (eat breakfast, wash face, brush teeth etc.). (Parent of a child aged 12 with APD)

Help them to do this at home as much as possible instead (more examples are provided later in the chapter, with regard to poor executive function and organization).

Some strategies are automatic and already with them from birth; others need to be learned. The strategies your child needs might be like the ones that other children use, or different, but there are commonalities that are sometimes grouped together as a generic list provided by some testing centres and schools. Remember that what suits one child might not suit others, and so their own unique methods must be developed. Generic support is limited support.

Some children might develop coping strategies automatically, without realizing it. Depending on age, self-awareness and capability, a child with APD might already have some in place even before diagnosis. But other children might need to find them, usually by trial and error. They might have some and need more, and will need to learn how to adapt the ones they already have, to allow them to cope in different situations and locations.

Parents, siblings, extended family (and even friends) can guide them by asking questions about what they struggle with and what they think might help, but ultimately they will all at some point need to know how to work things out for themselves. The difficulties listed on their diagnosis report are a good place to start.

> ...it takes a lot of effort to process what she's heard and then even

more effort to formulate an answer. It's draining. (Parent of a teenager aged 14 with APD)

In addition to everyday factors such as noise, illness, tiredness and stress can all have a negative impact on processing and coping strategies. If their personal coping mechanisms suddenly don't seem to be working, it can also be a sign that one of these three situations has arisen and needs investigating. Signs of being even less able to process than normal might include becoming disorientated, worried, and even a little scared (or even effectively deaf in severe cases). They will all need more support on these occasions, and so will adults. (APD should not get worse unless there is further neurological damage; it just appears worse in these circumstances because the individual cannot rely on their normal coping strategies to get around their difficulties.) A lot of the strategies in this chapter might themselves cause problems if the reasons for them are not understood, developing either as a result of having APD or as a result of trying to mitigate its effects. They can be automatic and the person with APD might be unaware that they act in this way. Some can be necessary yet often dismissed as behaviour problems and lead to criticism.

Communication and social skills

Many of the difficulties found in APD will naturally affect communication. These are caused by one of the most common difficulties diagnosed: auditory processing of speech. This can have an impact on receptive language (processing and understanding what they hear and acting on it effectively) and expressive language communication (expressing themselves clearly, both verbally and in written format). Ensuing miscommunication and misunderstandings can have a huge impact on all their relationships.

Following conversations can be very difficult, even with one person; with more people, it can sometimes become impossible. A small social network of good friends (whose voice patterns are familiar) is preferable to large groups, or even one or two friends, ideally socializing one at a time in quiet surroundings. Online friends are often preferred due to the lack of need for in-person interaction. Difficulty with using technology, phones, and so on can affect them socially due to degraded sound signals, as well as problems with chat programs like Skype. This can be especially upsetting if online friends are all they have. A problem with unfamiliar voices and accents can also cause difficulties in processing. Learning strategies early on can lessen the effects on communication.

Types of expressive language problems

As well as not understanding what is said to them, people with APD also have difficulty in making themselves understood, and might speak in particular ways in order to try to mitigate this problem.

Way of speaking

I have found that it is common for people with APD to communicate in one of two ways (but, as with everything APD-related, this does not affect them all):

- There are those who like to speak briefly, straight to the point, avoiding long, wordy explanations and unnecessary words. But this level of plain speaking can come across as flippant, curt, abrupt, or even rude or aggressive. This is not their intention, but it can lead to problems in relationships. It is just that it is an ideal way for a person with APD to be spoken to, because less speech with shorter words can be easier to process and understand, also aiding those with memory and sequencing difficulties. They might be instinctively speaking in this way without knowing it, simply because it is their preferred format.

- Others speak in a more roundabout way, which allows them time to find the right words (word retrieval) and to make sure that no detail is forgotten, maybe repeating themselves, too. This is to help them feel that they have explained themselves properly. It can be frustrating for them, but also for whomever they are speaking to. It is better, however, to respond in the shorter way described above. Interrupting those who speak like this can cause them to lose their train of thought, and they will need to start again.

Speaking style can run in families, so if the people around them also speak in either of these two ways, it may be learned behaviour. Some people with APD may use both styles interchangeably, possibly depending on how tired they are. They are all different, after all. Another common characteristic is that, whichever way they speak, they might dislike small talk, consider it pointless and don't wish to engage in it. This is because verbal communication is exhausting and they might automatically be conserving their energy for important topics, to say just what needs to be said. This can be perceived as dismissive, but it is a coping strategy and not a slight. However, interrupting a person with APD can cause them to lose their train of thought, and they might need to start again from the beginning.

Whatever their speaking style, people with APD can have difficulty in expressing themselves as they would like, and this can lead to other problems, including the following:

- Word retrieval is a common issue, not being able to remember the right word when they need it.

- Some children develop speech problems if they are affected by APD from an early age or have glue ear when learning to talk, so they fail to efficiently learn and remember some or all speech sounds, or accurately reproduce them.

- Some people with APD can develop a stammer due to processing problems, low confidence or even stress.

- They might forget what they were asked or the topic might have changed before they process it and they can plan what they want to add or reply. To cope with this, they often take the opportunity to speak when there is a lull in the conversation (but it can also be to make sure that no one else can speak, thus reducing the need to process additional information).

- They might not notice when they are being addressed and fail to respond unless the speaker first gets their attention, either by using their name or touching them gently on the arm.

One strategy to manage their word retrieval, delayed processing and response planning issues is by using various familiar words and phrases to give them more time before responding. This is a natural automatic strategy – for example 'er', 'well', 'oh', 'actually'. Or, as they get older, they might use phrases such as 'I was thinking that…', 'I don't know if you know this, but…', 'On the plus side…', 'Can I just add…', 'In reply to your question…' They are usually followed by a pause, adding more time. These are just examples, and any words or phrases can be used as a delaying tactic; they might also cough or clear their throat before speaking or replying, or between sentences. They are therefore unable to automatically self-regulate their volume, or tone.

Volume and tone

People with APD can speak either too loudly or too quietly (again, this may not affect them all). This can also cause a lot of difficulty at home, in social situations and at school (or work). Incorrect assumptions can be made about their intentions and/or personality, based on how they speak. This can be hurtful, especially as they are unaware of the impression that they give to others. A loud voice might be seen to indicate disruptive, aggressive or arrogant personality traits; a quiet voice can indicate that the person is shy, reserved or anti-social. In someone with APD, none of this might be true.

Speech volume, especially if loud, can be perceived as socially unacceptable, as can an unintentionally brusque or meek tone of voice. Other children or adults may also negatively interpret it.

> …no understanding of how her voice tone is coming across. She can sometimes appear aggressive or speak very loudly… (Parent of a child aged 12 with APD)

You will need to bring this to the attention of the person with APD. They might not be aware of this as something that they do (unless someone has told them before), but it is still not intentional – they have no idea that they are doing it unless reminded. Or it might be a surprise to them and they may even argue that they don't do this. Siblings or other children might complain that the child with APD is shouting at them, or get upset. It can also cause a problem at school. You should explain the cause (due to poor processing of their own speech volume). Or, if their voice is too quiet, they may not be heard, so just explain as before, and ask them to speak up. In either case, just explain why it is causing a problem in the current setting and ask them to speak more quietly or more loudly. Someone with APD who does this is not aware of their volume because they cannot process it.

Patience and understanding are therefore essential when conversing with a person with APD, as is making allowances for their communication preferences and difficulties, and not taking offence when none is meant.

Types of automatic coping strategies

The difficulties that a child with APD faces are many and varied, and so are the ways in which they might cope. I have listed them according to categories of common difficulties and strategy types.

Controlling behaviour, avoidance and reduction tactics

These strategies are practices that some people with APD manage themselves, often without knowing. These are what I would call active strategies, although the examples below concerning controlling their environment might not be conscious actions. Active strategies can be used to exert a measure of control over their environment and the actions of others. They are used to try to prevent problems from arising that could affect processing and cause exhaustion from listening for a long time, which can lead to sensory overload, or they are attempts to reduce the effects. They are a kind of pre-emptive damage control, making life easier for themselves, but it doesn't mean that the child is necessarily aware of them.

SENSORY OVERLOAD

This is a state that occurs when the brain cannot process due to being overloaded with stimulation by the senses. The child can appear to be daydreaming and stares into the distance, but this is not the case. Their attention can be recalled to the room by using their name or by touching them gently on the arm.

> She would 'zone out' occasionally. (Parent of a child aged 10 with APD)

[She is] sometimes unresponsive in lessons. (Parent of a child aged 12 with APD)

We make sure everyone...[is]...aware of APD and what it means when [she] switches off. (Parent of a teenager aged 14 with APD)

If a child cannot be roused, they might be having an absence (or petit mal) seizure, unrelated to APD and not caused by it. The child is unaware that this is happening or has happened, appears motionless, might stop speaking mid-sentence, flutter their eyelids and so on. No convulsing will occur. They should be left to come around on their own, but keep an eye on them. They might wet themselves; this is involuntary and should be dealt with discreetly later. Parents should make a note of what happened, any movements for instance, and take the child to their GP/family doctor. A child with absence seizures can also suffer from sensory overload, too, like any child with APD. Other adults/carers need to be informed.

SOCIAL ISOLATION

Many APD sufferers tend to avoid social events, especially where there are groups of people or crowds. They do this not because of their personality but to avoid anywhere with a lot of competing noise that makes speech discrimination more difficult, leading to sensory overload and exhaustion. It might not be because they don't want to socialize, engage with people or have fun with others. It is a method of self-preservation, becoming second nature as a vital coping strategy, one that can be easily misconstrued. It can manifest from an early age, and even the mention of family gatherings or parties can lead to tears and stress, triggering this form of avoidance. This is not bad behaviour; it is panic.

Parents might make their child go to a party fearing that they could be lonely. This may not be the case; they could just need peace and quiet. There is a difference between alone and lonely, and sometimes children with APD need to be alone, to rest and recover. They can have problems making and keeping friends because of their communication difficulties, but for any child with a disability, one true, loyal, supportive friend is worth a million who may turn their back on them.

The child might make a fuss in order not to go to such gatherings; if family and extended family do not understand, they might just treat this as defiance.

> I made the mistake of thinking my daughter was a 'naughty child' when she was very little; I would despair of her and make excuses not to take her out with us as she just didn't listen; it was only when I started to research about APD that I discovered it...eventually she got the diagnosis. (Parent of a child aged 12 with APD)

Parents might see a child playing up, feel guilty for not taking them, or take it as an insult to the hosts. They might make them go anyway, which can lead to the very distress the child sought to prevent, as well as the added disapproval of their family should the inevitable sensory overload, anger and frustration follow. It is a vicious circle born from a need that a child may not even be able to verbalize or explain.

Social avoidance will continue throughout their lives. This is not wilful behaviour; it is a necessary coping strategy. As they grow up, friends may eventually stop including them, invitations will stop, and social isolation begins. If a child doesn't want to go to an event or gathering, it is an attempt at self-advocacy and shows a glimmer of self-awareness, both of which should be encouraged and respected. Planning can help.

> He likes to know in advance if we are going somewhere new. We look it up, help plan what we think will be there, how to leave early if needed...he likes to go to places he knows well, normally in quiet times...prefers to stay close to people he knows well. (Parent of a child aged 10 with APD)

In contrast, some people with APD are more socially adept. Many people with APD automatically develop good lipreading skills from an early age, sometimes unknowingly, also learning to read facial expressions or body language. But others cannot read lips or other cues at all, and may benefit from online courses or training videos, even as adults.

Such methods all help to fill in the gaps in what they fail to process; those who are unable to process what they hear or read lips and body language can have more difficulty.

EXAMPLES OF CONTROLLING BEHAVIOUR

Controlling behaviour might involve actions like the following, many of which also affect expressive language (how people with APD express themselves) but also their receptive language (their ability to understand and respond appropriately). These are examples of situations which can all have an unfortunately negative impact on those around them, and need addressing. I have made some suggestions, but I'm sure you will find more to suit your child; social stories are always useful when explaining to young children.

Action: Needing to turn up the television volume, or listening to music at high volume.

Reason: Trying to make the speech or lyrics clearer and easier to process, especially when there is a lot of background noise (which, interestingly, runs the risk of triggering sensory overload, which can be counter-intuitive).

Solution: They can use subtitles/closed captioning while watching television (for those who read well) or plug noise-cancelling headphones into the television or DVD player (if watching it alone); noise-cancelling headphones or ear buds can also be used when listening to music.

Action: Not being able to understand speech when watching cartoons.

Reason: Lipreading is not possible; there are also minimal and unnatural visual facial cues and body language.

Solution: Using subtitles/closed captioning can help, or they can plug noise-cancelling headphones into the television or DVD player (if watching it alone).

Action: Insisting on watching the same DVD over and over.

Reason: This might be because it gives them a sense of achievement and familiarity to process what they hear by remembering the script, or the actors in the film are easy to lipread. Familiarity is comforting, and this can also apply to a favourite book which aids reading, again leading to possibly unfamiliar success that they will want to hold on to.

Solution: There is no harm in them doing this unless someone else wants to watch a different DVD or television programme, in which case, allow them to watch the DVD in another room, if possible, or take turns in watching DVDs. Similarly with books: children need to read a variety of age-appropriate books, but there is nothing wrong with re-reading familiar ones as well.

Action: Putting their hands over their ears when people are talking.

Reason: Possibly to block the sound if they cannot process what is said or if they are in sensory overload and don't want to listen any more, or if they have Hyperacusis.

Solution: Ask if they know why they do this and say you understand, but explain that it appears rude to others when they do this, and remind them not to. Instead, if they need to block sound, provide ear defenders or ear plugs for noisy situations, or seek a quiet place. (Ear pain can indicate ear infections as well as Hyperacusis and should be investigated.)

Action: Changing the topic whilst in the middle of a conversation.

Reason: They might do this because they have no knowledge of the topic and feel stupid, or find the new vocabulary difficult to process and it makes no sense. Alternatively, they might not know what the topic is. Or it might be because they miss their cue to answer while processing what is said, or forming a response (and don't realize that the topic has changed and they are, in effect, changing it back). This can cause great embarrassment and anxiety, often leading to not wanting to participate in conversations.

Solution: Be sympathetic, explain why this can be viewed as rude, and advise on taking turns (although if they don't realize that they are doing it, this can be harder to change).

Action: Interrupting when someone else is speaking.

Reason: This can be so that they can speak whilst they remember what they want to say, or to stop others speaking by speaking themselves (either because they cannot process what is being said or the subject is one that is unfamiliar to them or unfamiliar vocabulary is being used, making processing more difficult). They can then switch to a topic that they know well and which has familiar vocabulary. Similarly, if children with APD try to talk when it's quiet, they can get into trouble at school for doing this during lessons or at home when the family is watching television, or at mealtimes, and so on. Being controlling can be seen as bossy or manipulative and other situations can also arise from trying to maintain routine and predictability by e.g., controlling the other person's speech and actions; for example if they feel safe in the park where it is quiet and they can process better, rather than not going out at all they might try to prevent others from going to somewhere noisier, or including more people.

Solution: Try to explain that this sort of behaviour is seen as unacceptable but you understand why they do it. Ask them to be more aware when they do it; suggest that they should try to explain to people why they feel it is necessary and why they find conversation difficult, and to ask others to be more considerate of their needs too.

Many of the actions listed above are as a result of coping strategies that are often misunderstood, but the child with APD might not know that they are socially unacceptable or that they are upsetting others. They simply want to find ways to understand speech and be heard. Even so, some of these strategies are not always easy for others to understand or deal with. In children (or adults) with APD, these actions can cause friction in families and friendships and lead to sanctions at school (or at work). The child won't intend to be disruptive or rude, and although their actions can be interpreted as such, they might be unaware of them.

Children with APD can have some lapses in behaviour like any other child – it is normal for children to test their boundaries as they grow up. But in the instances mentioned above, their actions are more likely to be automatic self-protection.

If challenged, the child might become upset and embarrassed, deny that they do it or be aware of it and unable to explain why they do it, even failing to understand why it is wrong when it helps them. In all instances, it is best to gently draw the behaviour to their attention without blame, embarrassment or punishment. Explain *why* it is socially unacceptable and suggest a better course of action in those situations (like those listed above). What might be viewed as controlling behaviour from the outside can be essential acts of self-preservation to someone who sees the world as a very noisy, scary place in which they are constantly one step behind.

FURTHER CONTROLLING BEHAVIOUR AND PERFECTIONISM

This need for control can lead to a child or adult setting themselves sometimes impossibly high standards. Everything must be what they perceive as perfect, or it can feel 'wrong'. Failing to meet these exacting standards can add to their feelings of personal failure. They can also lead to unrealistic expectations of other people, who might not understand their need for control or perfection, and that the child might not understand why others don't feel the same way. Their actions might even be viewed as manipulative, even if they are unaware of them. I have encountered many cases of this need for control and perfectionism over the years, in various situations and at all ages. It can be particularly evident in dual exceptionalities/2E children who are painfully aware that they are failing to meet their potential.

This pursuit of perfection in some children with APD and/or the need for control might lessen or disappear as they mature. Or they might remain and go on to affect them at home, in school, in work and in inter-personal relationships. This level of perfectionism, need for routine, control, rules and familiar processes, and so on can be a good trait and an asset in the workplace. It can even be desirable in someone who wants a partner who likes to manage everything around the home. But it can also make them inflexible and unwilling to compromise.

This can cause problems, for them and for others. And if the other person later becomes too dependent on them and needs them to do everything, it puts further pressure on the person with APD to try to maintain the controlled environment. This might also happen if the person with APD is a young carer, or a parent relies on them too much. It is vital to try to understand why they do this and not add to their stress. Counselling can help.

Before reacting or punishing a child with APD or other difficulties, first ask yourself if their behaviour or reactions could be caused by their conditions. Be informed and be aware, and if you are unsure, always give them the benefit of the doubt. (This applies to teachers too.) Sometimes a child's behaviour is not just right or wrong.

NEED FOR ROUTINE

As mentioned, routine can be very important to a lot of people with APD, especially children. It brings a semblance of normality, reliability, continuity and safety. It provides a pleasant contrast to their usual feeling that everything is beyond their control, so they relish it and find it comforting. As a result, they might be very resistant to change of any sort, anxious and out of sorts when something changes at home or interrupts their routine in some way. It might be something small, like a negative reaction to changing their quilt cover, or brand of cereal, or ketchup, or wanting the same meal every day (possibly also due to sensory sensitivities). Anxiety might be triggered when changing to a different teacher or classroom routine at school. These children can go out of their way to try to ensure that their routines are not disrupted.

Because of this need for routine (as well as a fear of any new situations that might adversely affect their processing), the child might be reluctant to go on holiday or visit people. It might be misconstrued that they are being difficult or exhibiting obsessive behaviour, but this is not the case.

Not all children will need routines; they are all different, and sometimes it depends on their personality. Some children might be easy-going and not care about such things, but to the child with APD who needs routines, maintaining that sense of sameness is so important, even though they may not even be aware that they are doing it, or why they need routines.

They can develop routines and even rituals of their own, not unlike those of children with Autism. This habit can be mistaken as a sign of Autism, as can their obsessive traits, but they are usually simply coping strategies to maintain routine.

These forms of security are necessary and those around them can (and should) help to maintain them wherever possible at home and at school, always considering the needs of the rest of the family. Getting up at a regular time, having meals at a regular time, doing certain things on certain days might help if your child needs this sort of regularity (and school holidays might be distressing because the daily routine is often less rigid, or simply different). They are what I think of as both active and passive strategies, because some are managed by the person who needs them and others are maintained by others. They help that person to feel safe and can reduce feelings of anxiety and helplessness.

However, their parents, family and teachers should also help them to find active strategies that they can carry out themselves, to help them cope alone when change is unavoidable. It helps to explain why change can also be a good thing and will not necessarily lead to catastrophe.

Simple breathing exercises can help to lower anxiety and feelings of panic, such as breathing in to the count of four, holding your breath for four then breathing out for four, or breathing in for four and out for six (or you can use any low number, so long as the 'out' breath is longer than the 'in' breath).

Positive active strategies

What I call active strategies are all strategies that the person with APD carries out for themselves. They are positive, alternative ways to cope with the problems arising from APD (and ways around them) that have fewer negative effects on others. Parents, family, friends and teachers should always try to understand, accept and support these too, where possible.

Remember: Just because a child repeats something back it doesn't mean that they have processed or understood or registered its meaning, or implications, or will be able to remember it long enough to perform any required action. Every instruction and piece of information needs additional reinforcement.

Learning styles and strategies to aid auditory memory

The main types of strategies used by a person with APD are visual (needing information presented in writing or via images and diagrams) and kinaesthetic (using more hands-on methods). However, some children are auditory learners and will prefer information presented verbally, which can cause additional problems for learners with APD.

Visual and kinaesthetic learning styles can also aid poor auditory memory, as can playing memory games such as 'I went to the shop and I bought…' Also useful is 'chunking', which involves putting individual pieces of information together in larger groups (chunks), such as a telephone number. Instead of asking someone to remember 568293, ask them with a pause in the middle, that is 568 – 293, which can be easier to remember.

Grouping things with similar characteristics can also help in remembering a shopping list (fruit, bakery items, frozen items), or visualizing the aisle where they are found in the supermarket. Another option for visual learners is making up mental storyboards to remember a shopping list. For example, to remember bread, jam, milk and frozen peas, they might visualize themselves spreading jam on a slice of bread and drinking a glass of milk, then, as they open the freezer, peas fall out and they slip on them.

Mnemonics are visual, too – they can help for lists using the initial letter of a word to remember the word. For example, I was taught ROYGBIV to remember the colours of the rainbow: Red – Orange – Yellow – Green – Blue – Indigo – Violet. Mnemonics can also be used to help with spelling – for example, for the word 'because', 'Big Elephants Can Always Understand Small Elephants' (this is also a very visual example – they can try to remember the image of a big elephant with a small one). Auditory-based memory aids are those using sound or music, such as the 'ABC' song to remember the alphabet, and rhyme can also help in remembering spelling rules, for example, 'i before e except after c'. These are all strategies that parents can use with their child at home.

(I have also described learning styles and associated strategies in Chapter 7, which includes a section on supporting diagnosed APD difficulties in an education setting that parents may find useful.)

All children with APD and other additional needs can cope better with many aspects of schoolwork and further education by using their preferred way of information presentation and learning style.

Guessing

A child with APD might be able to guess what is said based on context, past conversations or experiences, which is very useful if they are correct. But quite often they get it wrong, further compounding their confusion.

Some people with APD can be very intuitive and empathic, sensitive to nuances in behaviour that others might miss, even from an early age. Being skilled at body language and facial expressions is part of this, but it also carries an element of guesswork.

They all have their own techniques, but some children have very few, and they will need even more support.

How to tell whether a child is mis-processing or misbehaving

This is a question that crops up a lot in my parents' support group. This is not an exhaustive explanation; the effects of APD are also not always the same for everyone because, as you will know by now, it affects everyone uniquely.

A child with APD can appear as having an 'attitude' or a behaviour problem for persisting to believe the accuracy of what they thought was said (when they had mis-processed it). It is natural to defend yourself when you think you heard something correctly and try your best to do as asked, but then it turns out you were wrong because it got muddled up on the way to your brain. Wouldn't you argue, too?

It seems that a person with APD can't trust their own brain. As a result, they may constantly doubt themselves, feel embarrassed or stressed more than any child can be expected to cope with. This can lead to a heightened state of anxiety and frustration, even anger, so they may act up or become labelled as having a behaviour problem at school, at home, or later at work. It can become a self-fulfilling prophecy. When a child is in crisis, a tantrum can be a cry for help. Worse still, they might become withdrawn, lost within themselves. People with APD can be misunderstood just because they have not understood.

In such situations, it is always better to be as calm and patient as possible, remind them that this is their APD and that it is not their fault. They trust you and rely on you for support. When their reality is crumbling, this is when they need you most.

Support in specific situations
Poor executive function

This is one of the many conditions that can coexist with APD; although it is not part of it or caused by it, it does seem to accompany a variety of conditions. It is not diagnosed separately in the UK, but it may be in other countries. One aspect of this that parents find difficult to deal with is their child's lack of planning or organizational skills (others have already been listed in Chapter 4). They might regularly forget to take things to school or bring them home. Complicated tasks including a collection of actions also cause them huge problems. If you asked a child with poor executive function to pack their bag for school, to them that is an abstract meaningless term. They would need more direct, individual instructions given in order. You would think that a detailed explanation would be more helpful:

> Get your school bag and put it on your bed. Then find your books for the day and put them on your bed. Find your PE kit, pencil case, lunch and drink and put them all on your bed too. Pack everything in your school bag, bring your school bag downstairs and leave it by the front door.

But for someone with APD, this set of instructions is too long, and they could also just process the words 'pack' and 'lunch' and miss the rest, packing only lunch. Giving a learner with APD a list of verbal instructions won't help. As well as not fully processing them, depending on their other difficulties they might not remember them all, or do them in the wrong order (and for some activities, the order is important). You could give them one verbal instruction at a time, wait for them to complete it, then give another, then watch them packing their bag and remind them what to do. But this ruins the main objective of encouraging them to do it themselves to promote independence.

> He likes to have a checklist to help him remember things in the mornings and once made one of these for himself. (Parent of a child aged 9 with Spatial Processing Disorder)

To help, it is best to prepare a numbered list of written actions, in order, like this:

1. Get your school bag and put it on your bed.

2. Check your timetable to see which lessons you have today.

3. Find your books for today.

4. Put the books on your bed.

5. Find your PE kit, pencil case.

6. Put them all on your bed too.

7. Pack everything in your school bag.

8. Go to the kitchen.

9. Find your lunch and drink/dinner money [delete as applicable].

10. Put the lunch/drink [delete as applicable] in your school bag.

11. Put your bag by the front door.

You could add a drawing or suitable clipart for each action on the list and ask them to put it up in their room somewhere. Put a copy on the fridge door. It could also help to copy their timetable, add pictures and leave a space for a reminder about additional items such as a sports kit. Your child can help, or they can make their own and put it up in their room too. They might also need reminding what day it is before they start. Morning and bedtime routines can be listed similarly; in fact, you can prepare as many lists as they need (put a header on each list). Over time, they might remember what to do when you ask them to complete a task. Or it might never become automatic and they will always need lists like these. Like APD, poor executive function does not affect intelligence.

Not processing alarms, traffic, school bells

This issue can be both problematic and dangerous. Some children with APD can block sound in order to focus or sleep (or maybe they just don't process these sounds). You will need to wake them up in the morning and tell them when alarms ring. A smartwatch with a vibrating alarm can help.

A child with APD may not be able to process the sound of approaching traffic or know how far away it is. You must teach them how to do this by looking both ways several times, and take extra care when crossing any road.

They may also not process fire drill instructions or be able to follow a verbal sequence of safety instructions on a school outing. Such instructions should always be provided in writing, and a buddy or staff member allocated to alert them to fire alarms, and so on. You will need to inform their teacher/s of any safety concerns that might occur at school or before they go anywhere (even for a day), and provide a list of their difficulties in writing with strategies that help.

Please make sure before any school trips that the school and other staff are aware to ensure that your child drinks enough, as dehydration can also affect concentration and processing and lead to headaches. This is also essential at home, and at school.

Attending appointments

Any medical appointment (either to visit a GP, Accident and Emergency department or for a dentist or hospital check-up) can be stressful and worrying for you and your child, even without any social anxiety and coping with APD. These tips can help reduce that stress, whether the visit was planned or not. Adults with APD can also use them:

- When booking an appointment, request a longer appointment than normal each time, to allow for delayed processing or communication issues and advocacy.

- Asking for an appointment at the start or end of the clinic can reduce the amount of people in the waiting room. It will be quieter, better for processing and help prevent sensory overload. If it does happen to be noisy when you arrive and this causes distress, you might want to re-book or ask for a quiet place to wait.

- Take ear defenders/ear plugs if noise is a problem.

- Carrying an APD alert card can avoid having to give explanations. It can save time with the receptionist or in the consulting room and help open a conversation about APD (they are available in various designs for all ages and can be downloaded free from the information page of the APD Support UK website).[1]

- Ask that APD and any communication difficulties be noted in your child's or your file, so that all medical staff will be made aware of it. When they are of an age to attend alone you might not always be with them and they may forget to tell people.

1   https://apdsupportuk.yolasite.com/information.php

- Parents should advocate for their child from the moment they arrive, unless they are able to self-advocate, in which case you should allow them to do so and just step in if they forget anything. You can note anything important they might miss or forget, to explain to them later.

- A teenager or adult attending alone can ask the receptionist to alert them if they don't respond when their name is called (due to background noise blocking out speech). You can ask that this be added to your/your child's notes and flagged on the system when you/they attend.

- If attending alone, in the waiting room, it helps for a person with APD to always sit facing the speakers if they use an intercom system or near where the person calling you might come from (near the desk or open door to the consulting rooms). Be watchful for someone about to speak to you – they will usually repeat your name if you miss it. You can also let the receptionist know that you need time to process and ask that whoever calls you should speak loudly, so they can be heard above all the waiting room noise. If you are called via intercom, you might miss your name as their voice will be distorted and it might not be loud enough to be heard over people chatting, so if you don't respond for any reason, the receptionist can tell you. It is better not to read magazines, call or text anyone, or chat much to anyone who is with you, especially if they have been tasked with listening out for your name.

- Make notes beforehand of anything that you might need to tell the GP/consultant/dentist. This might be a list of symptoms, notes on any deterioration or improvements, worries about your child or yourself, side effects from medication or anything else that you need to say. It can save time and prevent worrying when you get there about word recall problems or forgetting something (useful whether you have APD or are comforting a distressed child). Keep it in your hand to remember to give to the GP/consultant/dentist when you get into the consulting room (also show your APD alert card if it is a GP/consultant/dentist you have not seen before, or as a reminder if you have not seen them for some time).

- On your first visit, it might help to take information on APD to give the medical professional. This can include strategies such as what helps you, for example, facing the person with APD to allow for lipreading, making eye contact, speaking clearly, giving time to process speech and to formulate responses and allowing for word recall difficulties, whether repeating or rephrasing helps most, speaking more slowly and clearly to aid with lipreading or needing everything in writing. You could always email it to the surgery beforehand. Also include a preferred method of contact (by text/email/letter, but not by phone), and request that reminders be sent prior to any follow-up appointments.

- If you are alone, ask the GP/consultant/dentist to write down anything important that they need you to remember, or if you feel is appropriate, ask your family member/friend without APD to go in with you when you are talking to your GP/consultant/ dentist so that they can make notes. This also helps if the medical professional has an unfamiliar accent, is new to you or speaks very fast. They can leave the room if you need to be examined or treated.

- Parents can ask for leaflets/handouts/websites about their child's illness or condition to read later and explain it to their child. If you are an adult, you or your advocate can ask.

- If your GP/consultant/dentist will not comply with these requests, perhaps it would be better to see someone else in the practice or, if that doesn't work, to register with (or request a referral to) a more disability-friendly medical professional. A complaint can also be made, following the appropriate process of that medical/dental practice/hospital/relevant health board.

- Remember, it is your appointment and they are there to help you and your child: just make sure that they know how. Help them to help you.

Coping with family and group events

Decide carefully whether your child must attend a family event or party that they would find stressful. Will it cause them distress to go? Will it benefit them, the other people, or is it for your convenience? Are the people you're visiting, going out with or inviting into your home supportive of the APD and other difficulties? If you feel that your child must attend and want to go, it would help to follow these simple tips. These tips are applicable for any gathering where it is noisy; they are for parents but can be adapted for adults with APD too.

- When you arrive, make sure that your host/hostess knows about the APD.

- Ask your host/hostess to turn down music so that your child can process the conversation or not be distressed if they have Hyperacusis.

- If they refuse, or it is still too noisy to process conversation, move to a quieter room (you are also free to take your child home if it is too loud, or becomes unbearable, as the host/hostess has not taken your child's welfare into account).

- At the start of a birthday party or meal, make sure that your child is seated next to you, or someone they know and whose voice patterns are familiar.

- Make sure that your child takes frequent sensory breaks from all the noise, either in the bathroom/garden/kitchen or somewhere else that is quiet outside the venue.

- Send your child outside in the garden to play, or to a quiet room (for adults, offer to help in the kitchen to escape the noise).

- Don't feel embarrassed or guilty if you or your child needs to leave early because of the noise: your host/hostess will probably be glad that you took the time to attend.

Parents should always consider the needs of a child with APD (and other conditions) and how it might affect them in such situations. I don't mean to imply that you wouldn't consider your child; it's just difficult sometimes getting used to doing things differently, and your child might not be able to verbalize what they need.

Self-esteem and confidence

Self-esteem and confidence can be very low in a child with APD.

> She has low self-esteem... Her confidence was so low, because she struggled with maths and in the classroom generally. She thought she wasn't very good at anything. (Parent of a child aged 10 with APD)

> Extremely low self-confidence, low self-esteem, HATES her APD as it makes her different to everyone else and not 'normal'. (Parent of a child aged 12 with APD)

> He can feel a failure, call himself stupid, 'Thick, I can't do this, it's too hard'...can be very isolated in school...lack of confidence in his own ability, especially at school. Doesn't always want to try new things at first without a lot of encouragement. Self-critical of what he has done. (Parent of a child aged 10 with APD)

> [She had] low confidence, and due to a lack of knowledge of APD... [she] felt like an outsider who didn't fit in. (Parent of a teenager aged 14 with APD)

There are many ways to help someone to increase their self-esteem and promote confidence. These are just a few examples; they might seem like common sense and things you would do anyway, but it is easy to assume that your child knows that you love and support them, or that you think they are amazing. The child with low self-esteem might not realize it if you don't say it, and children who feel that they fail at everything might not even believe you. The same strategies can also help adults:

- A kind word or compliment can mean so much to someone who is lacking in self-esteem; your reassurance can boost their confidence too.

- Let them know that they are valued.

- Pay attention to their hobbies and praise them for every achievement, no matter how small, even if it is something that doesn't matter much to you; it does to them, and will mean a lot.

- Praise achievements at home, too, no matter how insignificant they might seem, for example, your child getting ready for school on time, putting toys away. Success breeds confidence as well as raising self-esteem.

- Don't give praise just for academic success; this might not matter to a lot of children.

- Sympathize if they don't succeed in something and tell them you love them anyway. Encourage them to try again; this builds resilience.

- Don't point out their weaknesses; just draw attention to their strengths (positive reinforcement).

- When they speak to you, give them your full attention; ignore your mobile phone/social media and turn off the television. Nod or smile to show them you have understood what they mean. Show that you are listening by repeating phrases back to them: this is called active listening (but try not to interrupt; as mentioned earlier, this can cause some people with APD to lose their train of thought).

- Look to your own experiences. If you also have APD, share your strategies with them, and even if not, when they have difficulty with something, you can always share ways that you have found best to deal with a similar situation.

- Try to put a positive slant on every situation; this can help them to feel more positive and to look at things differently. Negativity only leads to more negativity. Each morning, ask them to try and remember one good thing from their day and tell you when they come home. There will always be something positive, no matter how small.

- Mindfulness can help with this, too, helping them to focus on the present. After a bad day, remind them that what happened in school is over, and no one knows what might happen tomorrow because it hasn't happened yet. All that matters is now. (There are plenty of resources on mindfulness online.)

- Take small steps. Don't expect great improvements straightaway.

Any damage that has been done to their self-esteem and confidence might take a long time to heal.

- Seek help from others if you find this difficult or see little improvement (such as a referral to a child or family counsellor).

Family pets

Owning pets, caring for them and receiving their affection, companionship and loyalty can have untold benefits for a child, adult or the whole family, especially for those with additional needs like APD. There is no conversation to follow, and they expect nothing except food, love and a warm place to sleep. I have seen my children's affinity with animals bring them pleasure in a way that interaction with people often does not.

There are similarities between what our children and our pets need. With love, mutual trust and mutual respect given without judgement, they will all thrive and treat us the same way, even those who have been mistreated in the past.

A pet for a child with APD and other conditions is a companion that will love them unconditionally, a friend waiting at home at the end of a horrible day that will understand them without words. Because they don't talk, auditory processing is never an issue, taking away the communication barrier that can make a child's relationships with people so difficult. A pet is someone to share their fears and sadness with, someone to rehearse responses with, someone to cuddle while they cry. Whether it is a dog, cat, rabbit, bird, fish, horse, lizard or any other creature, a pet is a friend, and children with APD can find it hard to keep and maintain human friendships. A pet will never let you down or make fun of you.

Having a pet is not an undertaking to be decided rashly. They are just like children: when they are little, they need constant care, love and attention (and a lot of food). They are not toys for your children; they are living creatures. A dog, for example, will need someone to feed, exercise and entertain them, and they will need to be cleaned up after. This teaches a child responsibility. Choose one that doesn't bark a lot if your child or anyone else in the family has sensitive hearing, or one that doesn't shed much hair if anyone has asthma or allergies to pet hair.

A pet will take a lot of your time, and money (and may need neutering), but, like children, the rewards will be enormous if you are prepared to make the effort. Please consider all those abandoned pets in the refuges and rescue centres all over the world; they need a loving home, and if you can, look there first. Taking on the responsibility of a pet is like having another child, but, like children, they are well worth the effort.

Playing an instrument

It is common these days for audiologists to recommend that a child with APD takes up playing an instrument of some sort. It can help with processing difficulties with pitch, tone and rhythm, and is worth attempting. However, this should not put the child under any added pressure to succeed or be used as a subject in which to take formal examinations. It should also not take up time that is best spent resting. Children with APD, like any other children, will vary in their aptitude as well as in their choice of instrument. If one is unsuccessful, they can always try another, which might turn out to suit them better, and they can enjoy achievement in an area that interests them which will mean more to them than academic success. It can also be something that can lead to an alternative career path as a professional musician or tutor if they want to pursue it in that way, or it may just turn out to be a fun way to improve their processing and an enjoyable hobby. Instruments and lessons can be expensive, however.

How parents can help

The effects of coping all day with APD don't switch off when they leave the school gate. When they get home, they are drained, possibly in sensory overload, and their nerves are raw. They might have a headache from noise or processing or a stress migraine. (A child with frequent headaches should always be investigated by a paediatrician to find the cause.)

> Needs quiet times...[has]...exhaustion and headaches. (Parent of a child aged 12 with APD)

Children with APD might have a tantrum or angry outburst when they get into the car or arrive home because they have been holding in their anxiety and frustration all day, simply holding it together until they get home where they feel safe. This is known as the 'pop bottle effect'. Like an agitated bottle of pop, they will eventually explode under pressure. Sometimes they don't make it that far and it spills out at school, which can lead to arguments with friends, reprimands by teachers, detention, and so on. If they do make it home without incident, let their home be a sanctuary where they *can* let it all out.

They will need reassurance, then peace and quiet to relax and 'reboot' their brain, and process what they have learned in the day (not after-school clubs, parties, outings, therapies, extra homework because they failed to finish work at school or enforced socialization).

> She needed her time alone; we later found out this was to help her process the events of the day. (Parent of a child aged 10 with APD)

Another stressor that should be avoided is engaging the services of a tutor either after school or at weekends. It is awful to stand by and do nothing while a child is falling behind at school or might already be well behind their peers, but a tutor can add to their exhaustion at the end of a long, stressful school day (or week). If they are too tired or their brain is too overloaded, they will not learn from the tutor either, and this will add to feelings of failure. A child who goes to school needs to learn at school and not at home. If they are not learning or progressing at school, or just maintaining average grades when they are capable of more, parents need to fight for additional support to enable them to learn at school. If a child does improve as a result of the tutoring, the school will think that the child is coping and will have no reason to provide or increase support. It is the school and local authority's duty to provide the support to allow a child to access the curriculum (as explained in Chapter 6). Tutoring can lead to very real possibility of sensory overload and brain saturation. A child with APD (or any additional needs) who is failing at school needs far more than a tutor. Without help their daily struggles at school will still continue, with unnecessary stress added at home. This, in turn, will adversely affect processing and make them even more tired, making school harder and creating a vicious circle.

All these situations can put extra pressure on a child who might already be at their limit. They simply need to rest, play, just be a child, and be left alone. It is not wrong to let them decide to do that. They will make friends when or if they want to, with whom they choose. Please let them choose how they want to spend their free time. As we will see in later chapters, their interests might lead to a career in which they can be successful.

At the end of the day

Due to delayed processing, your child might not be able to tell you what went on at school when they get home, or say what is wrong; their brain needs time (possibly hours or overnight) to process it all, including what they learned, which might well have large gaps due to intermittent or incomplete processing. Their brain might be in overload or shut down after a busy day, and the same can happen if they are having a bad processing day (there will be good and bad days). What you say may make no sense and they may not be able to respond either.

Speak to them in a quiet place without the television on or other children interrupting, and wait until they are ready. Speak to them face to face, get their attention and use their name. Relate things one short, plain phrase at a time, and leave time for processing. Avoid lists of instructions: they could be forgotten or not remembered in the right order; they might get the first or last one, or none. Even doing this, they may still not understand. Give brief written instructions, worded as simply as possible (if they're old enough to read). For young children or those with listening difficulties, use pictures. Make flash cards with recurring themes of things you want them to do, in order, for example a child going into the bathroom, washing, cleaning their teeth, then putting pyjamas on and getting into bed. Even for those without executive function problems, it will help to keep it simple and make it visual, to aid their saturated brain.

> We get his attention first, wait, [and] then speak to him...use short, simple sentences, and try to check he's understood... We use lists and checklists to help him to remember which day it is, what's happening and what he needs to take...playing more games...as he learns a lot from these...giving him time to get his message out and

> not making him feel like he's taking too long...try to have a quietish home and keep the noise down when he's watching TV, but he still turns the volume up! (Parent of a child aged 9 with Spatial Processing Disorder)

Any homework can be a step too far. It needs to be appropriate and accessible, differentiated to their capability and only attempted for a set time. They might not have understood what was taught, or missed or mis-processed vital parts. If they can't do it, don't leave them struggling; stop there. Don't be tempted to do it for them. If you do, the school will think they are coping when they clearly are not. It might well be that they haven't understood what went on in class and they need written reinforcement of what was said, or a recording to play later at their own pace. Leave the homework undone, and explain to the school why it has not been completed. A child with APD should not be punished at school for not being able to complete homework, or work at it for hours at the end of the day feeling more and more of a failure. It should also not be a battle at home to make them do it. Home should be their safe place.

Parents can help in a variety of simple ways, as needed.

> [Have] conversations asking how our days have gone, any problems etc. where we can offer advice, or have a giggle at our own mistakes to show that she's not the only one to make them. (Parent of a child aged 12 with APD)

> [Having] Short sentences, quiet background...quality family time, especially at weekends. Making reading fun...a good bedtime routine. (Parent of a child aged 10 with APD)

Imagine what it's like living with this all day at school, and at home. APD affects them everywhere. It never turns off, never gets better. As mentioned earlier, you might ask yourself whether their behaviour is APD or 'attitude'. If it is attitude, it comes from a place of despair. It's that attitude that might just keep them going; it shows they still have some fight left. But it can also indicate that their support is inadequate, that their needs are not being fully met, that they could be at breaking point. Yet I would be just as worried about the quiet, compliant child. They are the ones who are defeated, the ones who are disaffected, depressed and who might be afraid of asking for help, or they are sick of trying and being dismissed or told off for asking questions, the ones who have lost any hope that anyone will listen or help them. Be the person who does.

Final tips

I know I have repeated this a lot, but the best and simplest advice that I can give is to make sure that everything that a child needs to know is always provided in the way that they prefer, whether in writing and worded as simply as possible, presented in diagrams, or recorded. But most of all, they need reassurance, someone who will listen and accept them as they are. Always remember, too, that a child (or adult) with APD can appear to be listening, because they are – it's just that what they hear makes no sense to them. They might nod and smile in all the right places and even repeat back what you said, but they may not have understood a word.

Living with APD is not easy, especially for the person who must live with it every day for the rest of their life. But it can have a huge impact on families too. Always remember that it isn't your child's fault: they didn't ask for it either. APD is a disabling neurological condition, not a choice. I cannot emphasize enough how important family support can be to a child with APD, particularly by being there for them, giving them that 'safe haven' away from the pressures of school. Acceptance, security and understanding are essential. Supporting them in any way that they need you to will lessen the stress for everyone and improve life at home too. Anxiety and stress can be extremely harmful and a happy, relaxed child with APD processes better.

> ...trying to get him the right help, researching, appealing things like EHCP [Education, Health and Care Plan]...and this eats into family time, down time...([my other] child with SEN [Special Educational Needs]...adds to the pressure)...very worrying and difficult trying to work out how best to help him. (Parent of a child aged 9 with Spatial Processing Disorder)

> ...we are still learning every day... It is hard when there is no one in this borough who understands and supports families with this hidden disability. (Parent of children aged 8 and 10, both with APD)

> It has caused a lot of stress with appointments, misdiagnosis, school problems. (Parent of a child aged 11 with auditory processing difficulties)

Support also needs to be provided at school, and parents will need to advocate on their child's behalf. It might be a continuous battle in some cases, but a battle that can be won. With the right sort of help, a child with APD can succeed. To be able to represent your child and speak up for their needs when they can't, at school and in all the other situations already mentioned, parents will need advocacy skills. The next chapter discusses how to approach it.

6

Advocacy

FINDING A VOICE

Advocacy as a parent

One of the most important aspects for a child living with APD is the development of self-advocacy skills: the ability to ask for the help that they need, when they need it. These skills may not come automatically, so most children will need to be taught them. Various factors can prevent this, such as anxiety, lack of confidence and fear of failure, ridicule or rejection. Schools, employers, family and friends cannot help if they don't know what is required, but until the child can ask for help, their parent or guardian must be their voice.

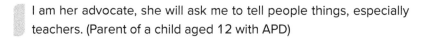

I am her advocate, she will ask me to tell people things, especially teachers. (Parent of a child aged 12 with APD)

The wider circle

After acceptance of the diagnosis, parents need to inform family members and family friends about their child's APD. Doing this and helping them to accept the diagnosis is part of advocacy. Many sections of this chapter will therefore address parents directly.

As already touched upon in the previous chapter, children will have contact with a variety of people outside the wider family, such as childminders, school, GP, dentist, hospital consultants, and so on. These people will need to know about a child's APD, and parents must explain it and what might be helpful (and what would not), expressing their child's needs until they are able to speak for themselves, if they can.

Need for school support

Apart from informing people about their child's APD, the most important purpose of a parent's self-advocacy skills is in obtaining suitable support for their child at school. It is also the hardest.

> When you have had time to come to terms with [an] APD diagnosis, start to educate people, especially school and the medical profession. (Parent of a child aged 10 with APD)

Some children may seem to be coping in the early years using their individual coping strategies, but they will only take them so far; the APD will remain and needs to be addressed and supported, as will all other coexisting conditions and difficulties. Some children will go to extraordinary lengths to mask their difficulties, for fear of not fitting in, of being told off, or looking silly. Even for these children who appear to be keeping their head above water, this may not be the case. Like a duck, they might be paddling feverishly underneath just to stay afloat. The need for support will become even more obvious as they get older and the workload and pressure increase. It is essential that support is put into place as early as possible, but no matter how much support is provided, it is also vital that a child with APD learns how to ask for help. It is even more important that the help is given when they ask, or the child will soon stop asking.

It is not easy for anyone to stand up and say, 'I have a problem and I need help', especially a child with low confidence. Neither is it easy for someone with APD to cope alone and hide their difficulties. This applies to parents or adults with APD, and it is harder for children. Adjustments need to be made, accommodations put in place and preparation made for the battles that you will have in order to secure them. It shouldn't be a battle for a child to access an appropriate education when they are legally entitled to it, but sadly, most parents will need to fight for it. It is difficult and it can be frustrating and distressing. You can do it: you are your child's advocate, and you are their best hope.

I know from bitter personal experience how hard it can be to confront professionals, whether teachers, Special Educational Needs Coordinators (SENCos), Educational Psychologists, Speech and Language Therapists (SALTs), local authorities, advisory teachers and so on. But there will come a time when it becomes necessary.

You should take the APD diagnosis report to your child's school as soon as you can after you receive it, and leave them a copy (not the original). After a couple of weeks, if you feel your child is not receiving appropriate or adequate support, or if the school ignores the APD diagnosis or fails to implement the specialists' recommendations, you will need to step in. The Education Act states that parents are legally responsible for their children's education, not schools or local authorities. You have a say, you are the ones held to account by law, and just because you enrol your child in a school doesn't mean you waive those rights or responsibilities, although the school is accountable while your child is in their care.

I used to do anything to avoid a confrontation, but there comes a time when you must be THAT parent. You may feel nervous, scared even, have a sick feeling in the pit of your stomach. Just remember – this could be the way your child feels going into school every single day without the help they so desperately need, dreading what each day will bring, lost and struggling. They may be labelled as lazy, bullied or ostracized by other children (or even teachers), kept in for unfinished work or for asking too many questions, or have that work sent home along with homework they can't do (and shouldn't be expected to do because they haven't got a clue what was discussed in class). These are children who can be constantly blamed for something that is beyond their control, because theirs is one of the invisible disabilities and people don't believe that they need help. It is up to you to tell them that your child needs help, and why.

> I had to battle by myself and stick to my instincts... I'm so pleased that I didn't give up. I nearly did so many times! (Parent of a child aged 10 with APD)

The stress factor cannot be over-estimated; the pressure on our children is enormous, struggling to do what other children do automatically. If you add to this their exhaustion and sensory overload, this can lead to a child in crisis. Support may also be needed to help them cope with the miscommunication associated with APD that can affect making and maintaining friendships, as well as the anxiety and stress that so often develops, which can be very stressful for parents, too.

Trust your gut... Don't take no for an answer. (Parent of a child aged 12 with APD)

The first step

The key to effective advocacy is information. If you are confident about what you are asking for and why it is needed for your child, you will have more chance of success. Familiarize yourself with the details of your child's APD diagnosis and any other conditions and what that means for your child. You will also need to understand the recommendations made by the diagnosing specialists for adjustments and support in the classroom, which the school should implement. If you do not understand the report, contact the diagnosing consultant, and ask them to explain the report in simple, everyday terms. Your own online research and joining relevant online support groups can also help with this.[1]

Other parents who have already been through the same process are always willing to help, and their experiences can teach you a lot. But most importantly, you must speak to your child in order to learn about how they are affected as an individual, with all their other differences and difficulties, quirks and struggles. You will need to know about any coping strategies that they use, too, their preferred way of receiving information (as discussed in Chapter 5), and pass that on to their school.

Children often have great personal insight, even from an early age. Some may not be able to put it into words; others may be non-verbal or have language disorders that make explanation more difficult or impossible. But most will know, and with time and patience, they may be able to explain. Keep asking. You will then be prepared to convey this information on their behalf, as needed.

Collecting evidence

After diagnosis, it can help to keep a diary of what your child tells you, just as you did pre-diagnosis, and ask their teachers to record what they observe too. Supportive teachers are your best allies, and they can also help to advocate for the children they teach. Having already discussed

---

1   My website has details of several online APD support groups I provide, both in the UK and internationally: https://apdsupportuk.yolasite.com/

and worked with your child on coping strategies and using your own observations and those of helpful teachers, you should soon be able to put together some idea of what they go through every day, at home and at school. Print out your notes and keep them in a folder, along with reports for all diagnosed conditions and any professional reports (basically anything relevant to your child and their difficulties).

A child who is not coping will come home and be upset, act up, and get angry and frustrated for apparently no reason. They might not be sleeping or eating well, or they are having migraines. These are all signs of anxiety and stress. Note their worries and fears, which might include an unfair reprimand for not listening, excessive homework based on school work that they haven't understood, and so on. This sort of incident might stem from a teacher's lack of knowledge of APD and needs to be addressed with information about APD. They can make a child dread school and even lead to school avoidance. It is so important to listen to your child. When they are upset or say they are struggling at school, please believe them, and deal with their concerns as soon as possible to stop anxiety building.

What does 'average' mean?

There is a misconception that a child who is meeting average school targets is not failing; this does not allow for the fact that all children have their own level of potential attainment.

'Average' is only a benchmark of generalized attainment, and not all children will be average. What might be the best level that one child can attain may be a gross under-achievement for another and totally unachievable for a third. All children are different, and the aim of an appropriate education, according to the law, is to make sure that they all reach the best level they can, whatever that means for them. Giving every child the same level of education, the same level of support, is inappropriate, because they will all need varying levels of support. Helping a child with APD and other difficulties to learn is not giving them an advantage; it is simply allowing them to meet their full potential. The purpose of education is not just to deliver a curriculum and leave it up the child whether they understand it or learn it. It should be to make sure that each child is understanding and learning, every day. When you know they are not progressing as well as they could, even if their grades are not falling, and your child tells you that they are finding school problematic, it is time to do something about it.

No support will be provided if the school feels that they are meeting average targets or making satisfactory progress. But 'average' is an arbitrary term, which may vary from school to school and does not consider children with above-average potential, or those who may be bright with learning difficulties: dual exceptionalities or 2E children.

Any child with additional needs might be capable of achieving far more than expected or attained. Their progress might be acceptable by school standards, but it might not be at a level that they should be achieving. Many children will know that they are not coping; they will be upset and frustrated. This is a sign that it is time to do something about it.

Approaching the school

When you have an idea of the problems that are affecting your child at school and you have collected evidence, it is time to approach the school. It is better to work with the school if you can. Most schools want to help all the children in their care, but they may be tied by funding restraints (although the support that a child with APD needs usually costs very little). You should:

- Make an appointment to speak to the school SENCo and class teacher (via letter or email, and keep a copy); this should be done as soon as possible.

- Explain your concerns clearly at the meeting; put them in writing and make copies to hand out along with information on APD (from the APD Support UK website) and any other relevant papers. This will also help if you also have APD and struggle with word retrieval. Take a friend or impartial advocate with you if you need support or someone to make notes. Pass around your handouts at the start of the meeting, or better still, email them beforehand so that people attending the meeting are familiar with the issues faced by your child, and time will not be wasted at the meeting while they read them.

- State your concerns clearly and calmly, and ask any questions you might have noted and brought with you. Ask whether the recommendations made on the diagnosis of APD have been put in place. If not, ask why not. Explain why your child needs support, and request that they receive it as soon as possible to avoid further distress.

- Send a letter or email after the meeting to all attendees. This is 'a letter of understanding', listing what was discussed at the meeting and agreed (or refused). Send one after every meeting or telephone call, and keep all emails to and from the school. You could write something like this:

> Following our meeting dated xxx, it is my understanding that you promised to supply/refused to provide yyy [add details of support] for my child.

Then add:

> Please could you confirm this in writing by [add date two weeks ahead].

It is vital that all communication with the school and local authority is in writing and that you keep a copy (in the file with your diagnosis reports, etc.) so that there is a verifiable paper trail of the support that you asked for, when, and their response.

I think school is the worst aspect... They do not know about APD or how to support a child with it. Ensure you know all the things that your child needs to do their best and insist that it is done. Never be afraid to contact school and say what your concerns are or that things aren't being done that ensure your child is on an even playing field with other children... (Parent of a child aged 11 with auditory processing difficulties)

Applying for an Education, Health and Care Plan, Special Educational Needs Statement or Coordinated Support Plan

You can apply for an Education, Health and Care Plan (EHCP) (in England), or a Special Educational Needs (SEN) Statement (in Wales and Northern Ireland) or a Coordinated Support Plan (CSP) in Scotland at any time, to secure additional support for a child with SEN at school or college, above what the school can provide or is providing. Parents also might apply if they feel that the support provided is not currently appropriate to their range of needs. An EHCP is not always necessary (i.e. if parents are happy that the school is providing adequate and appropriate support).

For example, parents in England can make a request to their local authority for an EHC assessment. The local authority must decide whether their child qualifies for assessment, i.e. whether the child has (or may have) special educational needs (SEN), or may need special educational needs (SEN) provision to be made via an EHCP. Those are the only stipulations. A child does not have to be working at any number of years below their chronological age, as some parents have been told. (Although provision is based on need and no diagnosis of anything is required, I would still recommend seeking diagnosis first for many reasons, particularly because to receive the amount of appropriate support that they need for all their difficulties, they need to be identified; without it, a child might just receive generic support.)

Parents are closely involved in the creation of the EHCP document which is legally binding, and the opinions of older children are also considered (and all children's views are considered, regardless of age). The EHCP should be monitored closely and reviewed annually; parents can attend reviews and raise concerns. If either the Assessment or EHCP/SEN Statement/CSP is refused, there is an appeal process and you can take the local authority to tribunal. An EHCP can include provision of equipment such as assistive listening technology. The APD Support UK website provides a guide to applying for assessment and links to other appropriate support agencies for advice.

It is advisable to check with your local authority and support agencies regarding the criteria and process to apply for a Special Educational Needs (SEN) Statement (in Wales and Northern Ireland) or a Coordinated Support Plan (CSP) in Scotland. Other countries should refer to their own SEN/additional needs legislation.

Other considerations

Here are some other school-related issues for which you will need to advocate on behalf of your child.

REASONABLE ADJUSTMENTS AND EQUIPMENT

Reasonable adjustments at school allow your child to access the curriculum despite their difficulties. Your child might require the use of an FM system for APD, or other equipment such as a laptop, recording equipment, certain software, for instance, depending on other additional needs. Teachers also need to support their use. The school or local authority might refuse, but your child is legally entitled to receive them under the disability element of the Equality Act (in the UK) as well as any other reasonable adjustments they need. Failure to provide this is disability discrimination (see Chapter 7).

> She has an FM system. She was made to feel different and sometimes laughed at by staff and pupils alike for using this. A common thread was that she wasn't deaf so didn't need the system. (Parent of a teenager aged 15 with APD)

TRANSITION OF SUPPORT FROM PRIMARY TO SECONDARY SCHOOL

Make sure that all support is carried forward to secondary school if your child is diagnosed at primary level. If you have a supportive primary school, don't expect that your child's secondary school will necessarily be the same.

> I'm still currently in meetings with the school to make sure ALL the teachers help and support her, not just a couple of them. (Parent of a child aged 12 with APD)

At secondary school, they will expect your child to be more independent, to understand and remember everything they are told, complete work at the same pace as their peers, be able to function in timed tests and in noisy environments, do things in the right order, and a range of other things that a neurotypical child does automatically but a child with a disability like APD cannot manage without help. Without adequate support already in place, no allowances will be made, especially if the new teachers are not aware of any need for support.

The transition to secondary school needs to be managed carefully for each child. Information on your child's additional needs should be sent to the secondary SENCo from the primary school. It is then the role of the SENCo at the new school to personally pass that information on to each of your child's teachers, but sometimes mistakes can happen. My advice is to inform them all yourself. Include a photo of your child and information on APD (available from the APD Support UK website), and urge them to read it and act on it, at every lesson, every day. (It might help to inform them that failure to support a child with APD or any other medical condition or additional needs is disability discrimination and therefore unlawful.)

In the UK, if your child is not on the school's SEN register, they might not be considered as entitled to any support, at primary or secondary school. If information is not transferred properly from primary school, your child may not be on the SEN register and will not be supported until the error is corrected. Schools receive funding per head of learners registered. Ask the SENCo, in writing, to add them to the SEN register, or get a reason in writing for the refusal.[2]

REPEATING A YEAR OR ACCELERATION

Depending on a child's performance at school, some schools might suggest that they repeat a year (basically keeping the child in the same class for another year because they haven't made adequate progress). However, for a child with APD, this will bring the additional stress of settling into a new class of younger children, getting used to their new peers' voice patterns and that of their new teacher. It would also separate a child from their friends, and it is not easy for children with APD to make and keep friends.

Holding a child back can also lead to bullying, making them appear even more different than their peers and compounding their feelings of failure.

But the primary consideration is that a child with APD and other difficulties kept behind without support will not succeed in the new year any better than they did the first time. If a child needs to be held back, the support they are already receiving is not adequate or appropriate and they are not learning. Without support they might fail the repeated year too, and they can't keep being held back every year.

Repeating a year puts the burden to succeed on the child, not on the school or local authority that should be providing support, thus putting the child in a further position of failure when it is the lack of support

---

2   If you are not in the UK, please check for similar measures in your country.

that has failed them. Even a brief trial of repeating a year can cause the child additional distress, facing the embarrassment of having to go back with their original class, not feeling as if they belong in either, with possible bullying from both.

If this is suggested, parents need to advocate for adequate and appropriate permanent support to be put in place for their child and leave them where they are, preferably with support guaranteed by an EHCP/SEN Statement/CSP.

The same difficulties will apply to a child who is accelerated (moved up a year) because they are found to be exceeding (average) expectations. Their ability might mean that they are dual exceptionalities or 2E, gifted with additional needs. Both the giftedness and the additional needs must be fully supported. It is also better to leave these children in their peer group and provide them with work to match their extended ability and full support, not add work or move them to the year above. Bullying and friendship difficulties can also occur for these children, as well as loss of self-esteem if they cannot keep up because of their APD and other difficulties, or fail and are sent back. These children might be more capable academically than some of their peers, but they still have additional needs that must be met; these children have double the needs (see Chapter 7).

> Be prepared to battle school for support for a condition that they have mostly never heard of. Be that parent who fights for your child in school, question school why they are doing things that way when it is clear your child is struggling, have a plan [so] that you are clear [about] the support you want to have from school and try and get the school to agree to it under reasonable adjustments. Don't listen to the school saying…that they have other children who need more support… No matter how hard it is, try and keep communication open with the school to support your child… The one most important thing I would say is believe your child, understand their struggles each day, help them to develop their ability and confidence to speak up and explain what APD is and how it affects them as it is different for each child. (Parent of a child aged 10 with APD)

Helping your child to self-advocate

It is essential that all children learn independence and self-reliance, and children with a disability such as APD are no different. Parents won't always be with their children (especially as they spend most of the day at school), and the child with APD will become an adult with APD. As for parents, for the child to self-advocate they must fully understand how they are affected by their APD (and any/all other comorbid conditions and difficulties), what sort of individual support they need, and how to ask for it. The work you have done with them on coping strategies will go a long way to help with this. As with adults, these skills may come easily for some children and they may take to it readily. In my experience, for many people of all ages, readiness to self-advocate often doesn't occur until after acceptance of their APD and other conditions has taken place. But even a young child should be encouraged to start as soon as possible. Linked to this is the development of self-confidence, which is often lacking in a child with additional needs.

With children for whom self-advocacy may not come naturally, this will need to be taught and encouraged.

> ...especially at school, he will rather struggle than ask for help as this might make him different from others. (Parent of a child aged 10 with APD)

Here are some strategies for developing self-confidence in a child:

- One of the best ways is to encourage your child to put their hand up in class if they don't understand or are having difficulty. Remind them to wait quietly until the teacher notices them (although if this takes some time, they may have forgotten what they were going to say or ask). They can practise this at home so that it becomes familiar and they will have less chance of forgetting what to say when the teacher sees they need help. It helps to keep it simple, so try phrases like 'I can't remember what you said', or 'I don't know what to do next', or 'I don't understand'. The teacher can then ask them what the specific problem might be. It is said that repetition of something seven times helps it to stick in the long-term memory, but for some children this may take more, or a lot less. So these techniques should be practised regularly until you know they are understood and remembered; every child is different. I would tell the teacher that you have encouraged your child to ask for help, and ask that they check that your child is asking. Ask your child if they are receiving help when they ask – a teacher who responds positively and consistently to the child's requests for support will help enormously in confidence-building. It should also not be assumed that help is not needed just because a child doesn't ask.

- Where understanding verbal communication is a problem, as is the nature of APD, it may help to use clipart to make colourful flash cards to reinforce what you are practising, such as an image showing a child putting up their hand. It will help the child to identify with the process if they help with choosing the clipart.

- For a young child or one who may feel embarrassment, lack confidence or not want to appear different, making a reversible card with faces or other symbols can help. It can be used discreetly in school, with the teacher's permission and cooperation. When the teacher goes around the class, your child can place the card on their desk showing how they feel at that time. The card could show a happy face on one side to show that they understand and do not need help, or a sad face on the other to indicate that they don't understand and are struggling or need help. Then, as they grow more confident and comfortable asking for help, they will begin to put up their hand, which should be encouraged (this practice will certainly need to be in place before they leave primary school).

- A child with APD and/or other sensory processing difficulties will need sensory breaks during the day (in a quiet place, to avoid sensory overload), so it is important that they have a way to indicate when this is needed. A similar card can help, with an agreed image to show the teacher that the child needs a break from the classroom.

- Another area in which a child with APD will need to self-advocate is in the use of an FM system (if they have been recommended one). They will need to be able to remind the teacher to use it and to tell them if it isn't working correctly, for example if the batteries have run out. At primary level, this is more straightforward because they usually deal with fewer teachers than at secondary, where they can have a different teacher for each lesson, so they will need to repeat the process every time. Again, rehearsal of standard phrases that they can use will help, or an appropriate flash card.

- It can be very useful for a younger child with APD to have an opportunity to explain to their teacher and classmates what APD entails and how it affects them. It will take confidence for a child to do this, and it should only be attempted if they are happy to do so. You can help them to prepare a short description with flash cards that they can use to practise beforehand, and then take with them to read on the day. A transcript for the teacher would be useful in case your child gets confused, or nerves get the better of them. Some schools will allow a parent to accompany their child, for added confidence and to prompt or intervene if needed.

- Self-advocacy with their friends can follow on from this, and this is another essential practice that should be encouraged. Letting a close friend or circle of friends know about their coping strategies, how they like to receive information and what helps them as an individual should be encouraged from an early age. It is hoped that a good friend might also act as an advocate. When your child is in sensory overload and needs a break, they can just withdraw into themselves and not be able to ask. A friend who notices and does so for them is invaluable.

However, both parents and teachers need to remember that it is common for a child with APD to mis-process what was said or asked of them, and they may not know it has happened. They would therefore not be aware of the need to verify it.

> ...it's something we are working on...but he often doesn't realize he's missed something or misunderstood which makes it harder... he really doesn't want to stand out. (Parent of a child aged 9 with Spatial Processing Disorder)

Bullying

A common factor among children with APD (like any disability), and one of the most difficult to deal with, is their vulnerability to feelings of low self-esteem and self-confidence. Their vulnerability can be like a magnet to bullies, who are quick to pick up on a child's weaknesses. The bullying will only serve to echo and seemingly validate the child's own doubts and fears, which, when emphasized by a tormentor's verbal taunts and insults, can quickly lead to feelings of hopelessness and frustration. If you get called stupid often enough, you start to believe it. This can, in turn, lead to further anxiety, fear and anger. If other children side with the bullies, maybe due to the fear of being the next target, the child with APD and other disabilities can lose the few friends (or maybe the only friend) they have and quickly become ostracized by their peers. It is a downward spiral that must be stopped as early as possible.

Any suspected issues of victimization should be raised as soon as possible with the class teacher, SENCo and head teacher. This situation requires them to have advocacy skills too, even to tell a parent about it, let alone a teacher. Encouraging open discussion at home can help and raising the topic occasionally in case they have been bullied and cannot verbalize it. Every school must have a policy to deal with bullying: ask for a copy and make sure that the school follows it. Don't let them label your child a victim because of their disability: it is not a forgone conclusion that vulnerable children will be picked on, and labelling the child as a victim only adds to their misery. It may even imply to them that they are somehow to blame.

> ...she doesn't even realize that the nasty things friends say to her all the time is actually bullying. (Parent of a child aged 12 with APD)

Erring on the side of caution in order to protect bullies may occur, and it is understandable that they will need help, too, for whatever makes them treat other children in that way. But the safety of all the children at the school must come first.

Bullying can take many forms; among children I have found that it is usually physical, verbal or emotional. Each is as damaging as the other, and all need addressing equally and swiftly, for the sake of both the physical and emotional wellbeing of the child who is being bullied. Every child has a right to feel safe at school, and it is the school's responsibility to make sure that they are safe. However, any bullying that occurs outside school is not deemed the responsibility of the school. This is a police matter and should always be reported to them.

A link to the world

Remember that, whatever the age of your child, until they are old enough, practised enough or have the confidence, a parent is normally their only advocate, often their link to the outside world. It can be a scary place for our children when they don't fully understand what's going on. As well as being their parent, we are their translator and warrior. They need to find their voice, know what they need to communicate with the world and how to ask for it, and fight for their right to receive it. As parents, we must be knowledgeable, prepared and resilient, and eventually, so must they. We need to boost their confidence at every opportunity, encourage them to practise these skills at home, where they usually feel safest. We must teach them to do all these things for themselves, because, one day, we will not be there. They must find their own voice.

> She never used to put her hand up or ask questions or ask for help; she is learning and growing in confidence...sometimes she will ask for help too. [Her self-advocacy is improving] but she still struggles... (Parent of a child aged 10 with APD)

7

Adjustments

The problems with APD and education

The previous chapters should have provided some insight into the needs of individuals with APD. Many of the problems and strategies used outside school will also apply in education. This chapter describes difficulties experienced by children with APD when learning (hereinafter referred to as 'learner(s)'), and it includes strategies to help. (These also apply to adult learners with APD.) What follows is a brief summary of the effects of APD that have already been explained, but with an emphasis on their impact on learning.

Education is a huge part of a child's life – most children spend more time at school than at home. Many also continue into further education and pursue studies as mature students. All education professionals need to know about APD because, as stated previously, it is thought to affect as many as 1 in 10 children (or 2 in 10 adults). It is therefore not unrealistic to assume that all educators might at some time be teaching children or adults with this condition. They may also have family members, friends or colleagues with APD.

---

1 Please note, whenever the word 'processing' is used, this refers to auditory processing; a person with APD may also have visual processing deficits for which other support will be needed, as well as for any other comorbid conditions. This chapter specifically addresses auditory processing and support needed for APD, unless otherwise stated. Readers outside the UK should check on the disability provision regarding education adjustments in their country of residence.

Lack of acceptance of a diagnosis

More diagnosed learners need support and this will increase, but in some local authorities, problems arise for learners when education professionals won't accept a diagnosis of APD or auditory processing difficulties from a specialist testing centre, despite the diagnosis being made by specialist medical professionals using bespoke scientific tests. This reluctance is especially evident when the diagnosis is obtained privately, yet it is just as valid. Where full testing is sought (and it should be), the same tests will be administered by the same testing centres. This failure to accept a diagnosis (either an NHS or private diagnosis) will only serve to prolong the period before that child with APD receives the support they urgently need.

> ...getting school support is a continual fight. (Parent of a teenager aged 14 with APD)

Need for support and the law

Early recognition of a child's APD (and their other comorbid conditions and difficulties) by teachers and Special Educational Needs Coordinators (SENCos) as well as acceptance of the diagnosis and its recommendations are vital to all learners with APD and other conditions. The earlier that adequate tailored support is put in place, the greater the number of children who are likely to succeed and gain qualifications.

Supporting a child with APD or other additional needs via reasonable accommodations by any member of school or local authority staff is not a choice; it is a *legal obligation*. The same applies to the provision of necessary equipment and software as reasonable adjustments.

If you think a learner might have APD

Only a parent can seek a diagnosis and only a specialist in audiovestibular medicine is qualified to diagnose APD, but teachers are in a prime position to identify a child who displays symptoms. Anyone who thinks that APD is suspected should mention it to the child's parent or guardian, and refer them to the APD Support UK website for information on APD and how to seek referral, plus access to support.[2]

APD and learning difficulties

APD is not a learning difficulty itself, but it can cause them in many learners as a result of their difficulties in processing, auditory memory and communication. The difficulties can appear like those experienced by Hearing Impaired (HI) learners, but those are mitigated when the HI learner is given hearing aids – they can then hear speech, but their understanding of what they hear is not impaired. A person with APD can normally hear perfectly well, but cannot understand what they hear because their brain cannot process it efficiently. This has a huge impact on learning. HI children can also have APD, making it harder to identify. If a child's learning does not improve when their hearing is improved, APD might be present and full testing is needed.

Inconsistent effects of APD

APD is also random and intermittent in its effects, which leads to further confusion for a learner (and their teachers). There can be good days and bad, and a child with APD should always be fully supported as if they were having a bad day, because neither they, their teachers nor their parents will be able to tell how much their APD is affecting them at any given time.

The child with APD cannot rely on what they have heard to be accurate, even when it might be; it's like a faulty lightbulb flickering on and off, and fatigue, tiredness and stress can make it worse, leading to failure of coping strategies and all of these can reduce their ability to learn. For a child with APD in an education situation, mis-processing an instruction and arguing that what they believed was said was true can lead to a teacher mistakenly assuming that the learner is being wilful, defiant or rude, when this is not the case. We instinctively believe what our brain is telling us, but children's brains with APD let them down, causing repeated instances of discord and distress in so many situations.

---

2   https://apdsupportuk.yolasite.com

As a result, the learner with APD may frequently doubt themselves and ask a lot of questions to ensure that what they heard was correct; this is not an attempt to be disruptive. This inconsistency is also one reason why educators find it hard to believe that a child has APD, maybe because they confuse it with permanent hearing loss, which is constant. A child with APD is not malingering when they appear to understand speech one minute and not the next. It is exactly what is happening. This can occur randomly throughout the day, every day. Every child is affected uniquely, so even if a teacher knows or has taught a child with APD, others will need different support to accommodate the child's unique APD profile. Glue ear can cause similar effects to APD due to intermittent hearing loss and can lead to APD in some children. (These children are also legally entitled to school support for this equally valid medical condition with a similarly huge impact on learning.)

Comorbidities

Learners with APD will also have any number of other potential conditions and difficulties that might affect learning – it can coexist with anything or everything. Education professionals also need to know about, look out for and support all their comorbidities.

APD can exacerbate other coexisting learning difficulties, especially where there are other existing conditions that APD can impact on (and vice versa). The effects of learning on each child with APD will depend on their individual APD difficulties, their severity, comorbid conditions and ability to use effective coping strategies. It never goes away; they just find alternative ways of getting around it and manage the best they can. A learner who will always need a wheelchair can get around, but never walk; similarly, a learner with APD must make do with the help of whatever tools they can find. In my experience, even one auditory processing difficulty can have a huge impact on a learner's education (as can even minor hearing loss without the use of a hearing aid, which also needs school support).

Awareness from education professionals

Learners can have a very difficult time at school when teachers (and other learners) don't know about APD, don't believe they have it or don't understand its effects and the need for support. Luckily, more teachers are aware of APD these days and are willing and eager to help, although sadly, the following scenarios still unfortunately occur too often. An education professional who might act in this way is guilty of disability discrimination and in some cases, harassment or bullying:

- Learners with APD are called lazy (by teachers as well as other learners) and made to feel stupid, although APD does not affect intelligence. The neurological damage causing APD means that they simply don't understand what to do; slow processing can also lead to slow working.

- Learners with APD might ask repeatedly for help, in vain. Without acknowledging the effects of APD, the teacher expects that (given their age and/or intellectual capacity) they should be able to understand what they have been told and complete their work accordingly, they should need no help and are time-wasting. With the effects of APD on learning, it's likely that learners with APD haven't fully processed the questions or instructions given, or even the information that they are based on. When other learners are halfway through a required task, learners with APD still don't know what to do and haven't even started. That learner might not have even understood the topic because, for them, the explanation had gaps and vital words were lost. New vocabulary can make no sense. If they think they are just words that they *should* know, they may waste valuable time trying to make sense of them, maybe guessing and trying to fit familiar words with similar sounds into the wrong context. This can cause further confusion and lead to them missing or misinterpreting sections of explanation or instruction.

- Constantly misunderstanding what is said in class can lead to other problems, too, such as if the learner mistakenly processes a negative instruction and does what they were asked not to do, for example, '*don't* call out', '*don't* stand up'. The '*don't*' might not have registered. Missing or mis-processing just one word can totally change the meaning of a phrase or sentence.

- The teacher might think that the learner with APD is choosing to be difficult, and decide that they have a 'behaviour problem'.

An unhelpful and unwarranted label like that tends to stick. Reprimands follow, even punishments like detention or extra work, and unfinished work might be sent home; more self-esteem and confidence are also chipped away. The child has a disability, not a behaviour problem.

- Learners with APD often cannot verbalize their thoughts or feelings, so the sense of injustice can build up, hidden inside. Situations like this destroy a child's love of learning, their self-esteem and their confidence.

- Even when a learner with APD is having a good day or time of day, and they *did* understand the relevant topic and the questions asked, they still might not be able to understand the inferences or nuances of the questions, depending on the type of difficulties they might have.

- A learner who is given a string of questions verbally might not be able to process them all. They might process the first and/or the last one, or none of them, and not get what they process in the correct order.

- At any age, it is natural for a learner to ask their classmates for help, especially if help is refused by the teacher or they are too afraid to ask for it, or they have been ridiculed for asking previously. They may then get into trouble for talking or bothering others who are working (while they themselves may not have even started the work). Even if the teacher doesn't notice, their classmates might become tired of being interrupted. This can lead to criticism for not being able to do the work, or even being bullied or ostracized by their classmates:

He gets told off for asking questions. (Parent of a child aged 10 with APD)

- If their requests for help are constantly ignored and they are just seen as a nuisance or criticized for asking (which is disability discrimination), the learner with APD might stop asking altogether and their work will be left undone or incomplete, ultimately affecting their progress and their grades.

...the first time she requested handouts as it was on her ILP [Individual Learning Plan], her teacher (in secondary) embarrassed her in front of the class by saying 'You've had nothing wrong with your brain from September until now, so why now is there something wrong with your brain?' This crushed her. (Parent of a child aged 12 with APD)

- If a learner cannot cope and has an outburst in class, it is seen a self-fulfilling prophecy of bad behaviour and a lack of self-control or immaturity, when it is, in fact, a cry for help from an unsupported learner for whom the pressure has become too much.

Underestimated academic level and poor expectations

The ability of a learner with APD can be underestimated because they fall further and further behind their peers. Their intelligence is not affected by APD. If the teacher recognizes their ability, they may be constantly in trouble for not achieving, for incomplete work, or pushed to their limits trying to maintain their grades or catch up with their peers. Or the opposite occurs – they are not expected to achieve anything and their ability is wasted.

The learner with good natural coping strategies might fare better; they can manage to appear average when they are capable of far more. They can maintain a situation whereby they are scraping by, so their teachers are satisfied that they are meeting the required targets, and no one sees how stressed and anxious they are (and that they are way below what they should be achieving). But average is not what should be expected of any learner; the target should be to support them to work to the best of their ability. Learners with APD can fall through the cracks.

She is not less able; she is very able and just needs to be taught in a different way...they underestimated her potential as they didn't support her in the correct way. They sat her by less able, disruptive children at the front (sometimes) and then wondered why she failed to concentrate. They gave her work that was too easy... If they had done as asked and...checked she understood the work, they would have realized she was more than capable – she just hadn't understood what she needed to do. (Parent of a child aged 11 with auditory processing difficulties)

Dual exceptionalities

If a learner appears bright despite having learning difficulties or appears to be struggling despite being bright, they may be what is known as 'dual exceptionalities': bright or gifted learners who also have learning difficulties.

Many learners with APD are gifted visual-spatial learners. These learners with APD and other difficulties need specific support. They could have a photographic or eidetic memory or other amazing compensatory gifts in different specific areas, like a savant (although they might not also have Autism). They will know that they are capable of so much more than their difficulties allow them to achieve.

Sometimes the happy ignorance of not knowing one's potential is a blessing, but not so for these learners. They might set themselves impossibly high goals that their intellect demands but that their difficulties render unattainable, all of which increases their feelings of failure and lowers their self-esteem. Or they might eventually come to think they are as stupid as others say they are, and lose all confidence in themselves and in their abilities.

Dual exceptionalities learners can easily be missed, leaving them without support for either their additional needs or their ability. Both aspects need addressing. The gifts might go unnoticed unless they are tested by an Educational Psychologist, because the learner with APD simply appears as average, and no one looks any further. Their results will show a pattern of both very high and very low scores, but they will come out with an average total score. They might be treated as average and overlooked, believed to be achieving satisfactorily, when they are, in fact, failing miserably to meet their potential. The low scores are clues to their additional needs and should be investigated accordingly; similarly, their high scores indicate their strengths. With the right combination of support, these learners can meet their full potential instead of just pottering along. Some learners can mask their high intelligence or gifts and their difficulties. However, struggling with both aspects without support means that they can be under double the pressure (or more, considering any comorbid conditions). Under no circumstances should these children be accelerated without adequate support for both aspects.

People have assumed he is not bright as he struggles to understand. (Parent of a child aged 9 with Spatial Processing Disorder)

Sensory overload and regular breaks

No matter what their type of difficulties, their severity and any coexisting conditions, making sense of what they hear and maintaining coping strategies can be exhausting. Fatigue then adversely affects processing and their natural coping strategies are less effective. Learners with APD therefore need breaks during lessons to avoid sensory overload. Some teachers view this as unnecessary, but a learner in sensory overload will not be able to learn. Their brain will be like a saturated sponge and no more information can be absorbed; it is like their brain is a PC in 'sleep' mode. They cannot control it and may even be unaware that their brain has effectively switched off.

Speech can sound like gibberish and they might not process or understand any more information that day, or retain what they might have managed to process and retain. The breaks are to avoid this happening. Many children with APD suffer from headaches due to noise or stress and/or processing, which can also include stress migraines. If they say they have a headache, this is not an excuse to get out of doing something. If a child has recurring headaches, I would recommend suggesting to parents that they seek referral for their child to a paediatrician, to find the cause.

They will be better able to process at different times of the day when they are less tired, or in subjects or situations where they feel less stressed or anxious. Processing is always poor at these times, and can easily lead to sensory overload because the brain is busy dealing with the effects of these situations and coping strategies suffer as a result, even if they are automatic. Reducing anxiety wherever possible can help.

When in sensory overload, a learner can 'zone out' in class and take nothing in. It is as if their brain switches off but they will usually become aware again if their name is called or their arm is touched gently. They cannot help it and may be unaware when it is happening.

If a learner cannot be roused in this way, they might be having an absence seizure (also known as a petit mal seizure), which is not related to APD, but is one of any other comorbid conditions that might possibly coexist. They may appear motionless, stop talking suddenly or flutter their eyelids. They are usually unaware that this seizure is happening or has happened. This is different to a convulsion; no convulsing will occur. They should be left where they are to come around on their own, but a responsible adult should monitor them and record any movements in order to inform their parents (in case they are unaware that their child has this condition). The parents should be requested to take the child to the GP/family doctor for further investigation. Urination can sometimes occur involuntarily, and this should be dealt with discreetly when the seizure is over. A child with absence seizures can also suffer from sensory overload and might 'zone out' for that reason too.

Unfinished work and distraction tactics

Unsupported learners with APD and other difficulties are often kept in to finish work at break or lunchtime, but with no extra help or explanation given, they would still be unable to complete the task. They will have missed their time to relax, de-stress and get some fresh air and receive the benefit of a sensory break This can continue and escalate, leading to being kept in the next day or the day after until the work is done, and they are still unable to do it.

A learner who cannot understand or finish work might act up or play the fool. in order to divert attention from the fact that they cannot cope. They might be embarrassed and not even want the teacher to know, and feel that even punishment is better than anyone finding out about their condition or potential failure. In my experience of working with learners with emotional and behavioural difficulties, a learner will not misbehave without an underlying reason. These children need help, not punishment.

I have seen comments such as 'you must complete your work in class' and 'less than 60% on spelling tests is unacceptable'. (Parent of a teenager aged 14 with APD)

131

Safety issues

Some learners with APD can block or 'tune out' background noise in order to concentrate. This is an advantage, but it can also cause problems, leading to missed information or additional instructions. It can even pose a danger if they block out sound so much that they don't hear or process fire alarms, for example. Teachers should always ensure that learners with APD don't miss or mis-process instructions where there are safety implications, such as in sports, swimming or using science equipment, instructions should be given in writing. On school outings, be aware, too, that learners with APD might not be able to tell the direction of approaching vehicles or their distance away. Some learners with APD may also need to be woken up each day because they don't process alarm clocks or phone alarms due to blocking all sound (like when they are working) in order to sleep. These issues should be discussed with parents before they sign the consent form for residential trips if they haven't already raised them, and appropriate safety precautions put in place.

Teenage stress and transition to secondary school

Secondary school teachers and other education professionals are used to dealing with teenagers, but may not have come across a teenager with APD (or they may not have been aware of it). There are specific issues that arise for the teenager with APD at school that need to be addressed.

Moving to secondary school raises new problems for which many children are unprepared. There is more work, harder work and more pressure to perform and achieve. This is worse for children with APD:

- Moving to secondary school with so many new teachers' and learners' voices to get used to can cause great difficulty, due to unfamiliar voice patterns. These will take time to get used to.

- SENCos need to make all teachers aware of the learner's difficulties and they all need to read that information, or the learner will be forced to try to explain in every new class why they can't do things and receive unfair punishments for what isn't their fault because the teachers don't understand or accept their explanations, and see them as excuses.

- As secondary schools are bigger than primary schools, even walking between classes there is no sensory break when traversing noisy corridors, with everyone speaking at once. There are also bigger classes and more classes, many more people making more background noise. Breaktimes and lunchtime can be a nightmarish cacophony of sound and a quiet space must be provided for them to avoid sensory overload.

- For a learner with APD in an education situation, mis-processing an instruction and arguing that what they believed was said was true can lead to a teacher mistakenly assuming that they are being wilful, defiant or rude, when this is not the case. We instinctively believe what our brain is telling us, but these children's brains let them down, causing repeated instances of discord and distress in so many situations. These situations need understanding, not punishment.

- A teenager with APD and other additional needs might be reluctant to accept support, or embarrassed to appear different to their peers. They might start to refuse it at some point from self-consciousness. Discretion is needed so as not to make them stand out, as refusal of support can seriously affect their education.

The effects of hormonal changes during adolescence can be enormous and worse for a child with APD because they also affect processing (see Chapter 9). All of this, coupled with getting lost and trying to make new friends, can be enormously stressful, apart from any work-related difficulties and a possible lack of school support. If a teenager or even a young child is displaying symptoms of stress, anxiety, self-harm, addiction or any other mental health or behavioural concerns, their parents should be advised on how to seek appropriate support from a mental health professional.

The importance of school support

APD can lead to learners having huge gaps in their knowledge and it puts their education seriously at risk, especially in subjects that build on prior knowledge, like maths or science. It is like a wall with shaky foundations and bricks missing; ultimately it will all come crashing down.

Listen to the learners in your class who ask for help; always provide it, even if you think they don't need it or are time-wasting. Believe parents who say their child is not coping. Educate yourselves about APD and how it manifests, and help parents to understand it, if they haven't noticed the signs. Advise them to seek a full diagnosis, support their requests for adjustments, and make sure that they are implemented in your classroom. Learners naturally want to learn, but that enthusiasm and enjoyment will gradually fade away in those who are left to fend for themselves. Children with invisible disabilities are not invisible. They all have a right to an appropriate education.

Ways to help

The support needed by a learner with APD and other additional needs allows them to do what neurotypical learners do naturally and automatically, leaving them better able to learn and perform at a level appropriate to their ability. The rest of this chapter includes examples of suitable strategies, reasonable adjustments and equipment that will allow learners with APD to do that. Every learner will need different combinations of them, or they could need different strategies.

Strategies to avoid distraction

Teachers often tell learners with APD that they're not listening or that they need to pay attention. But they *do* listen: it's understanding what they are listening to that causes them problems. Distractibility can also occur due to other senses being heightened to compensate. (This should not be confused with Attention Deficit Hyperactivity Disorder, ADHD.) Strategies to avoid distraction include the following:

- Learners with APD should sit where auditory and visual distractions are avoided or reduced. This should not be near windows, open doors or next to a chatty classmate.

- They need to sit where they have an optimal view of the teacher and/or whiteboard; despite common recommendations, this might not necessarily be at the front of the class, especially if the teacher likes to walk around the classroom when teaching.

- If an FM (frequency modulation) system (described later) is recommended, it must be provided, and its use supported and encouraged in class. Its importance cannot be underestimated for a learner who needs one – it can mean the difference between learning and not learning.

Reducing background noise

Background noise can be a big problem for learners with APD. It makes processing speech harder and can also add to distractibility. This should be addressed in the classroom. Adjustments to reducing background noise can also help other learners to concentrate better and be less distracted by ambient noise.

Research has shown that noise pollution in schools can even be above legal limits, causing auditory fatigue, affecting concentration for both learners and teachers, and becoming detrimental to every learner's performance. Those who also have Hyperacusis (hyperacute hearing or sound sensitivity) as well as APD find that it makes processing more difficult. They can even suffer from ear pain. Therefore, classroom noise should always be kept to a minimum. A quiet room might be devoid of ambient noise, but learners with APD who also have Hyperacusis may also hear sounds a long way away.

Noise can be reduced in several simple ways:

- Classroom noise can be muffled with carpets or rugs. A less costly option is to provide covers for the bottoms of chair and table legs to lessen the sound when they are being moved.

- Put posters on the wall as well as paintings and cork boards with pictures or notices on. None of these costs a great deal, and all are reasonable adjustments.

- Support the use of FM systems and other assistive technology that can block background noise.

- The use of ear defenders and provision of a quiet place to work is beneficial, especially to those with sound sensitivity.

- Working in small groups, to a maximum of four, can minimize sound during group work.

- Learners with APD should be provided with a quiet place to work, or given ear defenders or musicians' ear plugs to block sound when concentrating, and also to use in the hall for assemblies, the dining hall at lunchtime and outside during breaks (including sensory breaks).

- There should be no music playing during lessons (apart from during music lessons).

- Keeping a quiet, orderly classroom can help enormously when you are teaching and learners are working; also minimize noise when learners work in groups. Make sure that only one learner speaks at a time.

Pre-learning and pre-printed notes

A learner with APD should never have to write notes down, either by taking dictation or copying from a book or whiteboard. I cannot stress enough that the notes that the learner with APD makes can regularly be incorrect or incomplete. This is likely to happen because of the nature of APD, with its intermittent processing, memory and sequencing difficulties and other problems. Those notes are often all that they are left to work from at home and are used to revise for tests and examinations. Not ensuring that they have accurate notes can mean that a learner with APD is set up to fail, at every stage of their education, and this can affect other learners too. Their future depends on the teacher making sure that the notes they learn from are correct.

Dictated notes rely on accurate auditory processing and auditory memory, which will be lacking. Copying is a complex set of skills, all of which affect memory and processing ability. It is not easy – copying from the board involves looking, reading, retaining that visual information by transferring it to their working memory and then looking away from the board and writing it down. The teacher might be talking at the same time, which the learner is trying to process too, classmates might be making a noise, or there may be other distractions. Learners with APD might also not be able to listen or process speech while they are copying or writing, so any additional verbal information or instructions can be missed. Many children with APD also have VPD to contend with, or added writing difficulty. Therefore:

- Pre-printed notes should be provided automatically for all lessons, including any verbal information, anything that might be dictated or that they might be expected to copy from the whiteboard.

- They will also need printed lists for each subject or topic, containing any new vocabulary (which, as we have seen, can cause them a lot of difficulty). Meanings should be included.

- They will need a sheet showing the common, subject-specific lists of words that mean the same thing (for example, for maths this might be 'add, plus', 'minus, less' or 'multiply, times lots').

- Also essential are sheets with explanations for cue words in instructions letting them know what is being asked, such as 'find, list, describe, explain'. These might mean the same to some learners.

- The notes must be given to them as pre-teaching, at least a day before the lesson is due to be delivered, so that they can familiarize themselves with both the topic and new words. The topic (and the vocabulary that should be listed with explanations given in advance) will not then be new to them when they are introduced in class or have no meaning. Trying to decipher additional words for which they do not know the meaning without a familiar context to help them is pointless.

- Any announcements, homework, events and important reminders should be written down as a note to take home or sent via email or text to parents, in case the note becomes lost or left at school.

- Pre-printed notes must already be in place by the time they leave primary school. If not, secondary schools and institutions of further education still have an opportunity to implement them as a reasonable adjustment.

...she finds it difficult to remember her timetable...[she] will often forget what homework was set if she hasn't written it down. (Parent of a teenager aged 14 with APD)

Supporting learners in this way means that they can be less stressed in class, focus on listening and trying to process, and gain as much as they are able during each lesson. Without the added pressure of worrying about making notes, they will be free to learn and can revisit the topic at home later, to fill in the gaps. Even if they have written correct information, this doesn't mean that they understand the topic – they could have been so focused on writing it down that their processing of the meaning is lost.

This type of pre-teaching and note provision is essential and should be provided from as early as applicable in their education. Learners with APD, like other learners, should not be penalized for not being able to take notes. This is not what is being taught or tested, and it just adds to their confusion and the possibility of sensory overload. Other learners can also benefit from note provision, especially those with writing difficulties.

Homework and differentiation

Homework can cause many difficulties for a child with APD and other additional needs:

- Learners with APD need to be left to rest each evening. They cannot do this if they are working until bedtime, especially if they are in sensory overload after a busy school day. They also need time for the brain to process what they have learned at school, so they can be ready for the next day. They must be allowed to do this in order to build on it the following day.

- Delayed processing often takes place at night when the brain is rested; these children need plenty of sleep and rest without noise, in the evening and at weekends. Homework detracts from this process, leaving them unrefreshed the next day, which affects them taking in new information, further compounding their difficulties.

- Homework that takes a neurotypical learner half an hour might take them hours, if they can do it at all.

- Most of the time is spent with parents trying to make them do the homework, leaving less room for families to just spend time together. It also puts added pressure on parents to insist that the learner completes their homework in order to prevent them getting a detention, often not realizing that doing so is damaging to the learner and to the parent–child relationship.

- Some parents will complete the work for the learner to avoid them getting into trouble at school, but they do their child a disservice, because teachers need to see that the work is too hard and too much. The teacher should then differentiate it, or put more support in place if needed. If they think the child is coping, nothing will be done.

- Homework is not legally compulsory in the UK. The need to set it should be examined very carefully; it can easily be disapplied. It is up to each school to decide their policy. Only when it is necessary to the child's education should it be set for a learner with APD and/other additional needs.

- Homework is set as reinforcement of topics taught at school. If a learner has understood the topic, they might not even need homework as reinforcement.

- If a learner receives pre-printed notes, they will have understood the topic far better, and homework may not be needed. Homework is not the only method to ensure understanding, which should be done in class.

- If it is deemed essential, as with pre-teaching, homework should only be used to reinforce what was learned in class, not to introduce a new topic. Pre-printed notes should be used in place of that. No learner, even those without APD, should ever be expected to answer questions or write about something they haven't already been taught in class.

- Homework should always be explained in class first, then provided in writing for learners with APD (rather than just telling the class to 'Read Chapter 2 and do the first five examples on page 67'). Without written enforcement, they might misprocess or forget the chapter, the number of examples and/or the page number. If left to write it down themselves, they can so easily do the same, then be told off the next day and have wasted time working on the wrong thing, and then be expected to do the correct homework the next night, along with new homework.

- Any homework that must be set for a learner with APD and/or other difficulties must be suitably differentiated to the needs and ability of that learner. **SMART** targets[3] should be set, as follows:

  - Specific, easy to read: first state what the goal of the homework should be, which topic needs to be practised or learned, and then add the homework itself.

  - Measurable: state how many examples are needed.

  - Achievable: challenge the learner, but set the work at an attainable level.

  - Relevant: the work should be personal and relevant to the learner, in order to be more engaging.

  - Timely: to be completed within a set amount of time. When that time is up, no matter how much is completed, they should stop. The amount of work set should roughly be enough to fill that time for someone at their level and ability.

- 2E learners should also be set differentiated work that will challenge them, not additional work, or work that will take longer. 2E learners might not need more than three examples, or (for some reason) it can confuse them.

> We made changes to when and how we complete homework, using time limits agreed with school, ensure that homework doesn't become a battle and accept that he is over-tired and very 'processed-out' from school. (Parent of a child aged 10 with APD)

A learner who goes to school happy and relaxed, having rested well the night before and understood the homework that they were set (or has no homework to worry about because it was understood at school) will feel a sense of achievement and process information much better than

---

3   For any learner with additional needs, or 2E learners, differentiation and the use of SMART targets should also be applied to their classwork.

the learner who is exhausted and stressed, yet again having experienced failure.

APD and types of memory

There are different types of memory, and in my experience, all of these can be affected in some way by APD.

AUDITORY MEMORY

This is simply remembering what we hear. It is the type of memory that is *directly* affected by APD, but APD can affect other types of memory indirectly too.

Some people use short-term and working memory interchangeably, and there is some debate about this. But I agree with the view that they are not the same thing, and I will explain why. They are separate stages, and this is how the stages progress:

- First, we process what we are hearing/seeing/feeling and remember it for about 2 minutes while we decide what to do with it: this is short-term memory (when dealing with auditory information, it is referred to as short-term auditory memory).

- We might then reject it as not worth remembering and erase it from our memory.

- Or we hold it and use it; this is called working memory, because this is where we work with the information.

- Or we do nothing with it at that time and simply store it away for later in the long-term memory (when dealing with auditory information, it is referred to as long-term auditory memory).

One stage should flow easily on to the other if the information is not forgotten, mis-processed, confused/garbled, or has information missing. But all of this can tend to happen in a person with APD. If part or all of the auditory information is incorrect or incomplete at the start (due to APD), these processes will not work efficiently. Also, what you commit to the long-term memory is what will be there when you try to access or remember and use it later. Like a computer, the brain can only recall what we put into it. Furthermore, the person with APD will not even realize that the information they stored is faulty. Quite a lot of auditory information can also be discarded as nonsense, because it makes no sense as a result of the gaps due to the APD.

If people have Visual Processing Disorder (VPD), the same applies to visual information, and someone with APD may also have VPD (and have visual memory difficulties to contend with as well).

APD can also affect processing of speech and sound, which means that it can also affect musical recognition and recall.

RECALL OF INFORMATION FROM LONG-TERM MEMORY

For recall of information to function properly, the person must have efficiently and adequately fulfilled these three requirements:

- Encoding: this involves changing stimuli into a useable form so the information can be transferred into storage. This is just like a computer where information punched into the keyboard is transformed into an electronic code that the computer can store. In a person with APD, the auditory information encoded may be incomplete or incorrect due to not having been processed correctly or only part of it being processed or understood.

- Storage: this is the retention of information in our long-term memory, from which it can later be retrieved, in the same way as a computer. In a person with APD, due to delayed processing from the brain focusing on processing or understanding information before saving it (especially if it is incorrect, incomplete and makes no sense) information might not be stored properly, or only part of it is stored, or all of it is rejected as nonsense because it makes no sense (following the use/save/reject function of working memory). This is just like what happens to faulty computer files.

- Retrieval: this is the process of recovering information from the long-term memory. We retrieve information via cues or prompts, which is like how computers retrieve information. What has not been stored correctly cannot be retrieved easily, and information that has not been encoded or stored properly will make little or no sense due to being incorrect or incomplete. Also, the person with APD will not be aware that what they have processed, stored and remembered is incorrect or incomplete. It is therefore important

142

to use methods to help them to retain new information, especially if the learner has APD or other difficulties affecting memory.

The actions of our memory can be a seamless process in people without processing difficulties. But as you see, it can cause several problems when they have APD (or VPD). Therefore, multisensory input is so important to help people with these difficulties to remember things. Having more in-roads from the other senses to back up what is remembered in the short-term, working and long-term memory can go a long way to helping them to make sense of it all.

Supporting music and languages

Many learners with APD are very capable in music; it is thought to be processed by a different part of the brain to language and playing an instrument is often recommended these days to help improve processing. However, there are also those who find this subject extremely difficult as APD can also affect the processing of sound, affecting the recognition of tone and pitch, remembering notes correctly and so on.

Some languages are easier for some learners to master than others, so a choice should be provided. It can also be difficult enough for a learner with APD to process the sounds of their own language let alone master a different one. But there are those with APD who are very good at languages, even excelling at them.

Using more visual and kinaesthetic methods can help with both subjects; in fact, all subjects (and learners) can benefit from multisensory teaching. Learners with APD should be allowed to be disapplied from these subjects (as well as any other subjects with which they have a great deal of difficulty). They can then have more energy for the subjects they excel at, or at least have a better chance of obtaining a qualification, as subjects that put them in a further position of failure adds more stress and anxiety and increases exhaustion, and these can adversely affect their essential personal coping strategies and learning ability overall.

OTHER DIFFICULTIES

It is also worth noting that learners with APD can find either high- or low-pitched voices easier to process and a teacher of that voice range would be very beneficial; wherever possible, this need should be met for each lesson. It can also take time for learners with APD to adapt to processing new voice patterns.

Processing and understanding supply teachers can therefore also cause a great deal of difficulty, especially if this happens often with different teachers. Information must be provided to the supply teacher on the needs of all children with APD (and other additional needs) or they might fail to support them. Anything taught on those days may be lost altogether.

Use of assistive listening technology

Assistive listening technology might be recommended for a learner with APD. When recommended, it is needed and should be provided because it increases the volume and clarity of a teacher's speech when it reaches the learner, and helps them to artificially block background noise. (Please note that these devices only help people with difficulties processing speech in noise and spatial processing difficulty and do *not* improve processing.) Assistive listening technology is not a therapy or a cure, although it is reported to be very helpful in many cases, and allows children better access to learning. But it should not be used all the time, or as a replacement for developing coping strategies. It is also not the only support needed by a child with APD.

> ...school did provide this. However, they assumed that their job was done at this point. (Parent of a child aged 11 with auditory processing difficulties)

Care should be taken that assistive listening technology is not over-used. It has been reported that learners can become disoriented and less able to process in noisy environments. With over-use, coping strategies can fail when not using the technology (because the learners have come to rely on it). It can take some time for coping strategies to fully return, leaving the learners disorientated and unable to process.

The types of assistive listening technology include the following.

AN FM SYSTEM

The teacher wears a microphone linked to a headset worn by the learner or ear buds, as preferred (or to a speaker on the learner's desk, which may not be as effective). What the teacher says is transmitted direct to the learner's ears, therefore reducing background noise, and providing better speech clarity. It only amplifies the teacher's voice, so whole-class questions and responses may still not be heard as clearly. It is quite often recommended by an audiovestibular specialist in their diagnosis report for children with an auditory figure-ground problem (that is, difficulty in processing speech in background noise) or in spatial processing (telling the direction of speech and/or who is speaking, which allows them to process the teacher's voice from all the voices in the room from the one they are supposed to listen to). It is recommended for use in limited situations, such as in the classroom, to help a learner to better access lessons, but not at lunch or during sport where the use of a microphone for just one person is not possible. An FM system can, and should, also be used by a teacher or head teacher in assembly, and where the child has trouble understanding (especially as school halls tend to have an echo, adding to all the usual noise). An FM system also has settings for partnered and group work. Under no circumstances should an FM system be used with only one earphone or earpiece; this can cause damage to dichotic listening and have a further detrimental effect on processing.

An FM system can have varying degrees of success:

- Some learners gain no benefit at all.

- Some learners, especially teenagers, think that using one will set them apart from their peers and fear bullying because they don't want to appear different. They may refuse to use them, although ear buds are more discreet than headphones.

- Secondary school learners must transport the system from class to class and it needs to be set up at the start of each lesson; it may end up being left behind or lost.

- Teachers can also be reluctant to use them.

When considering an FM system, as they are expensive, try to borrow one from a neighbouring school or local authority sensory support team first, for the learner to trial before purchase, as there are different brands, and one might suit one learner over another.

SOUND FIELD SYSTEM

Another similar type of assistive listening technology is a sound field system. This is an amplification system that improves the learning environment for the entire class by improving the sound environment in all classrooms. Designed specifically for speech sounds, these systems similarly enhance speech volume and clarity, although they are neither a treatment nor a cure for APD. A sound field ensures an even distribution of sound from the teacher, the learners and any multimedia equipment. The teacher wears a microphone, the learners wear headsets and speakers are placed around the room.

COMPARING FM AND SOUND FIELD SYSTEMS

A child with hearing loss can link their hearing aid to either an FM system or sound field system. Sound field systems are far more expensive and are usually often only found in schools for Hearing Impaired (HI) children or those with a lot of HI learners, and are usually funded by the providing institution. Schools might decide to install a sound field system to benefit all learners; they can also refuse an FM system where they already have a sound field system in place. A sound field might not benefit some learners, and where it doesn't benefit a learner with APD, an FM system trial should be arranged to see whether it works better for them.

Parents have found that funding for an FM system can be very difficult to obtain. Certain schools and local authority sensory teams refuse to buy them, leaving parents to bear the cost, if they can. But for those children who have trialled an FM system and benefited even slightly from its use, it has to be remembered that it qualifies as a reasonable adjustment under the UK Equality Act 2010, which means that all local authorities have a legal duty to provide them to allow a learner to access the curriculum. A refundable trial should be approved in all cases where recommended by the specialist in their diagnosis report. Funding for equipment that provides reasonable adjustments can also be requested as part of an EHCP (Education, Health and Care Plan), Special Educational Needs (SEN) Statement or Coordinated Support Plan (CSP). (Other countries will have different arrangements.) (See Chapter 10 for information on such systems for adults.)

HEARING AIDS

Some children with speech in noise difficulty/spatial processing difficulty have also been found to benefit from programmable low-gain hearing aids. They work in the same way as FM systems and sound field systems by increasing the volume and reducing background noise, thus improving speech clarity. However, only the more expensive ones from private providers appear to be effective in blocking background noise. Hearing aids are also not routinely recommended in the UK for children without hearing loss, but are being trialled by some hospitals. *They should only be bought and fitted in person from a qualified audiologist (not online) to prevent damage to the child's hearing.*

MOBILE PHONE APPS

Another recently available method that helps some learners with a speech in noise difficulty is an app used with a type of proprietary ear bud via a mobile phone or tablet. This method is a lot cheaper, but some schools will not allow a mobile phone in class, even as an assistive listening device, although there are also teachers who have recommended this method. The system can be managed by the learner, with no teacher participation.

Please note, with all these devices, however, some children with APD and Hyperacusis have developed headaches after wearing headphones for long periods, probably due to the increased amount of speech they can now hear.

As with everything APD-related, learners are all different, and must find what works for them as individuals.

APD and difficulties in producing written work

Learners with APD and other additional needs often have problems in producing written work, and these should be investigated. They also need strategies to help them. If a learner has problems getting their thoughts onto paper, there can be several barriers to overcome.

For some learners, the mechanics of writing things down can cause problems. This might be due to Dyspraxia or Developmental Coordination Disorder (DCD) or joint problems, an unusual grip, pain on writing and so on. For these learners, typing can help, as can provision of a scribe. Those who need to use a laptop should be provided with this as a reasonable adjustment and given lessons in its use for classwork, homework (if applicable), for tests and examinations. The learner should be allowed to type out a draft first, which just contains their responses, essay or coursework. They should then be given extra time to complete the work, including a re-draft with attention to grammar and spelling. Recording their work and typing it up (if the type and severity of their APD allows them to process what is recorded) might help, or the use of speech to text software (although it can take time to get used to the voice of the user, and this needs to be practised).

When the learner has correct and complete information to work from, an appropriate method of recording it and they still can't provide a good response, other issues might be to blame.

A learner with APD might simply have not processed or understood the question or essay topic correctly, so questions should also be presented in writing or typed up.

Focusing on spelling, grammar and spacing are needed, as well as the demands for neat writing.

The learner may take longer to write things down (or type), so they may not have time to finish their work. With VPD, they can also have difficulty in filling in tables. Extra time should be allowed.

If the problem is around writing long replies to questions, it may be an organizational issue because the learner might have problems organizing their thoughts due to word retrieval, or simply because APD has meant that their notes are incorrect or incomplete, which is unfortunately often the case, and they may not even be aware of it (although, as mentioned earlier, pre-printed notes and vocabulary lists should be provided in order to prevent this). If replying to a question, memory can be an issue.

Sometimes people with APD and other difficulties have a problem knowing how much to write or how to pick out the relevant details from the text. Comprehension skills do not always come naturally, and may need to be taught. With learners with additional needs, nothing should be assumed. Learners with VPD, for example, can miss the little words that give meaning to what they are asked to do (or the text that they are reading). For some learners faced with a wall of text to pick out answers from, it can be terrifying, and appropriate differentiation is needed.

Sometimes any learner, even without any difficulties or additional needs, will not be able to tell from the question whether they need to produce a short answer in a sentence or just a long list, a simple response or an explanation, a few words or a paragraph. These things are often covered at GCSE level, late on in the year and usually after the curriculum is finished, as examination skills. But this comes too late for many learners. They need to be taught this early on in their academic career, especially those who are whole picture learners. Some will automatically always produce a response of a few words, maybe a correct but too succinct answer without explanation, and not understand why it was criticized when the answer was right. Others will write pages and still miss the point.

Learners might need to be taught how to find the answers they are asked for, find the information requested in comprehension tasks (using scanning and skimming skills), how to respond appropriately, recognize cue words in questions to work out what is being asked and understand words that mean the same thing. As stated earlier, lists of these words as pre-teaching can help the learner to answer appropriately. Lack of these skills can seriously affect a learner's education.

Creative writing poses its own problems. Planning can be another problem for some learners when producing a piece of free writing – where they should start, what form it should take, how to end it, how to pad out the story, grammar issues, use of similes, metaphors, adjectives, and so on. Planning takes a lot of work, especially for a learner with APD. Mind maps can help some learners, while others don't find them useful. Using printed templates is another method, starting with three boxes for the beginning, middle and end of a story. Some learners haven't even grasped that a story needs this basic format, even by secondary school, because they may never have been taught it. Once they have learned this, more boxes then come, padding the story out, splitting it further into paragraphs. How to describe a person, develop a character, set a scene, plan a plot: all of this might need to be taught. Holding all these ideas in your head is an impossible task for those with a poor working memory, especially if nobody tells them they don't have to, that it's perfectly acceptable to make notes. Visual and hands-on (writing) is particularly helpful to a learner with APD. Word retrieval can be more of a problem if they must just write it out, as in a test, so extra time needs to be given for this (and for planning).

In creative writing, learners can also have a confidence issue about 'doing it wrong'. Most works of fiction have common themes and there is no copyright on ideas (although learners must avoid plagiarism). Quality over quantity should be encouraged, and appropriate differentiation should allow for shorter responses rather than no response at all because the learner is overwhelmed. Learners can learn to write more when they are confident that what they have written is correct. It is common for such learners to be criticized for lack of effort when all they might lack is confidence.

As you can see there are many barriers to writing in different formats and any learner may have more than one. The best way forward is in finding how each learner is affected and helping them to develop ways around the difficulties by whichever methods they need, developing the skills they lack, using assistive technology, accessing scribes, provision of pre-teaching and written notes, and building their confidence.

Preferred learning styles

Every learner should have full access to learning in whichever way works best for them – this is the purpose of education for each of them, according to age, ability and provision of support for all their additional needs. Part of this will depend on their natural (and therefore preferred) learning style.

Because people with APD struggle with understanding verbal communication, they need to learn how they prefer for people to communicate with them (see 'Alternative methods of presenting information'). Learning styles are part of this, to complement their understanding as well as providing revision methods (which might also need to be taught). Children with APD regularly exhibit more visual and kinaesthetic strengths, like HI children:

- Support visual learners by providing written messages or in-structions via notes, texts, email or diagrams. This form of communication can also help those who have difficulty expressing themselves verbally. Using colour is another example, such as, colour-coding or highlighting passages of text to learn.

- Children with difficulties in processing verbal communication might also benefit from writing things down, or having them recorded to replay later at their own pace. Learning Makaton or sign language can also help, but families need to learn them too (and teachers, too, if they don't teach at an HI school and know it already). These strategies can help with visual or tactile learners or those who are both (visual-kinaesthetic learners, also common with APD) and those who struggle with speech. But it is very important that this method should not prevent the child from also practising speaking and listening skills where possible.

- Many children with APD need kinaesthetic input (sensory touch or movement) in order to help them process. This might be swinging on a chair when learning or twirling a pencil. Some even find it helps to pace up and down when talking, to aid focus and remember what they want to say. Fidget toys can help. Schools tend to frown on this type of activity, but it is necessary for some children to be able to process.

- Some children with APD can be auditory learners, which might prove more difficult. Using mnemonics or rhyme, or putting things to music, or revising while listening to music can all be useful.

Multisensory learning and revision

Whatever type of learner your child happens to be, learning and revision should be complemented by the individual sensory methods mentioned above, to provide a multisensory approach that can assist with the learning deficits that can be caused by APD and other difficulties. This route to learning can also aid those with literacy difficulties.

When learning or revising, they should try a combination of activities such as writing things down in point form (kinaesthetic), drawing diagrams or mind maps and highlighting/colouring (visual) plus recording it, and using mnemonics, rhyme or adding music (auditory). Some find listening to music when studying helps (music is processed in a different part of the brain to speech). Some children with APD still find studying or playing music difficult due to problems with rhythm and tone.

There are also other learning styles that you can investigate, and combinations of them, but those mentioned here are the most common.

Other multisensory methods might be using flash cards for each point learned, with a pictorial clue, highlighting words or paragraphs or colour-coding as well as writing in different-coloured gel pens. Anything that allows them to engage other senses as cues to aid memory can be used (particularly things that are visual and hands-on).

Compensatory gifts

These are natural attributes that the children are usually born with. What makes them different also makes them special, especially those who are also gifted or 2E. These gifts can be used to aid learning. For example, some children with APD and other difficulties (such as Autism) can have an eidetic or photographic memory. They might be creative thinkers, finding intricate alternative ways around their difficulties. Such methods of coping should be encouraged, as they are unique to that learner.

Alternative methods of presenting information

Providing an alternative, preferred method of information delivery to replace speech can help with most APD difficulties – confirm with the learner with APD which they prefer. Examples to use, as appropriate, include:

- Written instructions or information, or simple diagrams, sketches or clipart (which can also be used as reinforcement).
- Communication by email rather than by telephone.
- Communication by text rather than by telephone.
- Use of voice to text software or apps on mobile phones.

If speech cannot be avoided:

- Speak at your normal volume, but clearly.
- Attract the learner's attention and face them when you speak so they can lipread and use facial cues and body language; ask if they need something reworded or rephrased.
- Give short explanations using simple language and avoiding unnecessary words.

- Avoid small talk – stick to what you want or need to say.

- Ask one question at a time and allow time for a response.

When teaching any subject, make sure that each stage of learning is completely understood before building on it and that nothing has been missed out or misunderstood. There should be consistent provision of pre-printed notes, subject-specific and new vocabulary, as pre-teaching will help with this.

Remember that a learner with APD might repeat something back to you, word for word. They might say that they have understood and they might think they have, but they may not have understood at all, or they may have missed important facts. Even if they understand, they might not remember.

> I'm not sure if he has strategies...as I'm not sure how much he realizes he's not following things. (Parent of a child aged 9 with Spatial Processing Disorder)

Specific support for individual APD difficulties

These difficulties have already been discussed in Chapter 5, with the emphasis on how to help at home and elsewhere. Education professionals need to know and understand those strategies, too, and the reasons behind them. The difficulties are listed again here and briefly explained, but this time the focus is on how to provide specific support in an education setting.

Considering the unique nature of APD, as well as the compounding effects of so many other difficulties and conditions, each learner with APD a teacher might encounter might have any combination of these difficulties, so they need to know about them all and how to support every learner with APD appropriately to their needs (also taking into account any and all other comorbid difficulties).

These are the most common APD difficulties that can be tested for and form part of the diagnosis, available in the report provided to parents (and given to schools) with recommendations for support. They are explained in simple terms, along with ways to help. These can also be applied to adult learners in further education or training.

AUDITORY MEMORY DIFFICULTY

This is not remembering what was said, which might be a short- or long-term problem (or both):

- Auditory short-term memory difficulty: not remembering what was said a few moments ago. This leads to not being able to respond appropriately to a question that they have not understood, or do what was requested, or doing one or more of a set of directions but not all. Support the learner by providing all verbal information or instruction in writing for them to refer to later, and include images or diagrams where possible as visual reinforcement. A recording can also help. Provide multisensory teaching, and use methods to aid short-term and working memory, providing visual cues that don't involve verbal delivery. Exercises to strengthen auditory memory can help improve this area, such as 'I went to the shop and I bought…' but they will not lead to full remediation. This can also cause problems with aural comprehension.

- Auditory long-term memory difficulty: not remembering what was heard more than a few minutes ago. Again, the person with APD needs a written version or a recording of what was said for them to keep and refer to later. If this is not given, they will not be able to remember it fully or accurately later.

AUDITORY SEQUENCING DIFFICULTY

This is not remembering the correct order of multistep verbal instructions and therefore not being able to carry out a sequence of verbal instructions in the right order. (Long lists of things are difficult enough for someone with APD to understand or remember, let alone in order.) Give instructions one at a time and write them all down as reinforcement. A problem with auditory sequencing can also affect sound blending, reading or spelling.

AUDITORY FIGURE-GROUND DIFFICULTY

This is being unable to process speech in the presence of background noise and not understanding or having sporadic comprehension when there is even low-level background noise. This can lead to problems with processing what a teacher says in class amid ambient noise, or following a conversation with friends when it is noisy, when in a group, or with more than one person speaking at once. Minimizing background noise can help, or chatting in a quiet location; only one person should speak at once. This can be more difficult among young learners who have difficulty with taking turns (and with speaking quietly). Assistive listening technology (as described earlier), if recommended by an audiovestibular specialist, can be vital in the classroom or workplace as a reasonable adjustment, although some types can be costly and must be trialled to find out which option helps most.

SPATIAL PROCESSING DIFFICULTY

This is not being able to tell the direction of the person speaking, which can lead to difficulty knowing which voice to listen to when more than one person is speaking or locating the speaker's voice, especially when it is noisy. Attract the learner's attention and face them when you speak so they can lipread and use facial cues and body language. Ask if they need something reworded or rephrased. Assistive listening technology can help them to know which speaker they need to listen to and locate where they are. This difficulty can also have safety implications if the learner with APD cannot process the direction of approaching vehicles, for example. A teacher or responsible adult should hold their hand while crossing the road when they are little. As they get older, repeatedly reminding them to look both ways a few times before crossing can help with this (and with their independence). This can be a danger for school outings – don't rely on their age as a guideline and don't let them cross roads alone. In time this should become automatic, but for some learners it may not. Diagrams and written explanations are helpful alternatives.

AUDITORY DISCRIMINATION DIFFICULTY

This is having difficulty processing the difference between words or sounds that sound similar, for example, cook/book, goat/coat, or ch/sh, f/v (as they have poor phonemic awareness). A learner with APD can also have problems learning new vocabulary. Poor recognition of speech sounds can cause speech acquisition problems. The learner might be unable to relate phonemes or sounds to the written format or graphemes, which, in some children, affects spelling and/or reading, causing auditory Dyslexia. Speech and language support can help with this, although for a learner with APD, phonics may never work because their brains are not wired to recognize the differences between sounds, and so this cannot be remediated – it can cause extreme distress to make them continue with phonics for that reason. Whole word and multisensory methods for reading and spelling should be used instead, such as flash cards with whole words and pictures as reinforcement, felt letters, letters made from sandpaper, magnetic letters, scented pens and drawing letters in water or sand.

GAP DETECTION DIFFICULTY

This is not processing the gaps between words efficiently, making it hard to separate the words they hear from one another. It means that words can merge as one long sound and speech may not make any sense. A written transcript is needed; recording speech and slowing it down may also be useful to some people with this difficulty.

AUDITORY COHESION DIFFICULTY

This can lead to:

- Having a problem processing when undertaking higher-level listening tasks. This leads to problems drawing inferences from conversations, which can be improved by the speaker using simple language and explaining clearly what is inferred because the person with APD will not be able to make those connections themselves. A written version or a recording of all verbal communication is always advisable. Attract the learner's attention and face them when you speak so they can lipread and use facial cues and body language. Also ask if they need something reworded or rephrased.

- Understanding riddles – these will need to be explained or avoided because the person with APD will not understand what is needed or be able to work them out.

- Comprehending verbal maths problems: these should be written down or recorded for them to do later, at their own pace. For mental maths tests, allow extra time. Ensure knowledge of tables and number bonds and teach strategies using their fingers.

- Prosodic difficulty is a type of APD difficulty where someone might not be able to process or distinguish the tone, mood or inflection of what they hear. The words and tone used might be very emotive, but someone with this difficulty cannot process the nuances in speech, although this doesn't mean they couldn't feel or understand the emotions if they were explained. Prosodic difficulty can also affect understanding of sarcasm and humour. This difficulty is made harder to deal with in people who cannot read facial expressions and body language. Many people with APD do this automatically and without realizing, but if not, learning them can add essential strategies to help them interpret what might be intended and interact with others effectively (which helps with interpersonal relationships and acceptance by others).

[She] Cannot read body language, sarcasm, tone of voice or understand jokes. (Parent of a child aged 12 with APD)

He doesn't pick up on tone of voice and gets very upset if he thinks people are shouting/angry when they haven't raised their voices... (Parent of a child aged 9 with Spatial Processing Disorder)

She struggles with sarcasm and doesn't always understand if people are joking. (Parent of a child aged 10 with APD)

Strategies for associated difficulties caused by APD
SLOW PROCESSING SPEED OR DELAYED PROCESSING

These difficulties can cause problems for many people with APD and are currently not part of the diagnostic criteria. Those who have a slower processing speed will need to be allowed extra time to process speech. Someone with delayed processing might process what is said later than is normal or it could be hours later or even the next day. This can be helped by having everything written down or recorded, texted or emailed for them to review later. Some learners, especially those with a photographic memory, might have a video-like replay of events later that can help make sense of what was delayed (when they finally process it).

WORD RETRIEVAL PROBLEMS

This is problems finding the right word to say or write. It can help the learner to try visualizing the word that they are looking for. If it is a noun or object, they could think of its colour or shape. They could also try to recall a related sound, or smell, or how it felt to touch. If they are trying to remember an adjective used to describe the appearance of something, or an adverb to describe its movement, visualization of the object in motion can also help. The more senses that are used when trying to learn something, the easier it is to remember it; therefore, the same strategy might help someone to access the word in their long-term memory, which might be stored somewhere less accessible than for other people.

REMEMBERING WHAT THEY WANT TO SAY

It helps people with APD to practise what they want to say beforehand in certain situations, or to rehearse responses. Encourage them to write it down, too, if appropriate. A similar problem can occur with understanding and remembering unfamiliar words and names. Again, this is where pre-learning and new vocabulary sheets can help. If applicable, having them recorded can help here, too. At school, teachers use name badges for the pupils in their class for the first day or two or until they are familiar with them; this can also help learners with APD. Where this is not an option, the person with APD can always be discreetly advised to apologize if they try and get it wrong, or asked to explain that they are not good at remembering names (which can affect people without APD too).

PROCESSING UNFAMILIAR ACCENTS AND SPEECH PATTERNS

Some people have more trouble processing the pitch of people of one gender over another. Strong accents can also be difficult to process. Not much can be done for this difficulty if the person interacts with them frequently, apart from hoping to get used to their accent or speech pattern over time. If it is a short-term acquaintance, such as a supply teacher, asking them to speak clearly and face the person with APD and addressing them by name can help. Also ask them to write important information down. A supply teacher should also be advised to differentiate work (if not already prepared), give the learner the usual teacher's pre-printed sheets for the next day and allow extra time for planning work and for writing or answering. Learners with APD can also have problems with processing inarticulate speech and people who speak very quickly. It helps in these situations to speak clearly and at a slower pace.

POOR EXECUTIVE FUNCTION

This can coexist with APD, like other conditions, yet is not part of it or caused by it. This deficit is not diagnosed separately in the UK, although it is in other countries, and can cause planning and organizational skills (see Chapter 4). Learners with this difficulty can be forgetful about packing books and equipment for school and can also leave items behind at school. Planning and self-organization skills and remembering routines and using timetables can also be affected, and more. Written information and diagrams can help.

Access arrangements for tests and examinations

Depending on their individual difficulties, a learner with APD and other difficulties might need the access arrangements listed below. They are entitled to be assessed for their provision in all tests and examinations, whether internal or external, written or aural/oral (including tests and examinations of speaking and listening, oral language and mental maths). The arrangements they might need include the following:

- A quiet room, preferably with no other learners and the use of ear plugs or ear defenders, in order to minimize background noise and distractions, allowing them to concentrate better.

- Twenty-five per cent extra time to take into consideration the time needed for a learner with a slow auditory processing speed and poor word retrieval, especially for aural/oral tests and examinations because timed activities, test and examinations put learners with APD with a slow processing speed at a disadvantage.

- A reader, if they also have reading or spelling difficulties or a slow reading speed. As mentioned before, learners with APD will often be able to process low- or high-pitches of voices more easily, and this preference must be respected with the reader or it can adversely affect processing and test or examination results.

- Verbally providing their responses uses different parts of the brain to writing and might be more appropriate for a lot of learners with added writing difficulties.

- Use of a laptop if a learner has writing difficulties. This can help for all the reasons given above. The learner must be familiar with using the laptop, and it should always be used, in class and at home, as their preferred method of producing work. As per normal guidelines, their laptop's spellchecker and all other programs will be disabled for the duration of the test or examination, but ideally they will use a similar laptop that just includes a word processor and is kept for learners to use in this situation.

- Frequent breaks might be needed and access to water. The learner should be permitted to ask for a break at any time, within reason.

All readers and scribes must be fully trained and their support administered properly and consistently. The learner will also need to train to work with them. The same reader should be used every time, or at least one of a couple with whom the learner has trained. It takes time for the reader or scribe to teach the learner how to master the skill of using a reader or scribe if they are to benefit from it, and to build trust and confidence.

This support should start for internal tests and examinations in primary school and continue when they move up to secondary level; it is imperative that none of the access arrangements are withdrawn at any time. The learner will rely on them to access an appropriate education, and every effort should be made to ensure the learner is never left without this access. To withdraw any such adjustments puts them at a distinct disadvantage, and their results will not be a true reflection of their ability. If a learner is unable to process the voice of the reader effectively, or any of the support is withdrawn, it will put the learner in a position of failure, negating the support and adding to their stress. It can affect their self-esteem and knock their confidence, thus discriminating against a learner with a recognized medical condition or disability.

For external examinations, schools should ensure that these learners are registered with the relevant external body for appropriate adjustments. They should also be re-assessed each year to ensure their difficulties have not increased (as can often happen during adolescence due to hormonal changes, re-occurring glue ear etc.). Processing can also be harder to deal with at times of stress such as these, so even if a learner appears not to need adjustments in class, they might do during a test or examination or in an external examination.

Pastoral care, social skills and external support

Stress at school can affect learning for those with APD, and anxiety is common. They will therefore need emotional support, reassurance and patience. Learners with APD and other difficulties who are unsupported at school have even more difficulty with stress, anxiety and even depression. Referrals to appropriate mental health services can be vital for so many learners with such difficulties. Sadly, it is not always recognized that, for some learners, the anxiety can be caused by trying to cope with their additional needs, especially if they are not supported appropriately or fully. Waiting lists for this sort of agency support are also very long, and some learners simply cannot afford to wait. Each day puts them under unbearable pressure, and this can lead to school avoidance and refusal. Provision of on-site counselling, where possible, is far more immediate and can help stop things spiralling out of control. It is also vital that schools have greater awareness of APD and other difficulties at a far earlier age, as well as where to obtain a referral for diagnosis and how to provide support.

Social skills can be a problem, too, for many learners, due to the communication problems caused by the APD. Both new and existing relationships can suffer as a result of this. Relationship problems can add to their anxiety and make coping with APD harder. Social anxiety, school stressors, low self-esteem and confidence can also prevent them making and keeping friends, worsening the effects of their APD. Their lack of social skills can make some learners with APD appear naïve or immature, or they might be perceived as lacking in intelligence (or all of them).

It is advisable not to force a learner with APD to make friendships with peers unless they want to. Being alone and keeping to themselves is a recognized strategy for self-protection; it can be preferable to shame or ridicule. It is self-isolating in order to avoid the upsetting situations that can arise (as described in Chapter 5). These are the APD-related miscommunications and misunderstandings that lead to embarrassment, distress and continued feelings of failure.

Learners with APD can be vulnerable and targets for bullies. Some learners with APD don't even realize that people are making fun of them until it sinks in later. Bullying should always be taken seriously and acted on, by parents and schools – believe the learner. Explaining to the class or whole school about APD can help to break down barriers and ignorance, and that people with APD just process information differently. It can help to encourage the learner with APD to talk about it themselves, explaining how it affects them as individuals and how others can help them. It can also improve their self-advocacy skills, but they should only discuss it if they want to, or it may cause them further distress instead.

The services of a Speech and Language Therapist (SALT) can be invaluable to many learners with APD. As well as helping with difficulty with verbal communication (both receptive and expressive) and social skills strategies, they can also help with speech delay, caused by APD, or due to glue ear when learning to talk, because of not being able to process or reproduce speech sounds (phonemes) accurately. In some learners this can also lead to what is known as 'Auditory Dyslexia', the other one being VPD (see Chapter 4).

Support and understanding: cooperation, not blame

For a learner with APD and other conditions to leave school having met their potential, it takes a combination of parents and teachers understanding APD and the provision of fully tailored education support. Each needs to understand the wide-ranging, lifelong effects of APD and all that it implies, and the effects that other conditions might have on it, in all situations. Education is the legal responsibility of parents, sometimes undertaken themselves, or, more often, by placing their child in the hands of the professionals trained to do so. All schools need to be able to teach *all* children, and those who teach children with additional needs must know how to do that.

Children are neither the property of parents nor schools; these are all temporary carers with similar, yet different, responsibilities. In some cases, parents often notice more than teachers, and in others, teachers will see more. All are busy, rushed and stressed. But information-sharing benefits everyone, especially children. A short chat at the end of the day, or a text or email, is all that it takes to keep each other updated on what is working and what is not. It should be a partnership and not a competition to decide who knows best or most. Parents blaming schools and schools blaming parents does nothing to help the child – it is a situation that needs everyone working together for the benefit of the child (who is also not to blame). It is a difficult situation for all concerned. But only when we can achieve that will each child with APD and/or other difficulties have access to the full and appropriate education that they need and must receive.

Ways to help a learner with APD: a summary

- Limit classroom noise as much as possible; encourage other learners to work quietly.

- Minimize distrations, because the learner with APD's other senses can be heightened (this is different from an attention deficit).

- Attract the learner's attention and face them when you speak so they can lipread and use facial cues and body language. Also ask if they need something reworded or rephrased.

- Speak to them somewhere quiet – the less background noise the better to avoid speech getting mixed in with other noise.

- Be patient if they misunderstand what you say or ask them to do. Ask how you can help them to understand you better, possibly by verbally repeating or rephrasing, in written format, by recording, by gestures, or via diagrams; using text or email instead of phoning can help.

- Give all information in writing as pre-teaching, as well as any new vocabulary and subject-specific words and meanings for them, guaranteeing that their notes are always accurate.

- Give instructions one at a time, allowing them time to process each one and then carry it out, or put them in writing and word them as simply as possible, or record them for the learner to replay later at their own pace.

- Any questions, homework, reminders, notices and other information should also be provided in writing.

- Allow frequent sensory breaks in a quiet place; encourage the learner to take them and also to hydrate (as dehydration can also affect concentration and processing and lead to headaches).

- Provide somewhere quiet to complete work, tests and examinations.

- Allow extra time to process and complete work, including all tests and examinations (as well as any other appropriate access arrangements).

- Group work should include no more than four learners; encourage turn-taking.

- Make allowances when they are tired, ill or in unfamilar or stressful situations, when APD symptoms will be harder to cope with.

- Allow and encourage the use of assistive technology.

- Support the learner's natural coping strategies and preferred learning style.

- Encourage self-advocacy at the learner's own pace.

- Make sure that they are coping. For younger children you could use a discreet card system (green for 'I'm okay', amber for 'I need help', red for 'I'm really struggling' and blue for 'I need to go out', which means 'I'm in sensory overload' or 'I need a drink'). For older children, when they put up their hand, instead of explaining in earshot of the whole class, they could be allowed to come to your desk and discreetly explain what is needed.

- Don't send unfinished work home or keep learners in at break or lunchtimes. In the evenings, they need to rest and post-process information.

- Homework should be disapplied, or at least kept to a minimum;

it should always be relevant, accessible, timed and suitably differentiated.

- Support requests for disapplication of other languages and/ or music. Or BSL might be a suitable replacement as a second language.

- Never ask a child with APD a question in front of others. Ask them individually or if they put their hand up, also be kind if the answer is incorrect due to mis-processing or misunderstanding the question.

- For communication difficulties, using Makaton can help with younger learners.

- Full support from a Learning Support Assistant, reader or scribe can be vital for many learners with APD.

Children with APD and other difficulties may seem to need more time and effort spent on them. but if the appropriate support is in place, eventually they can become successful independent learners like any other child and fulfil their potential, at whatever level that might be. However, for some children with APD, mainstream education is not an ideal environment. The next chapter discusses the alternatives.

8

Alternatives

FLEXIBLE EDUCATION

Changing schools

If your school is not providing the education and/or pastoral support that your child needs, you might want to consider finding a more supportive or appropriate school to better meet your child's needs. As upsetting as change might seem to a child with APD, leaving them to struggle unsupported in an unsuitable school situation can be far worse. The local authority should support you in finding a more suitable school. If a child has an Education, Health and Care Plan (EHCP), Special Educational Needs (SEN) Statement or Coordinated Support Plan (CSP) (or you are applying for one), you can request that the school or academy of your choice can be added. However, that school or academy might refuse and you would have to appeal and explain the reasons why you feel that your child should be admitted.

A specialist school or special academy might be an option, but it all depends on the school, the child's individual array of needs and the school's criteria (and also whether they have a vacant place). A school for hearing impaired (HI) children might seem like an ideal placement because teachers are aware of hearing impairments and how to support them, but they might not be willing to accept or support a child with APD.

Many of the strategies for children with HI are similar to those for APD, but not all are suitable and might not help the child develop their own coping strategies. For example, HI schools might teach British Sign Language (BSL), and although it can be helpful in some situations, such as if a child is also HI or has speech problems, for those who don't it can be isolating, especially if parents, family and friends do not know BSL. It can also put added pressure on parents, family and friends to learn it, as well as on the child (who has enough trouble coping without the addition of another language). The only way to know if BSL will benefit your child is to try it.

Many mainstream schools, academies, HI teams and local authority sensory support services for HI in the UK still do not accept APD as being a hearing disability, and refuse to support it or provide reasonable adjustments. Therefore, you might not be permitted to enrol your child in such a school unless your child is also HI, even though this is discrimination. Another option, if a more appropriate school cannot be found, is home education, which a growing number of parents are now undertaking.

Home education

Having taken this route myself, I know that the decision to home educate is not an easy one. Home education is chosen for many reasons, and some parents choose to never send their child to school.

> Learning has been primarily on a one-to-one basis... I do not think my daughter's education has been adversely affected [by APD] because she has been home educated. I started home educating all of my children when my daughter was a baby, so [she] never went to school...[it] was a lifestyle choice... (Parent of a home-educated teenager aged 14 with APD)

Some parents decide to withdraw a child from mainstream education because of their school's failure to stop bullying, for many it is due to lack of support or another suitable school. For the child with additional needs, it often comes as the last resort. However, I know many children who have thrived after such a move.

A lot of children with APD and other difficulties often reach breaking point when they are unhappy at school, stressed or anxious, not coping, and their grades are failing because they don't have adequate or appropriate support. Their self-esteem and confidence are also suffering. They might not be sleeping or eating well and something must be done. It is important for their mental wellbeing and physical health that they are removed from a damaging situation, that they are free from as much stress as possible, and that they are happy and well (for more on stress, see Chapter 11). A child under such pressure and without support cannot learn.

The child's mental health and happiness must be the priority. School avoidance can be an indicator that this is approaching, as can a change in behaviour at home or at school (the child may act up, be more anxious or withdrawn, or become disaffected due to continued feelings of failure, and give up altogether). Teachers can simply put this down to a behaviour issue, but they should see this as a sign that something is wrong.

Parents or guardians will usually look for another suitable school as soon as it becomes clear that the school their child attends is no longer an option, but one may not be found that can meet the child's needs, or a place at an ideal school might not be available. The local authority can sometimes offer a home tutor, but in many parts of the UK this is just provided as a temporary measure for a few hours a week (usually when a child is ill or has school avoidance but they expect the child to return to school at some point). This option by no means provides adequate coverage of all lessons, which leaves the child with further gaps in their knowledge. (However, this might be a helpful addition if you just intend to home educate while you wait for a place to become available at a new school of your choice.)

There may also be financial implications to home education if a parent or guardian has to give up work to teach their child. A drop in family income can be difficult (especially for a single parent), and the options need to be carefully considered. There is normally no financial support available to home educators, who will need to buy all the textbooks, other resources and necessary materials. But there are affordable ways to manage this additional expense (see below), and parents will save on any childminding costs, travel expenses, school uniform, lunches, and so on.

Considering your options

If you are a parent or guardian in the UK who wishes to home educate, once the decision is made, you must formally de-register your child from school by sending a letter to the head teacher of their school with a copy to the local authority. Ideally send the letter recorded delivery or, if you deliver it in person, request a receipt. But if a child attends a specialist school that is local authority-funded or arranged, local authority consent is required to delete the child's name from the school register. Write to the school in the same way as above, and request that the school inform you in writing when this has been done. In this case, make sure that your child attends school until you are certain that they have been removed from the school register. If a child is too ill to attend school for whatever reason (including stress or anxiety), a sick note from the child's doctor or consultant must be provided to cover the period until they are formally de-registered.

The officer with responsibility for home education at the local authority will then arrange a meeting to discuss the format that the planned home education will take (whether following the National Curriculum, child-led education, plans to do GCSEs, etc.). The local authority might want to hold this meeting at your home, but you can refuse to hold it there; you can also refuse for your child to participate if you feel that it might distress them.

There is also the option of part-time home or school education, and at the meeting you can discuss your options with the local authority, for example, if your child wants to just take science lessons at school in order to be able to use the school's laboratory facilities, learn languages, or continue with art or music, or maybe they might want to participate in sports. Some children choose this option to maintain contact with their friends, or because the pressure is less if they only need to go into school for a few lessons or a couple of days a week. But parents or guardians should ensure that appropriate and adequate support is still put in place, however short a time they spend at school.

The choice is yours and your child's, but it is advisable to have some idea of how you want to proceed before the meeting. The officer can advise you if you are unsure, but even if they try to persuade you to return your child to mainstream education, it should be your decision, although your child's input is vital.

Ongoing local authority supervision

The local authority will normally want meetings periodically to monitor your child's progress, but they vary in the amount of supervision they wish to provide. It is best to establish the level of their intended supervision at the first meeting. Remember that legal responsibility for a child's education in the UK lies with the parent or guardian, and you can educate your child in the manner you choose. In England and Wales, according to the Education Act 2011, it is a parent's responsibility to ensure that a child of compulsory school age attends and receives a full-time education, either in a mainstream school or by any other means that is appropriate for their age, ability and aptitude, while also taking into account any additional needs they may have. It makes no difference if the child has an EHCP or SEN Statement; it is still your choice as to the form that this education takes.

Choosing a curriculum

As mentioned, for a child in the UK the decision will need to be made whether to follow the National Curriculum or a more child-led education, letting the child study what they are interested in with no aim to study for any qualifications, or how many they wish to take. For those who choose to take the National Curriculum route, home education provides the added benefits of being able to pursue the subjects your child wants to study and the ones they can excel at rather than those that must fit into their school's timetabling restrictions. The formal examinations themselves (for example, GCSEs, A-levels) can be taken at local schools or colleges for a fee per examination taken. The local authority can advise on the procedure in your area, should your child take that route.

There are also online courses that lead to both academic and non-academic qualifications, recognized accreditation or certificates of competency. Depending on the age of the child and their ability and aptitude, this can be a suitable option for some children; they provide all the tutorship and learning materials necessary.

> My daughter is now studying for five IGCSEs to enable her to access Level 3 studies at college. This is a route my three older children took and were all successful. (Parent of a home-educated teenager aged 14 with APD)

Some of the courses are free, but some must be paid for (particularly those that lead to qualifications). Do your research online before deciding. Include your child in any decision, bearing in mind their ability in certain subjects and their personal interests, as well as any future career aspirations or aptitude. For some children it might be better to start with non-academic subjects or basic skills so that they can get used to the examination process.

Adjusting

Home education works well for a lot of families, but it can take a period of adjustment – it is not always easy for a parent or guardian to take on a new role with their child, or being at home all day with their child, especially if they are used to going to work. The child also needs to get used to the change. Children with APD seldom take change well; they find comfort in routine and sameness, so it is advisable to roughly plan your days and set up a home education system as soon as you can, bearing in mind that this should be as flexible as your child needs.

> My daughter enjoys learning... She has plenty of free time outside her studies to explore and pursue her own interests... It gave us the opportunity to spend more time as a family, and to lead a more relaxed, less pressured life. I think all of my children think home education was beneficial to them as individuals and us as a family on many levels... (Parent of a home-educated teenager aged 14 with APD)

Often jaded by mainstream education, it may take time for a child to get used to not being in school, with its rules and regulations and having their day regimented. They will probably relish being at home and try to avoid work of any sort, especially if they had distressing experiences at school. Stress can also affect processing. Learning might now be associated with failure or ridicule, which can be distressing, almost like Post-Traumatic Stress Disorder (PTSD) (which is possible in children; if suspected, you should take them to see their GP and arrange to consult a mental health professional).

They may need persuading in order to engage with learning again; their self-esteem and confidence might have been badly affected by past failure and they might fear even attempting anything in case they fail again. It is best to start with something they like, a favourite academic subject or topic, or something hobby-related. Also, home used to be the safe space away from school, so make sure their bedroom remains a lesson-free zone.

Teaching materials

I always found it useful to prepare simple lesson plans and resources in advance, simply stating the learning objectives and what resources and materials were to be used (listing the subject, textbook, topic, chapter, page, etc.). This could be recorded week to week, or day to day, remembering to take account of their good days and bad days (and including contingency plans). I used a lot of second-hand textbooks, ensuring that they came with no answers written on the pages (those with answers in the back were useful). These can be bought at minimal cost from websites and auction sites. I also bought CD-ROMs with visual or hands-on exercises and games to reinforce different topics, and we used a lot of free online games that are readily available. I would just look for the topic I wanted to practise and listed the school year/age/academic level, and there were usually several choices. My son preferred textbooks, CD-ROMs and sites with a lot of visual representation, images, games, and so on. If you belong to a home education group locally, there is always the possibility of sharing resources too.

For reluctant and less able readers, free (age-appropriate) online comics, graphic novels and manga can encourage and support reading skills. Anime with subtitles can help, too. This is due to the inclusion of images to reinforce the words (and there are far fewer words than in a book). In books for younger children images are included and they can be a great help for a struggling reader. For some reason, pictures in books are frowned upon for older readers (and in schools), although it can be of so much help to them. The wide variety of topics can also be more of interest than those found in more formal texts. There are also more books available now with a lower reading level, higher interest and less words. These can be bought online and some are available in the children's section of libraries.

Learning style and gifted visual-spatial learners

As already discussed, It has long been recognized that we all learn in different ways and that everyone has a preferred learning style. At schools, teaching is 'one-way-fits-all'. At home, however, a child with APD can be taught in the way they learn best. So, in order to teach your child, the first thing you will need to know is how your child prefers to learn.

Many people with APD tend to be either visual or visual-kinaesthetic learners. These learning styles help to compensate for poor auditory processing skills by people employing their strengths in vision and hands-on learning.

There are also gifted visual-spatial learners who do not learn in a sequential way; these are the 'big picture' learners who prefer to know the end product first and work their way back to the start (these so-called 'top-down' learners need the outcome before the steps). My son is such a learner, and I had to tell him every day what we were studying, why we were studying it and what the outcome was expected to be; only then did we discuss how to get there. He also has an eidetic or photographic memory, which is quite common in visual-spatial learners. It is one of his compensatory gifts. (Having APD and other difficulties while being able/talented makes him one of the dual exceptionalities/2E learners mentioned in previous chapters and below.)

Where a learner has a learning style that is also affected by their processing, you would think that this would cause additional problems, for example, the auditory learner with APD or the visual learner with Visual Processing Disorder (VPD). But it must be remembered that APD doesn't affect listening, only auditory processing, and VPD doesn't affect vision, only visual processing.

Support for learners with APD at school can easily be adapted at home, such as pre-learning and pre-printed materials (see Chapter 7, the section on pre-learning and pre-printed notes), and can include more visual and hands-on learning.

> ...she has not had issues around accepting support, but this may change in college. I think she wants to feel more 'normal' and will try anything that might achieve that goal. (Parent of a home-educated teenager aged 14 with APD)

Reinforcement and repetition are used in school to ensure that a child remembers what they learn. It involves giving the child many questions in class, for example 15 sums, plus homework. This method may help a lot of children, but not all, so different methods need to be found. Gifted visual-spatial learners do not often need repetition or reinforcement to help them to remember things (or at least very little). My son learned best if I introduced a new topic one day, discussed briefly what it was about, and then left it until the next day to start teaching it. On the third day I would give him three or four questions on the topic or three sums in order to remember a mathematical principle, and that would be enough for him to remember it. After that he would become confused and we would have to start the topic again from the beginning. That is the way he learns, but it is up to you to find the best way for your child.

The benefits of home education with APD and other difficulties

Apart from having the time needed to allow a child with APD and other difficulties to work at their own pace and use their preferred way of learning, there is far less background noise at home due to fewer children and less general bustle. There is no need to worry about appropriate and adequate support or the benefits of one-to-one instruction, because you are providing it. You have time for detailed explanations, questions, discussion. Your child can take as many breaks as they need, and you can accommodate their bad days. They can also have greater access to the outdoors, fresh air and exercise. There is no need for additional homework, and you can go over things as often as your child needs.

Without competition with peers, fear of failure can be turned into feelings of success, especially when a child feels less pressured and anxious. One of the bonuses of home education is that there are endless learning opportunities out in the wider world, ones that a child would not get in a classroom all day or from following a rigid curriculum. There are more opportunities for independent learning, one of the main aims of any education. This can bring learning to life and reignite your child's passion to learn, which may well have been lost after their negative school experiences. Seeing your child want to learn and relishing it again is a wonderful thing. Their confidence and self-esteem will also grow with every small achievement and, as a result, they will become more relaxed, stress will be reduced, and less stress aids processing and improves their wellbeing.

When to teach

Teaching a child with APD at home is all about making the most of good days and bad days. With APD being random and intermittent, some days processing will be minimal. There can also be additional difficulty due to illness, fatigue and stress. APD will still be there. They will still be exhausted from the effort of processing, but this can be minimized in a quieter environment with more breaks.

Certain times of day will be better for your child than others; my son was always more alert in the morning, and his processing waned as he tired through the day. So most of our studying took place in the morning, with the afternoons usually consisting of less academic subjects such as arts and crafts, music, and so on. Your child might be better in the afternoon or evening, although tiredness makes a big impact on processing, so teaching hours should be a lot fewer than at school – how long depends on your child. You will find that on a good day you will get a lot more done and it will be remembered better. Home education is all about finding your own path to suit your child. On poor processing days, I knew that my son would not take much in. So formal teaching was abandoned in favour of less academic subjects and enjoyable educational outings, but he was still learning.

Learning opportunities can be found anywhere and everywhere, if you are prepared to be versatile. Mental maths can be practised when out shopping, historical facts can naturally be gleaned from visits to museums, and various art styles can be discussed at art exhibitions and then copied at home. Media studies can be incorporated into a visit to the cinema, concert or show. This can be followed up at home that day or the next with a written review, listening to albums by the musicians or singers they saw and learning their songs, by watching videos with the same actors or with similar themes (in order to develop comparing and contrasting skills).

You can use these visits to find out what your child likes and have in-depth discussions about the reasons why and why not (leading to the development of analytical and debating skills). They can take photographs on these outings and use them to accompany a written account, or draw the aspects that they most liked, all of which they can then use to compile a scrapbook or portfolio of their visits. The possibilities are endless, and the world is now their classroom.

Teaching 2E children at home

A dual exceptionalities child will benefit from home education, although it is essential to address the difficulties as well as the giftedness. Both aspects must be equally supported, and this is something that schools find difficult to reconcile (how a child who is so bright can struggle, or how a child who needs so much support can be capable of great academic success). They might either push the gifted aspect or support the child's difficulties without considering the need to accommodate their intellect and help them reach their potential. At home, it is easier to be flexible, to give them projects to extend their interest and capability whilst knowing that you have already put in place all the appropriate support your child needs in order to learn efficiently. It may be trial and error for a while to find the level to work at, but you know your child; you understand them, and if they are struggling or become bored with the level of work provided, you will soon find out. But be sure to increase the difficulty without increasing the quantity of work or time taken. Independent learning can be encouraged by giving your child free rein to study something that interests them, maybe a topic or subject that might not be on the National Curriculum (or whichever curriculum or route you have taken) or they could learn a different language to that taught at school, one they find easier.

Social implications

One criticism that is always thrown at home educators is that they are taking away their child's access to social interaction by home education, or denying them access to their peers. But the opposite is the case. They can always see their school friends after school and at weekends and holidays. Also, enforced peer friendships are unnatural and not always beneficial; they do not reflect 'real life'. After we leave school, we no longer go around in peer groups. We become independent adults who mix with anyone and everyone, and the sooner we learn how to do this the better. Someone who is home educated will still need to learn to self-advocate and can also have difficulty or be reluctant to do so.

> She is embarrassed that she can't understand what people are saying to her and it makes her want to avoid social situations... In the past she has 'coped' by relying on us as parents to be her 'interpreters'... This has felt awkward, especially as she has grown older. (Parent of a home-educated teenager aged 14 with APD)

There are local home education groups that offer the prospect of meeting up with other home-educating families and interacting with a wide variety of people of all ages and experiences.

In a similar way to attending after-school clubs for sport or music, for example, there are also groups, classes and societies where they can still engage with people with similar interests. However, there are still those who don't understand and who can be discriminatory towards home educators.

> People are quick to judge and to assume that her problems are due to her having lived in a 'bubble', and not having had the opportunities to learn social skills...she grew up with three siblings, living in a busy household with lots of comings and goings, travelling, visits and interactions...her home-educated siblings, now grown, never had any of the same problems and progressed fairly effortlessly to college, uni, post-grad courses and jobs. As a mum I feel like I have to explain all the time. (Parent of a home-educated teenager aged 14 with APD)

Being home educated doesn't mean you will automatically become a hermit; the sociable child will always seek out interaction, and a child who has social anxiety because of their APD will still avoid social contact as a method of self-preservation – avoiding situations where they feel they will have difficulty is a normal coping mechanism for so many of them, and being home educated will not change that. Also, with APD, social skills are often absent due to their processing deficits, not from the lack of opportunity to socialize.

> Sadly...the lack of understanding on the part of those around us has probably been the worst thing to deal with. Is it any wonder that my daughter avoids social situations when she feels people see her as 'weird' because she has to keep asking them what they have said over and over...? (Parent of a home-educated teenager aged 14 with APD)

But your child will now have opportunities to make friendships wherever *they* choose and not be restricted to the children within their classroom.

If home education doesn't work

Some home educators find that home education doesn't work well for them and for others it may not suit their child. Or they find that, after a period of de-stressing, their child is ready to return to mainstream education. This is always possible but it can take time, and there may be a waiting list for the school you choose, but always be open to all possibilities.

9

Adolescence

TEENAGE YEARS AND LIFE SKILLS

In addition to all the difficulties that a child with APD must deal with, as they become a teenager with APD, they will have a totally new range of difficulties to face and overcome as well as the APD itself. I use secondary school-age pupils here as a roughly average demographic, although in some children, the difficulties discussed in this chapter may happen sooner (as can puberty).

Academic success is not always the best way forward for some children. If they are unable to take formal examinations, perhaps apprenticeships and vocational training might suit them better. As they get older and their interests come more to the fore, you can help them to explore their options. There are also children who may never be able to work if their difficulties are extremely severe, and it is wise to manage their expectations and your own as early as possible, as well as considering their need for housing, income and any potential care needs. This chapter discusses these issues, as well as the need to develop life skills.

Teenage support at home
Hormones and changes at home

Some teenagers go through puberty easily, with little outward effect. But for others, especially those with APD or other disabilities, their lives seem even more out of their control. The age at which puberty starts varies from person to person. Their bodies are changing and their brains are raging with an influx of hormones, so while they try to get used to their new situation, anxiety might be more common, as well as anger and frustration. Tears and emotional outbursts are more common at this age for any young person, but this is worse for a teenager with APD. Hormonal changes during puberty can make coping with APD much harder.

> Puberty, bodily changes and moods have been a little rocky. She... coped better than we thought she would...bodily changes have needed to be explained lots of times...self-confidence has hit rock bottom... Memory and concentration are also affected. (Parent of a child aged 12 with APD)

Many people with APD are averse to change – they take comfort in routine and if they are prone to anxiety or depression, anything unforeseen can be blown out of proportion. If they are diagnosed with APD (or anything else) at this time it may also be harder for them to reconcile the news with everything else that they have to deal with, so acceptance can take longer.

Major changes to the body (and the brain) during puberty can have knock-on effects on many aspects of an adolescent's life. Anything that affects the brain can make APD seem harder to deal with, even though it hasn't actually become any worse – APD usually only worsens when there is further damage to the brain (from certain illnesses, injury, stroke, epilepsy or by the neurological effects of prolonged alcohol or drug abuse etc.).

The teenager's personality might seem to change, too; they may become more negative, lethargic or even defiant as they struggle through the minefield in which they suddenly find themselves. They need guidance in order to fully understand why they feel or react this way. Remember that they are still the same child they were when they were younger, even if this child seems to have been taken over by an alien entity set on challenging you at every turn, and determined to avoid you. But they need you more now than ever, even if everything they do appears to indicate the opposite.

Supporting teenagers with APD at home

There is little information available on supporting a teenager with APD. This is a particularly difficult time – parents need to be prepared and find ways to help their teenager (and to cope themselves). Some common problems and difficulties are discussed below.

ROUTINES
Be more aware than ever of keeping things the same; if routine is important to your child, it will be of even more comfort now as it provides a sense of security at this very confusing time.

PRIVACY
Respect their privacy and help them to be more aware of the need for modesty. As you would expect from them, you should knock before entering their bedroom. If your child was used to taking a bath or shower without locking the bathroom door, they should start to do so (considering any safety factors if they also have physical disabilities). If you want to speak to them, wait until they allow you into their room, or come out of the bathroom. A conversation through a door, especially with the shower or taps running, is much harder to process for someone with APD.

SPACE
The child who used to spend a lot of time with you might now want to be alone more, or spend more time with friends or peers. They are finding their place in the world. They might draw away from parents and siblings, spending more time in their room or preferring the company of friends (or a particular social circle). Many teenagers are more conscious of needing to belong, seeking the company of others outside the family unit, even if just at school or online. For outgoing teenagers with APD who struggle to fit in socially, this can be particularly hard.

Other teenagers with APD might seek peace and quiet, often preferring their own company or one or two supportive friends, so it's best not to try to enforce peer relationships or push them into situations they are actively trying to avoid. They do this for good reason, even if they can't express why they need to do so.

In some cases, this separation from family might be because of peer pressure and not wanting to appear different or being seen as a 'baby'. They might develop new interests and wish to follow them (although they may still look to their parents for transport until they have their own, which is cheaper, safer and can be more reliable than public transport later in the day). Whatever the reason, they are growing up and need their independence, which should be encouraged, even with APD, although parents should always be mindful of safety concerns (as discussed below).

> Learning how to get the bus to and from school...a HUGE step... (Parent of a child aged 12 with APD)

SLEEP

It is a scientific fact that teenagers need more sleep (estimated as 9–10 hours) in order to cope with the changes occurring to their body and brain. This is not laziness.

The adolescent with APD will use far more energy than neurotypical teenagers to do what their peers do automatically, to understand what they hear accurately and respond effectively in a timely manner. Tiredness adversely affects APD (and can lead to struggling more in school), so try to encourage them to go to bed earlier, even if this is met with opposition.

Coupled with the normal level of tiredness experienced by teenagers, they will be exhausted. They will therefore need additional and frequent sensory breaks during the day, in a quiet place. If this is not already one of the accommodations that should be provided, now is the time to ask that it be included.

Not processing clock or phone alarms is common with APD, and this can cause them to sleep late, so maybe setting more than one alarm might be the answer. Buying a smartwatch with an alarm and a vibration feature can aid independent waking. Even though a knock on the bedroom door would be less expensive, they need to find a way to wake up independently.

SUBSTANCE ABUSE AND MENTAL HEALTH

Although teenagers can self-isolate for many reasons, if they become increasingly withdrawn and appear overly anxious or depressed, as is quite common when coping with APD and other difficulties, it is wise to urge them to seek professional support to help them get through this (see Chapter 11).

The pressures of adolescence can lead neurotypical teenagers to self-harm, eating disorders, alcohol or drug use and so on. Teenagers with APD can be very vulnerable to them too, maybe to help regain control, to hide from their feelings of inadequacy, or maybe to punish themselves for failure or feeling different. These can all arise in younger children too.

Drug and alcohol abuse can also be because of peer pressure (the 'Try this' or 'Take that' scenario). The unrealistic demands imposed on young people by social networking are a dangerous trigger: the pressure of trying to attain the impossibly unobtainable façade of a perfect person with a perfect life that is all too often perpetuated online. Whatever way their stressors manifest, they need help.

A vulnerable or easily led child with APD is not likely to change much when they are a teenager; in fact, more so. Anyone who exhibits concerning behaviours does so for a reason. The reasons can be as unique as the person themselves, but they should be looked out for more in those for whom disabilities like APD can make life seem out of their control and success and happiness out of their reach. Whatever way their stressors arise or manifest, these young people need help.

These are mental health concerns that need professional support, no matter what has triggered them. Parents and schools should be vigilant, take them very seriously and act (more on this in Chapter 11).

If children of any age are not given the support that they need at home and at school, for these difficulties as well as their education needs, the situation can worsen. This is especially relevant, given that APD and other difficulties do not go away when you leave school. They are present throughout life, in all aspects of life. So, too, are the feelings of failure, helplessness and resentment, which may carry on into further education, the workplace and in relationships (as discussed in Chapter 10).

SAFETY

Although teenagers usually strive for freedom from their parents and want to do things independently, measures must be in place to make sure they also do so safely. Even if they seem capable, they might not be; similarly, children who are vulnerable will become vulnerable teenagers.

> We have worked hard on stranger danger...strangers have always been an issue. She will talk to anyone. (Parent of a child aged 12 with APD)

If a child with APD or a spatial processing difficulty cannot tell the direction of an approaching vehicle when crossing the road, this will not improve as they get older, unless they have learned how to cope. Strategies should already have been taught and practised, such as looking left and right more often than normal before crossing and while they cross, because a parent won't always be with them to hold their hand (literally). Curfews, appointment times, reminders and so on. can also be set up on their phone or smartwatch. As I have already mentioned Chapter 5, these should be taught early because the hope is that, after practising, they will become automatic. For some children, depending on severity of the APD and other coexisting conditions, this may not happen as they might fail to learn them or remember to use them.

COMMUNICATION DIFFICULTIES

Miscommunication can occur at any age, leading to disagreements at home and at school, too, sometimes resulting in potential over-reactions and outbursts that might be out of character. This is because any teenager might be more sensitive to casual comments or light-hearted teasing that they may have previously dismissed with a smile. However, those with APD might not understand that the comments were meant as humorous or sarcastic. In an adolescent/teenager, this can add to their frustration.

Many people with APD cannot express themselves fully or fluently, even without additional speech problems. They need patience, and other children, teenagers or (even adults) might not make the effort needed to understand their difficulties or make allowances for their very real individual needs. Any of their potential relationships can be fraught with arguments and misunderstandings. For example, a person with APD might argue that what they thought they heard was correct and the other person knows they are wrong. In these situations, if those around them understand why it is happening, allowances can and should be made.

Autonomy

A teenager with APD and other difficulties might suddenly decide that they want to deal with any issues that arise themselves; they might resent parental interference, which will be seen by some as embarrassing because they feel that they are mature enough to solve their problems by themselves. They might want to rebel against home or school rules and must deal with the ensuing reprimands, like any child. Truanting might be another result. Defiance is a rite of passage that so many teenagers can go through in some form. Those who have APD and other additional needs have additional difficulties.

Misbehaving at school can be a form of attention-seeking, or to deflect from the fact that they are struggling. They would rather be excluded than feel ashamed or be seen to fail. As well as those who act up, which can draw attention to their difficulties, there also those whose difficulties are missed due to them *not* being viewed as a behaviour problem. They are the ones who simply withdraw and become almost invisible. This can be even more worrying.

School avoidance can develop from lack of education-based support, bullying, anxiety, fear of failure, and so on. If the child is not helped with these enormous feelings, it can develop into a very real and distressing school phobia. They might become disaffected and abandon any hope of achieving anything. Sadly, for those with additional needs this can be perceived as a behaviour issue and disruptive rather than a young person who needs help. Both home and school support are needed if the child is to feel safe at school again. However, as discussed in Chapter 8, it is always best to remove a child from a distressing and possibly damaging school environment that is not likely to improve. Alternatives are available.

An adolescent with additional needs might suddenly decide that they no longer need any school support, or refuse to use an FM (frequency modulation) system. The need is still there, but they might decide that they are old enough to manage alone, or feel that accepting these things makes them appear different to their friends. They might feel that they will fail anyway, so why would they need them? But learners with APD can and do achieve with the right support, and refusing it can be a major setback. There is a big chance that their grades will soon start to suffer as a result, especially if they also refuse examination adjustments.

Forcing them to accept support will not work and they may well dig their heels in further and become defiant. For many teenagers, fitting in becomes even more important, especially for those with an already poor self-image, low confidence and few friends. But sometimes, compromise can help.

...in primary school, she was so proud of her 'super ears' [FM system]...used them every day and they helped a great deal. Secondary school was a different matter. She would hide them, lose them, not wear them, leave them around the school...[she] said they made her look different and stand out. She just wanted to be the same as everyone else. We agreed she could wear her hair down to cover them, and put them in before she left for school...no one could see them. She has since been wearing them because she said that she noticed a difference for the good. (Parent of a child aged 12 with APD)

Children with APD soon become aware of how they struggle academically and socially (and how others perceive them). By the time they reach adolescence, this has become ingrained and they can struggle greatly with their self-image. (Teenage difficulties at school are included in Chapter 7.)

It is important to encourage the development of decision-making and independence in preparing a teenager for life as an adult. But even if a teenager appears to be mature, they might not be. It is thought that the pre-frontal area of the brain is the last area of the brain to be fully developed, at around the early twenties. This affects executive function (planning, organization, response inhibition, assessing options, decision-making, mental inflexibility, etc.). Executive function difficulties can accompany APD and other conditions. It might therefore take a lot of persuasion from parents and teachers to induce them to continue with support (or accept new support). It can be a dilemma between seeing them fail, or playing a part in further damaging their self-esteem. If they flatly refuse support, their personal coping strategies and ways around their difficulties will become increasingly important, yet these are being adversely affected by hormones and increased exhaustion. But they are no longer little children. Preparing them for adulthood might also involve letting them fail then helping them to pick up the pieces, although gentle, tactful guidance is vital, supporting them as they make their decisions and hoping that they make the right ones. School can help with this. Inform them of the potential outcomes of refusal, and the same applies to any disagreements you might have with them. Remember that a heavy-handed approach might adversely affect your relationship with them; they need to know that whatever they decide, even if you don't agree, your love and support is unconditional and ongoing. Sometimes a teenager will 'push the boundaries' just to find out how secure their relationships are, and to make sure that their parents still accept them, just like when they were little. When they feel so out of control, half a child and half an adult, they need that acceptance more than ever, even if they don't show it.

Strengths, skills and career choices
Hobbies and interests

APD can also affect enjoyment of hobbies and leisure time, for example, those that involve verbal teaching of sequences, such as martial arts, gymnastics or dance, if they have problems with auditory sequencing. But reasonable adjustments must be made and success can be reached.

> She loves gymnastics and [is] doing well... (Parent of a child aged 8 with APD)

> She received a medal for her dancing during the last show. (Parent of a child aged 10 with APD)

However difficult the challenges are, all children and teenagers with APD should always be allowed to choose their own hobbies and interests and encouraged to use these areas of interest and natural abilities to aid in their career choices. I have seen young people who struggled at school come to excel on their own terms in various ways, by using their strengths.

But it isn't just about the enjoyment; their hobbies and interests can provide a far more practical and satisfying career path than academic qualifications. Although APD does not affect intelligence, just like children without APD, not all are academically brilliant. If those who have academic potential are left without adequate, appropriate support, they may never attain it, but with the right sort of support and coping strategies, qualifications can be attained. For some learners, however, depending on other coexisting conditions affecting their learning, this may not be possible. They may need to look at different routes into employment, and, of course, full support is also needed if a learner with APD is to find and maintain a job.

Children with APD will usually have compensatory gifts and skills such as an excellent visual memory or be skilled in art, the performing arts, music, woodwork, metalwork, sport, and so on.

> Naturally gifted at most sports...plays for a football team and often wins the trophy for 'Girl of the game'...won the sports trophy at her last school. (Parent of a child aged 10 with APD)

They could have an affinity with animals, or might have an empathic or caring nature.

> She is extremely caring and loving to others...loves animals. (Parent of a child aged 12 with APD)

> Strong empathy for young children and animals. (Parent of a teenager aged 14 with APD)

Their interests and attributes should be maximized and applied to help them find a way in the world (along with their coping strategies, preferred learning style, reasonable adjustments and self-advocacy skills).

Some careers may cause more problems for those with APD than others. Although they can achieve success, it also depends on their individual difficulties, level of ability in their chosen area and the effort they put in (like anyone else). The effects of other comorbid conditions, their individual coping strategies and support also play a part, as always. This is discussed further in Chapter 10.

Managing expectations

Everyone is entitled to dream and to try to make those dreams come true. At least if you fail, you will know that you had the strength to aim for what you wanted. Failure is part of learning, an opportunity to use your mistakes, grow and succeed next time. But part of preparing any child to cope in the world is also helping them to manage their expectations.

How many children want to be a pop idol, rock star, or sports celebrity? These are their dreams and no child or adult should be discouraged from dreaming, but there comes a time when they must be realistic. Rather than dissuade or disillusion them totally, they should be encouraged to look at alternative ways of reaching their goal, or maybe alter their aspirations a little to something that might be more achievable and practical for their abilities and needs. For example, a child who dreams of becoming a vet might be able to find work as a veterinarian nurse or assistant or someone who looks after animals in another way. It may be the care of animals that draws them to that career, not necessarily the surgery side of things, or the many years of study needed to get there.

Currently common in young people is the lure of fame and fortune as professional gamers. It might seem like paradise, but they will need to practise constantly, the profession demands an extremely high level of skill and determination, and it may take them a very long time to be one of the best. Also they might not be gifted gamers. The path is fraught with opposition and success is fleeting. Only the best win tournaments and earn good money, and it is rare to see a pro-gamer in their 30s. There is also a lot of travelling involved, crowds, strange voices to get used to every day and noisy venues to deal with. It is a highly-stressed environment and not for the faint-hearted.

I know that a lot of parents are concerned about their child's love of gaming and I used to be the same until I realized the benefits. For a child with social anxiety and few friends (or none), gaming friendships with like-minded others can be as fulfilling and supportive as in-person relationships, and just as lasting. They can communicate in text without the need for verbal communication, or they can just as easily play alone. But parents also need to ensure their child's online safety and that they are aware of security issues.

Transferable skills

Even if they don't become a professional, the skills that a gamer must develop are transferable to many areas of employment. They include hand–eye coordination, timing, strategizing, proprioceptive skills, attention to detail, auditory and visual memory skills, mental maths, typing and teamwork. Some children can also have a variety of interests, gifts and aptitudes seen from an early age.

He can think outside the box, look at the problem and find a solution, especially using a practical approach. Builds fantastic models that

189

> you think are a kit you have bought...extremely good at swimming
> and wishes to either swim the Channel or swim at the Olympics...
> lots of empathy with children younger than him; he seems to know
> that they need support and friends...will go out of his own comfort
> zone to help them, so they don't feel like he does. (Parent of a child
> aged 10 with APD)

The same applies to many interests – all can have transferable skills. Whatever they like, excel at or are drawn to should be used as a basis from which to help them build a career.

Using gaming as an example again, a love of video games might be useful towards a career that involves skill at creative writing, drawing, music composition or programming.

> [He] enjoys his computer work – coding and video games. (Parent
> of a child aged 10 with APD)

They may wish to pursue these other preferred skills as a career. These are quite hands-on activities and more qualifications, apprenticeships and vocational training are available now for a variety of professions that test practical skills and attributes and involve less written work. This approach is well suited to someone who is not academically gifted and can apply to a variety of careers.

Sensory attributes and career options

In someone with APD, their other senses are often heightened to compensate for their deficit in processing auditory information. This means that children with APD need to fight distractions, which can lead to misdiagnosis of Attention Deficit Hyperactivity Disorder (ADHD). But those heightened senses are also what make them special, leading to the development of amazing skills.

For a lot of people with APD, their auditory memory may be poor, but they might have an excellent visual memory, excellent for postal workers or delivery drivers (good at remembering routes).

> ...she has an amazing ability to remember routes, places. (Parent of
> a child aged 12 with APD)

Highly visual people might excel at photography or other visual arts, architecture, graphic design or interior design, and some have amazing attention to detail. They may have an excellent sense of smell (useful for a sommelier or perfumier).

A person with APD can even have heightened ability in perceiving music (processed by a different part of the brain to speech) and be suited to the role of a sound recordist, singer or musician.

> [She] Plays the piano and won several local competitions...love of acting, singing and West End musicals. (Parent of a teenager aged 14 with APD)

> [She]...plays the clarinet... (Parent of a child aged 10 with APD)

A person with a good auditory memory may be good at languages (while others may struggle) and could make an excellent interpreter or journalist. A good sense of touch or dexterity might help with someone wanting to teach braille or even sign language, or become a wood carver, sculptor, potter or another crafts-based role.

> ...she is always making things. I...signed her up for sewing and crochet club this term and she loves it. (Parent of a child aged 8 with APD)

> [She is] very good with her hands using tools. (Parent of a child aged 12 with APD)

These are just a few examples, but parents should find out what their child is good at or wants to explore. Empathy and intuitive skills can also help those who are interested in counselling, nursing or social work (as well as being visually observant). The innovative person with APD might look to be an entrepreneur, or even an inventor.

> ...very empathetic, caring and kind...a deep thinker and notices things...can express himself quite poetically...loves art, making, inventing etc. and is imaginative in these areas. (Parent of a child aged 9 with Spatial Processing Disorder)

Children who are gifted in other ways often see 'outside the box' and that can be the way for them to find happiness too: not by giving up on their dreams, but by finding a different path to the sense of fulfilment that their chosen career path appears to offer. These children often find unique ways of working around their difficulties. This skill is not just for the gifted; finding ways around things is a common APD coping strategy, after all.

Teenagers with additional needs might choose teaching as a profession and people with additional needs can make excellent teachers of children with additional needs. Because of their empathy, they understand how to reach them and how to teach them as they need to be taught. Instead of expecting them to be the same as other children, they know that individuality is a cause for celebration, that their uniqueness is what will help that child most.

> [She] would like to be a PE teacher... (Parent of a child aged 10 with APD)

Understanding your weaknesses is what helps most, in all aspects of life:

> He is developing a musical ability by working within his limitations and understanding what he can and can't do. (Parent of a child aged 10 with APD)

Other qualities

Many people with APD fare better where there are rules, policies and procedures set out by others, needing order and routine. But they can also be very adaptable. They can be resilient, overcoming obstacle after obstacle; after all, that is what they must do throughout their lives. They also tend to be focused, committed and hardworking (putting in more effort than those without their difficulties to deal with). These are all excellent qualities and desirable to many employers. Struggling to do what other people take for granted, they must listen well, pay attention and give 100 per cent every day, just to get through the day. People with APD can and do achieve great things, with the right support.

Whatever they choose to pursue in their spare time, it is important that they choose it. Parents and schools should also make sure that the APD teenager is not pushed to pursue a hobby or interest as a career, or become exhausted with the effort, become bored with it or no longer find it enjoyable. There is a fine line between encouragement and being overly forceful. For some, what is a hobby might result in being unsuitable as a career once they think of it as a chore, or if they are over-immersed in it. They could lose interest and enthusiasm for it altogether, thus defeating the objective of using the hobby as a career. It is a realistic option, but it must be their choice, at their pace, or they may decide to just keep it as a hobby, and that is okay too. Whatever they choose to do, they will need to consider all the advice that is available, both from career professionals and online sources, although it would be helpful if those professionals knew about APD and how to support it.

Volunteering

We all need to do jobs we don't like at times, in order to earn a living, but spending most of our day doing something we like is more likely to bring job satisfaction and lead to remaining longer in a post. Choosing a job that suits your skills is the best way to do this, and work experience and volunteering can help. A work placement as a volunteer is an excellent way to 'test the water' and to find out whether someone will like a chosen profession, and whether they might be capable of doing the job with the appropriate training. It will also help them to gain valuable work experience that can help them to get a job.

Also vital for someone with APD and other difficulties is the reassurance that the employer will provide the necessary reasonable adjustments they need to enable them to do that job, even if only volunteering. A suitable work environment is essential, and workplace support is discussed further in Chapter 10. As well as work experience and voluntary work, parents can help their teenager with APD to know what to expect from working life (and help them learn in advance to self-advocate for the support that they will need).

Preparing for adulthood

Before we know it, our young child has become a young adult and is leaving home, for college or university, or just to rent (or buy) their own space and start work.

As well as preparing our young people for the world of work, parents and schools also need to teach them the skills needed for everyday living. Some schools do this already but all teenagers will become adults who need to navigate real life outside the sheltered environments of school and home. It cannot be left to schools to do this; parents must teach them to lead an independent life, and this must start well before they are of a legal age to leave home. As parents of children with additional needs, we will have learned about their difficulties and which strategies they need to use to help them, but this is new territory, and preparation is even more important.

I have listed several skills below that teenagers will need to master when living as independent adults. This list is not exhaustive; whatever you do as an adult they will need to replicate, and you can add other skills. Parents can't rely on schools to cover this type of learning – their focus will be on academic needs – and with APD, all these tasks will be harder.

Life skills

I'm sure that a lot of teenagers will already know how to perform at least some of these essential tasks, but for those with APD, the instructions will have to include coping strategies and ways around the many challenges they might face:

- Verbal explanations will obviously prove ineffective when you consider mis-processing, memory issues and problems with sequencing, so parents should prepare typed sheets containing instructions.

- Note at the top of each sheet that they should perform the actions in the order given, and create a separate instruction sheet for each task.

- I would have two columns or a table: type each instruction on the left and on the right add appropriate coping strategies where needed.

- Discuss the strategies with your child and use their input on the sheet. It must contain what they would do, in the way that suits them best (which may not necessarily be the way that you or I might handle the situation). Ask how they would cope or get around each challenge that they foresee, step by step. By this age they should be quite self-aware about their coping strategies.

- You can add more tasks or sheets as you think of them, and ask your child to think of some, too, although they may not know what to expect or prepare for, but you can always help them as new situations arise.

- The instructions should be simply worded and easy to follow, numbered rather than using bullet points, and provided with a box at the end of each instruction for them to note as they go along that they have completed each step.

- Add illustrations or clipart to aid understanding, or if they have literacy problems.

- These sheets can then be put into a folder for them to keep.

- It would help if each sheet was laminated (in case they need to repeat the activities often) or several copies given. Even with practice, they may still miss steps out if they have organization or visual memory difficulties.

- You can also include recipes for their favourite meals.

- I would also add a list of useful telephone numbers (GP, dentist, hospital, etc.), or make sure they put them in their mobile phone.

Important tasks

They will also need to know how to carry out these tasks:

- How to shop for food, clothes, appliances, and so on, either online or in person.

- How to prepare and cook a meal.

- How to do their washing and washing-up.

- How to clean their room/home.

- How to deal with their finances (managing a bank account, receiving pay and paying bills).

- How to manage a household budget.

- How to put a CV together and apply for a job or voluntary position.

- How to paint/decorate or maintain a garden (or engage the services of a professional, as below).

- How to manage travelling alone, to and from work, further education or socially (read a timetable, buy a bus pass, etc.).

- How to apply for a student grant or benefits.

- How to study for a driving test and how to drive and maintain their vehicle and fill it with fuel.

- How to ensure that their vehicle is taxed and insured and has a regular MOT test.

- How to find a suitable place to live, whether rented, bought or student accommodation, going through the legal process, and so on or communicating with their landlord.

- How to obtain life insurance, contents insurance and even buildings insurance if they own their own home.

- How to communicate with companies to set up a home phone line (if needed) or converse with internet providers, pay for a TV licence or find a plumber, electrician, and so on.

Some coping strategies for these tasks

- Online ordering might be better wherever possible. It avoids verbal communication and they can add their email address instead of a telephone number. This also applies to other processes such as applying for grants or benefits, insurance, bus passes, car tax and job applications. Brochures and leaflets are often available online, too, and you can print out instructions.

- When dealing with people providing services, repairs or other professionals, it is always best to use email or text rather than verbal communication. Most companies now provide an email address as well as a contact number.

- When face-to-face communication is unavoidable, they can carry an APD alert card (provided on my website). On the front it explains what having APD means and on the back there are some tips on how others can help. It can be adapted or reworded to fit their needs.

- Practical activities such as cooking, washing, washing-up and cleaning should be practised at home before moving out. Where possible, these tasks should be rehearsed several times. Encourage and support them to be self-sufficient before they leave home, which will add to their confidence, lessen their anxiety and ease your worry. You can also prepare instruction lists for these tasks, too, as needed.

- Professional contracts, for example, rental agreements, should be read carefully before signing. For example, many landlords include home garden maintenance in their contract, and failure to do so can lead to breach of contract and termination of the contract. If they have reading or reading comprehension difficulties you can help with this (or ask someone else to help if you also have similar problems).

This list of skills and tips is not exhaustive, or exclusive to teenagers and young adults; older adults can benefit from them too and might find it reassuring. If you know an adult with APD, ask them if they feel it would be useful and (with their permission) help them to compile their own lists or folder.

Preparation and support

Watching your child leave home is like seeing your toddler ride a bicycle for the first time knowing they may fall off, but sometimes all you can do is give them a helmet, knee and elbow pads and hope for the best. It is also exciting, and part of growing up, another milestone for them (and for parents too) but reassure them that although they may be independent, they are not alone and your door is always open: that they can always move back home again.

Teenagers with APD will need your continued support as they make their way through the unpredictable and troubling duration of their teenage years and beyond, much more support than for a neurotypical teenager. You can still act as their advocate if or when they need you. They will always be your child, whatever they do and wherever they go.

10

Adulthood

PROBLEMS AND POSSIBILITIES

The story so far

Much of what readers will need to know about adults with APD has already been covered in the previous chapters, from childhood to teenage years, but there are certain topics that are only applicable when they reach adulthood and the APD is still there. By now, they will normally have learned how to employ coping strategies, use their strengths to offset their weaknesses, have a range of hobbies and interests, found ways around a variety of challenges, and formed relationships. But for some, this will not have come easily. The journey will not have been free from difficulties and distress at some time, or maybe often. It is likely that none of them will have come out of it unscathed. As with children, self-esteem and confidence will have taken many blows and left scars. Stress and anxiety might be all too evident, even depression. Some may have a diagnosis but most may not, for various reasons; they might not even have realized that they have APD, and there are those who don't acquire it until they are adults. However, there is hope for them all. This chapter covers these topics as well as discussing career options and further education.

Congenital and early-onset APD

Like adolescence, adulthood brings difficulties of its own. Many adults with APD will have had APD from birth or childhood, either because it was congenital or acquired at an early age (but it can also arrive at any point in life). Depending on age and location, there are those who will have received an early diagnosis, but for some, testing may not have been available to them because APD was little known when they were children. This 54-year-old man from Japan was diagnosed in the UK at the age of 53 with auditory processing difficulties.

Since I was a child, I was aware of something strange in me with other children... I now guess that because of my APD, I was not able to catch up with the speed of the conversation between them, I could not follow what they would be doing next. I was often told by them, 'you are slow!'... I believe that the sooner being diagnosed, the better the quality of life would be...

I was invited to several job interviews. When I was provided feedback on why I was not successful, the one specific comment was always standing out, 'We were wondering whether you could understand what we asked you to answer?'... I started to seriously wonder what's wrong with me...similar comments have always been given since I was young...

I prefer to be alone because I do not want to worry about not being understood by other people...

When I have to attend seminars in a big room, I try to get there early in order to locate and keep the best seat for me to listen to the speakers. I tell my friends why I do not want to see them in noisy places...

...my friends look confused when I try to tell them that I am diagnosed with APD...

I come to believe that I cannot achieve no matter what I long to achieve...

...I tend to blame myself even when I knew a mistake was made not by me...

As soon as I was told about the result of the assessments by a doctor, I was in tears because I was clear that...it was not my own mistake to have APD. I would not need to blame myself anymore. Since then, I have been feeling better about myself because I have been in the process of discovering who I am!

The more our society understands what APD is, the better the quality of our life will be...for the moment, APD is not curable, but definitely manageable, with proper diagnosis and continuous support.

For others, for whatever reason, their parents may not have sought testing for their child's difficulties (as discussed in Chapter 3). Perhaps they were diagnosed and their parents never told them about the APD and they may not have known back then why they struggled with so many things that their peers could do so easily.

Without diagnosis, they would never have received the support that they so greatly needed, either at school or later at work, simply feeling stupid, failing time and time again, blaming themselves and never knowing why this was happening and that it was not their fault. This scenario damages a child and can leave emotional and psychological scars that can stay with them into adulthood. Therefore, accurate early diagnosis, support and telling the child about their APD are so vital. The feeling of something being wrong, of some reason as to why life was so difficult, will remain with them.

However, even with diagnosis, early-onset APD can still be difficult, especially where there is lack of understanding and acceptance by others. This 24-year-old woman in the US was diagnosed with APD at the age of eight.

I'm glad I found out when I did because it just became a part of my life... Growing up I've done my own research about it to find other ways to cope in school...

People often get aggravated when I ask 'what?', [not] catching onto sarcasm and jokes. I have trouble telling tone of voice and I never know if people are mad at me or not. I am a teacher and having to constantly listen to respond gives me a headache...

I did tell a few of my co-workers and they are really supportive...

[A friend] told me that it wasn't my fault and and to never let anyone make me feel dumb. This is something that I really needed to hear and I am so glad she said it. She also told me that when these situations happen to explain to people that I have [APD] and that I am doing the best that I can...

I am always scared to do something wrong, make mistakes...

I am just really good at not giving up... I recently started running and I like it because unlike school I set goals for myself and I actually see myself achieving those goals. That has been a huge self-esteem and confidence booster for me. [Another friend] tells me that if I can

> run whatever distance I can do anything... I noticed that I am starting
> to actually believe it...
>
> I want to be a Special Education teacher... I would say learning
> how to advocate is super important in all aspects of life.

Late diagnosis

Undiagnosed and unsupported adults, even those with great potential, can lack the qualifications they might otherwise have gained and be forced into low-paid or menial jobs. They might also have had any career aspirations dashed from an early age, either by their school or their parents or guardians. Unaided, they may have simply given up on achieving anything, or given up on themselves. Even with a high level of intellect and ability to do far better, success will have been denied to them. There are also children with amazing coping strategies, resilience and imaginative ways around their challenges who will succeed without help, never knowing about APD, but these children are rare.

Late-onset APD

Living with APD at any age comes down to personal coping strategies to help you deal with what you cannot change and ways of avoiding those situations that you cannot control, as well as asking for (and receiving) tailored support. By adulthood, coping strategies and workarounds are usually well ingrained and can help adults with APD to overcome a wide variety of challenges via strategies or avoidance. But this only applies if you have had APD since birth or since childhood.

We know that APD poses great obstacles to the child with APD, but it can also pose great challenges to those who acquire it later in life. Late-onset APD can be acquired in several ways, such as via head injury, road traffic accident, illness, stroke, sepsis, drug or alcohol abuse. The causes might improve and so might the APD. For some sufferers, it might even go away as the brain heals. But for others, it will remain in some form for the rest of their lives, maybe minor effects, or those that are debilitating. Other difficulties might occur after the same neurological damage that caused the APD, such as Visual Processing Disorder (VPD) or speech problems, which make it all worse.

Whatever the cause, it can come as a great shock to find that you can no longer do what you used to do, what most people take for granted. Late-onset APD can be life-changing. The person affected might have a successful career that they may no longer be able to cope with, initially at least. For some, this could mean financial insecurity, low-skilled or lower-paid jobs, even unemployment. Going from being successful and competent in the workplace to coping with a disability can be devastating, as it can for those used to being effective communicators, or those who used to be socially adept. Even those with less challenging jobs or none can find life much more difficult, even impossible, until they learn to adapt. Those with late-onset APD will need to learn to cope, do things differently and learn strategies that the child with APD has developed over decades, and this is not easy. Children adapt much more easily than adults, and faster. It is also hard to learn to ask for help for those not used to needing it, and pride, shame and embarrassment can get in the way. But it is not their fault – disability and chronic illness can come to anyone, out of nowhere, at any time.

Whatever the cause, there are many challenges for adults with APD to face and overcome. This 50-year-old man in the UK has late-onset APD, believed to be due to a stroke in 2007. He also has aphasia and mild hearing loss.

Originally, due to aphasia, I could not explain the hearing processing problem. I researched my symptoms on the internet... I could not follow questions on the telephone, and could not follow audible stories.

[Others thought he was just] slow to understand...

I just do not follow music at all. I use subtitles with TV. I avoid the telephone if I can...

I have taken a course at university as a mature student... I am too conscious to use a microphone [FM, frequency modulation] at university...

I avoid large numbers of people. I miss much of the conversation. I follow the gist but not the detail.

I just cannot do things I used take it for granted: organize utilities, banking, arrange things... I used to be good self-advocacy (I was a solicitor) but now I do not. I cannot follow long questions.

Late-onset APD and relationships

With late-onset APD or a diagnosis later in life, family and friends must also get used to this new version of the person they know and love; they, too, need to learn to adapt, and this doesn't happen automatically, readily or easily for some. It can also affect their relationship with a partner. Each partner must make allowances and compromises, as with any other aspect of a good relationship. Either partner wishing it was different won't help; both partners must find a way round it between them. This will often involve the person without APD changing how they perceive things and accepting their partner with APD as they are, not as they were, also respecting their need to do things a certain way in order to understand and communicate. It isn't that they aren't trying or don't want to communicate or remember what was said, for example. They are simply unable to do so without certain adjustments, patience and support. It can be a shock and a trial for all involved.

Adapting to the new situation can cause friction and frustration for all concerned. Relationships can become strained, and may even come to an end.

Miscommunication is a major contributor to this, as is the reluctance of the other person to accept, adapt or support. The same difficulties can also apply to the relationships of those with congenital or early-onset APD. Adults with APD can find that those closest to them are dismissive, lack understanding or are unwilling to deal with the APD, ignoring it or pretending it isn't there. This all adds to the pressure that they must already deal with. But the person with APD should also realize that other people may find it hard to understand APD and its effects. They may want to help but not know how, unless the person with APD tells them (which can be hard if they have difficulty communicating their thoughts, feelings and needs effectively). Self-advocacy skills are just as important in adulthood as they are to a child, and those with late-onset APD will not have had the same amount of time to learn to convey what they need, adding to the stress in relationships. Therefore, time, compromise and patience are needed on both sides, as well as alternative forms of communication.

Social impact

As I have mentioned previously, people with APD often choose not to socialize in order to avoid miscommunication, misunderstandings and the possibility of resulting arguments. But some can become withdrawn and avoid social contact rather than admit they cannot cope with noise and social interaction. Restaurants, bars, and so on can have a lot of background noise from multiple conversations and music playing. It is difficult to ask for the music to be turned down if you have communication difficulties and social anxiety, or when the people around you are not unduly bothered by it.

Others might become isolated because they have declared that they have APD, ask for help and are refused it. They might fear (and indeed suffer) rejection, ridicule and a sense of failure. Yet it is not their fault: it is simply as a result of their APD and the thoughtlessness and insensitivity of those around them. Whatever the reason, this situation can lead to loneliness. But unless they try, they will never know how much better life can become. If they don't admit there is a problem, they cannot even begin to solve it. They say nothing about the APD and other conditions, settle for their lot and hope it will go away, but sadly, it won't. Sooner or later there may come a stage when they may be unable to cope alone. As mentioned previously, coping strategies can fail when a person with APD is stressed, tired or ill, and trying to cope alone can make people even more stressed, which can keep them awake at night and even lead to physical or mental illness. Everyone needs help sometimes. There is no shame in that, only in denying who they are and what they could be, and no one should settle for less. If you are an adult with APD, it may be hard to tell people, but it is better to be honest. You might be pleasantly surprised at the response, and there is just as much chance of receiving the support and understanding that you need and deserve. Despite any previous bad experiences, there are good people in the world.

Declaring APD to family, friends and partners

Some people try to hide their APD for many reasons. One of the most common is fear that others will view them differently. This is particularly true for those who have acquired APD later in life, and also for those who have had a late diagnosis – they don't want their partner, friends and family to think less of them. But if they have always had the APD and other conditions, their loved ones will have noticed that they have problems with communication, which can affect their relationships, further education and work. The undiagnosed APD may already have led to misunderstandings and arguments, and it can also be a great source of stress and anxiety trying to keep it hidden.

Any of these reasons (and more) can be what prompts an adult who suspects APD to seek diagnosis, either by their own instigation or that of a partner or someone else who is worried and wants to help them find the reason for their difficulties. So it may be no surprise to others when they find there is a reason behind their struggles. If the APD is declared to these people, they will often be relieved that the person with APD finally has answers and they will want to help. There may be others in their lives who are less than supportive, but in my experience, they are not the sort of people someone with a disability needs in their life. What they have gained from diagnosis will outweigh what they have lost.

There is also a fear of rejection when declaring a condition or disability at the start of a new relationship – we always want to appear at our best when meeting new people. But any relationship based on lies, half-truths and hiding who you are is not one that is based on solid foundations. At some point the APD will become apparent and those foundations can crumble. A caring partner, friend, employer or colleague would much prefer to know from the start, and many people dislike being lied to, even if it is a lie of omission. If they turn out to be unsupportive once they are told about the APD and any other conditions or difficulties, it is far better to know what sort of person *they* are and end the relationship early on before any further damage is done to the confidence and self-esteem of the person with APD. But whether to declare is a choice to be made by the person with APD.

In my experience, those who choose not to share that they have APD are often those who have not fully accepted it themselves, whether they were diagnosed as a child or later. As with a child with APD, the first step is acceptance. This 49-year-old woman living in the US was diagnosed when she was about 43. She also has slight hearing loss. She believes that her APD was possibly due to several childhood concussions from the age of two.

> I don't make sense of what people are saying unless I'm already tuned in... I lipread a lot... my partner accused me all the time of not caring enough to listen/remember what she said... I was always frustrated...because my parents told me I was playing 'the dumb game'. As I got older, I felt isolated in larger groups because I couldn't

follow the conversations...my partner gave me no end of grief even after my diagnosis... My slight hearing loss made it worse.

[She has not declared her APD at work] I do not want my competence called into question. I do fine with my coping mechanisms. I have hearing aids... I find that they do help in crowded places or with multiple people talking at once... I still use CC [closed captions/ subtitles] even with them because I will still miss stuff... I have asked people to please say my name or at least get my attention before talking to me and, in some circumstances, to please face me while speaking...

I was always being punished or singled out for not listening. I found that embarrassing and frustrating...

Just be patient. You don't have to be a saint...just realize the strategies are quite simple and will make EVERYONE'S lives easier.

Declaring APD at work or in further education

Not everyone with APD will need help at work or in further education, some might need a lot, and others could need very little; it all depends on the severity of the symptoms and the job itself, as well as whether it is a suitable workplace for a person with their difficulties.

If you let your employer/place or education and work colleagues/ fellow learners think that you are incapable of doing your job/course because you keep making mistakes or don't know what to do because of your APD, this can lead to suspension/demotion/dismissal or removal from your course, just for the sake of asking for support which can help you. These outcomes can be avoided.

Career choices

Someone who changes their job frequently might have an interesting resume, and it can broaden their experience and variety of job choice. But it may also appear indecisive and unreliable to an employer. For people with APD, this can be common. Moving between jobs might be because the employee doesn't like the work or is not progressing in the role, or they are unhappy there, for whatever reason. But for a person with APD and other difficulties, it can often be due to the workplace environment being unsuitable, the employer not providing reasonable accommodations, or the employee not coping and leaving instead of asking for them.

Interacting with work colleagues can also be problematic if they don't know about (or understand) APD, the nature of the difficulties that can arise in that environment and the effects on the person with APD that the job, or their actions, might cause. This is another reason to declare it at the earliest opportunity and to share information with work colleagues (where they think it is appropriate for them to know, and if they feel it will affect them if they don't know).

Therefore, the ability to self-advocate is so important, as well as declaring the APD and other conditions as early as possible. If not declared, their difficulties can severely hamper their job options and career progression. They might love the job, but if they appear to be unable to do their job properly, they will not be kept on by an employer, especially when they may not be able to understand why a suitably qualified and intelligent employee is struggling to keep up, achieve time-based targets, follow instructions or communicate efficiently. If the employee doesn't declare APD or ask for help, it is natural for people to make assumptions without knowing the facts; unfairly believing that an employee is lazy or unmotivated is incorrect and hurtful, taking the person with APD back to the feelings of inadequacy that they felt as a child. They may then leave the job out of embarrassment before they are fired.

Below are some examples of jobs that can be problematic for people with APD (depending on their individual difficulties, severity and coping strategies or workarounds). While it isn't practical to list all job types here, some tips are also given which can be adapted to other roles.

- Any customer-facing role such as reception work or retail can be difficult, unless there is no customer contact. Roles such as warehouse or delivery work are better, where instructions can be given in writing.

- As a barista, it can be very difficult if you have to engage with customers, and the working environment can be noisy. Taking orders can be problematic but manageable if you ask customers to speak clearly and to order one item at a time, allowing time for you to write it down. You should always read it back to them, too, to ensure that the order is correct. Such roles can be good, especially for those who need and enjoy the security of routine.

The same applies to waiting staff, counter staff in takeaways, cafes and restaurants. Kitchens follow set procedures and routines which may suit some people and not others: you can read the orders that need to be cooked, but they can also be busy, noisy and tasks will be time-sensitive.

- Roles that depend on using the telephone, such as call centres and customer care, or dealing with enquiries and complaints can be extremely difficult with no way to support this because there can be no alternative to telephone use. However, such communication-based companies might have roles that only involve replying to customers via email or letter.

- The armed forces, emergency services and other posts need employees to verbally take orders or instruction, understand them the first time and act on them quickly. Whether communicated in person or over a telephone, radio or other electronic equipment (which can be even harder to process), this can be impossible for a lot of people with APD. But an office-based role in these services can be more manageable, so long as it isn't working as a call handler or dealing with the public (however phone use is not problematic for everyone with APD). Similarly, any role that includes time-sensitive actions, working to deadlines, and so on can be difficult and extremely stressful for some people with APD, especially if they have problems with memory, word retrieval or slow processing.

- Any role that requires effective auditory sequencing (being told to do things in in a specific order) can be overcome by having instructions in writing.

- Working in the medical profession, for example as a carer or counsellor, naturally includes a lot of verbal interaction with patients/clients, possibly with speech or communication problems, and some of these jobs can also require acting quickly on instructions and what patients tell them. Misunderstanding speech, for example, in a hospital setting, can have serious consequences.

- Factory work can be noisy and repetitive, but offers routine and limited communication with others. Here, too, instructions would need to be written down and checked with the person giving them.

- There are also jobs in which rules and routines can change from day to day, such as working different hours/shift patterns, which might be a problem for some people with APD and associated executive function difficulties.

- A minute-taking role might be unsuitable for some people with APD, unless adjustments are permitted, such as a voice recorder, to allow the minute-taker to check that what was written down was correct and to help fill in any potential gaps. However, recording might need permission of the meeting participants under data protection legislation. Provision of a laptop instead of writing can help, too, for those who have additional writing difficulties. If taking part in a meeting, it can be made easier to process if one person speaks at a time, assistive listening technology is provided and the person with APD is addressed by name when their input is required.

- Office work might need reasonable adjustments, provision of certain equipment and limited use of telephones, or none. People with APD and any disability, difficulty or health condition are legally entitled to support in the workplace and their requirements and entitlement should be discussed with their employer or Occupational Health Adviser.

- Writing things down is a common solution to many challenges caused by APD. However, for those with writing or reading difficulties or Dyslexia this might not be a viable strategy. Use of diagrams might help in certain situations such as providing order sheets with items listed for customers to tick or illustrated menus to point to, but these might have to be requested as a reasonable adjustment. Noisy situations are worse for people with APD, although failure to process speech effectively can also occur in a quiet setting.

Support with telephones and video conferencing

With home-working on the increase and places of education running more online courses, classes and tutorials, communication difficulties in these areas are becoming more of a problem for people with APD. Some of the issues can affect anyone, but are usually worse for those with APD. The difficulties need to be addressed, to provide support in education, in meetings and when socializing with friends or family too. The outcomes can include improvements to working and teaching practices, productivity and inter-personal relationships. This support can be included in the reasonable adjustments requested from an employer or place of education; friends and family can help, too, when they use this form of communication.

Support for the workplace and in further education

The correct choice of career can be vital to a person with APD and other difficulties, and with support and some outside-the-box thinking, it can be possible to find ways around the problems in most working environments. However, if you can find a suitable working environment from the start, this is a bonus. I would consider an APD-friendly work environment to be one that is as quiet as possible to help employees with APD process speech better without background noise, although processing can still be a problem even when it is quiet. For those who also have Hyperacusis or sound sensitivity that makes processing more difficult, noise reduction can also help them as well as reducing ear pain. There are simple modifications that can be used to reduce ambient noise (just like the APD-friendly classroom described Chapter 7).

People who may have learned about APD as adults and those who have late-onset APD might have found it extremely difficult at school, without any understanding of APD or any form of education support, especially if they also have other conditions that may or may not have also been diagnosed late for some reason. This can limit their career options, especially if they don't realize that workplace support can and should be provided. After diagnosis, especially if they have had difficulty finding a suitable job and need qualifications, maybe for career advancement or to finally support the career they dreamed of as a child, they might decide to turn to adult education. Whatever they decide to do, at any level, they will need and deserve support and reasonable adjustments.

Reasonable adjustments can be requested for adults with APD in the workplace or adult education, as well as any adjustments needed for other conditions and difficulties. Listed below are examples of the sort of adjustments that might be appropriate. This is not an exhaustive list by any means; as with everything related to APD, the reasonable adjustments will depend on the specific needs of the individual.[1]

- All equipment required as reasonable adjustments for the workplace or place of education, such as assistive listening devices (for example, an FM system and other equipment like a speech recorder, speech to text software, noise-cancelling headphones or whatever is needed, and provision of items to minimize background noise with carpet/rugs, notice boards, noise-cancelling headphones etc.).

- Frequent breaks in a quiet place to avoid sensory overload and access to water to prevent dehydration.

- Use of text or email instead of telephones where possible, plus provision of an answerphone for messages and to record calls to replay later (this may need permission regarding data protection).

- Home-working, if/when appropriate to the job or study, and all necessary equipment (as above) to aid the employee/learner while working from home, plus a laptop and anything else needed.

- Provision of a note-taker, or pre-printed materials before meetings/lectures.

- Extra time to prepare reports/assignments.

- Reasonable adjustments for tests and examinations for learning/training such as a reader or scribe or a quiet room in which to take them (preferably alone with an invigilator).

- For video conferencing required for work meetings, tutorials and lectures, all necessary equipment and support that the employee/learner needs should be provided.

---

1   If you are not a UK resident, please check in your country for relevant disability rights information.

Legalities

With diagnosis of a disability in the UK the law is on your side in requesting reasonable adjustments in work and further education. Employers and places of learning are legally obliged to provide support and reasonable adjustments. (They also have a duty of care to protect all employees/students from harassment, bullying and discrimination.)

But support and reasonable adjustments for condition/s and difficulties cannot be expected if they are not declared or an education establishment or employer doesn't know that an employee is struggling, and they could not reasonably be expected to know that.

Not everyone with APD will need help at work; it depends on the severity of the symptoms and the job itself. But if you need or expect reasonable adjustments to be made in your workplace environment, it is advisable to declare your APD on appointment, or immediately after diagnosis, if this takes place after appointment. According to the UK Equality Act 2010:

- You must inform your employer of your APD, other difficulties and conditions if you want them to provide support, and if your duties or work conditions are changed, thus causing you difficulties that were not present on appointment.

- You must inform your employer if problems arise that you had not anticipated on appointment.

- You must inform your employer if the nature of the work for which you were appointed is different to that which you were expecting (and if what you expected would not cause you any problems with your APD or the perceived post that you accepted did not affect you anticipating having any problems when you accepted the post, but they do now).

Barriers to declaration of APD

Other barriers to declaring APD might be related to problems that have developed over time, such as with self-esteem, confidence and trust.

Whether or not they had been diagnosed in early life or were aware of their APD and other difficulties, adults with early-onset APD would have been struggling since childhood. Depending on age, testing might not have been available to them as a child, or, as discussed in Chapter 3, their parents may not have taken them for testing and support was scarce (in fact, both are still not widely available today).

By the time they reached adulthood, their self-esteem and confidence might have already been badly affected, possibly leading to anxiety and depression. The impact of poor self-esteem and low confidence is another factor that can make adults reluctant to tell anyone about their APD for fear of more ridicule and dismissive behaviour that may have been common, even a daily occurrence when they were growing up, as well as constant feelings that they were a failure at whatever they tried. I have known adults with APD to describe themselves as 'useless' or 'worthless'. They are neither of these things; people with APD are just as capable as anyone else in a sympathetic environment with the right support.

Feeling anxious at the thought of being further belittled by those who didn't understand them, these adults can be reluctant to try anything new and settle for menial jobs because without support, what they want to do seems beyond their reach. Yet what is holding them back is the very thing they fear: telling others and asking for help. It takes a lot of courage to do that. Lack of trust of strangers may also have developed over time and self-esteem and confidence issues provide further barriers, in addition to their existing communication issues. A partner, family member or work colleague can do a lot to improve the self-esteem and confidence of a person with APD, using the tips given in Chapter 5.

Residual resentment and Post-Traumatic Stress Disorder

Over the years, during my contact with innumerable adults and parents with APD in several countries, I have encountered a lot with residual resentment towards family, friends, colleagues, partners, medical and education professionals and even employers. There can be many reasons for this.

Resentment towards immediate family, as a result of:

- Parents not seeking a diagnosis when they were a child.

- Parents/siblings not trying to understand or accept their APD.

- Parents/siblings not providing emotional support.

- Parents/siblings unwilling to support essential coping strategies.

- Ridicule by parents/disability discrimination.

- Parents not telling anyone they had APD, appearing as if it made them feel ashamed of their child, something to be hidden.

- Parents not seeking or ensuring full support at school.

- Reluctance or failure of parents/siblings to defend the person with APD when faced with other family members/people they met who didn't believe that they had APD, or who needed help.

Resentment towards other children and adults, either peers/colleagues and/or those they considered as friends, as a result of:

- Being teased by other children or even adults, or being rejected for being perceived as 'different'.

- Reluctance or failure by others to support essential coping strategies and alternative methods of communication.

- Disability discrimination and/or bullying by children/adults.

Resentment towards medical professionals, as a result of:

- Reluctance or failure to act on parents' suspicion of APD (as a child with APD or later as an adult seeking diagnosis).

- Ridicule by medical professionals (as a parent or when seeking referral as an adult); some medical professionals have even suggested that people seeking referral had imagined their symptoms or simply had mental health problems.

- Reluctance or failure by medical professionals to refer for testing (as a parent or an adult with APD).

- Reluctance or failure to support essential coping strategies and alternative methods of communication in a professional consultation, or afterwards.

- Disability discrimination towards them and/or their child.

Resentment towards education professionals, as a result of:

- Lack of support in school or further education.

- Reluctance or failure to acknowledge the validity of their specialist APD diagnosis report (and other diagnoses).

- Reluctance or failure to implement the specialist recommendations in the diagnosis reports.

- Reluctance or failure to support essential coping strategies and alternative methods of communication.

- Reluctance or failure to implement requested reasonable adjustments.

- Ridicule or bullying behaviour by teachers.

- Unfair punishment for incomplete work or homework or not answering questions correctly (due to processing and communication difficulties caused by APD).

- Reluctance or failure to stop bullying by children.

- Reluctance or failure to learn about or support other conditions and difficulties.

- Disability discrimination.

Resentment towards employers/supervisors and work colleagues, as a result of:

- Lack of support at work.

- Reluctance or failure to acknowledge their specialist APD diagnosis report as valid (and other diagnoses).

- Reluctance or failure to implement the specialist recommendations in the diagnosis reports.

- Reluctance or failure to support essential coping strategies and alternative methods of communication.

- Reluctance or failure to implement requested reasonable adjustments.

- Ridicule or bullying behaviour or disability discrimination by other staff members and supervisor's/employer's reluctance or failure to stop it.

- Unfair censure, suspension or dismissal for incomplete work or other issues caused by processing and communication difficulties (due to APD, or as a result of other difficulties and exacerbated by lack of support or reasonable workplace adjustments).

- Being passed over for promotion due to disability discrimination.

Resentment towards a partner/spouse, as a result of:

- Reluctance or failure to understand or accept their APD and other difficulties and decision to seek diagnosis (and those of their child/ren).

- Reluctance or failure to discuss problems arising from a lack of understanding or acceptance.

- Reluctance or failure to provide emotional support.

- Reluctance or failure to support essential coping strategies.

- Ridicule, bullying, disability discrimination or abuse by a partner/spouse as a response to APD and other difficulties.

- Reluctance or failure to support the person with APD when faced with other family members/people they meet who don't believe that they have APD/other conditions, or need help.

As you will see, there is a pattern of similar ways in which those with APD can be let down by people around them. Some experience it on one or two occasions and not everyone they meet might behave in this way. But for too many people with APD, it can happen again and again throughout their lives. It is therefore no wonder that feelings of resentment can build over the years. It is not just a question of feeling sorry for oneself. The reasons, where present, are usually due to the other person's lack of knowledge of APD, refusal to accept its existence and lack of support when they needed it most.

Resentment can eat away at people and ruin relationships; they can also develop into mistrust of others, another factor preventing disclosure of their APD and other difficulties, which can also lead to reluctance to seek support. These feelings should not be dismissed or minimized, and counselling can be beneficial.

My personal advice to anyone who has residual resentment, who is still holding onto that pain, is that forgiveness will help. Letting go of anger and resentment and forgiving those who let you down can only heal those wounds and free you from that burden. It is their load to bear: you have held onto it long enough.

Discussing these issues with other like-minded adults with APD (in whichever format is best for the individual with APD) can help a lot too. This is why online support groups work so well for people with APD, largely due to the ease of communication without the need for verbal interaction, thus minimizing the effects of APD to a large extent. There is also the relative anonymity of online contact, allowing people to express their feelings and experiences more freely, as well as sharing coping strategies. Such information-sharing can, for some, eventually lead to adults with APD learning strategies to be able to talk about these feelings and other issues with partners, family and friends. 'That happened to me and this is what I did' is a very useful method for dealing with such problems and leads to finding compromises and ways around them (when they feel ready and able to do so). Having APD is nothing to be ashamed about.

Discussing such topics with those close to you and whom you feel resentment towards can be difficult and may increase anxiety. There are also situations whereby a casual word or action by others can make you relive past insults, belittling behaviour, bullying and so on, leading you to lash out at that person who meant no harm and who is confused and hurt by your reaction. If they don't know about the APD they wouldn't know how you have been treated in the past, or the reason for its lasting effects. It is like a type of post-traumatic shock and therapy might be needed to help you to deal with the trauma. These incidents can be distressing for the person without APD too. Partners find that couples therapy can help too.

Many adults have reported improvements in their relationships as a result of being honest about their APD. In this situation, too, people cannot help or understand if they don't know there is a problem. It is a case of those with APD needing to spread awareness of the condition one person at a time, instead of expecting the people they meet to know about it. The very nature of the condition makes explanation difficult, although carrying an APD alert cart (available from my website) can help with that, as an ice-breaker to help raise the topic.

One day APD may be better known, like Dyslexia or Autism. But today, APD is *not* widely known, and until that day comes, anything that an adult can do to spread information will ultimately be a step towards helping themselves, their children (if they also have APD) and future generations with APD so that they won't have to suffer the ignorance and misinformation that currently exists and has caused them so much pain.

A summary of ways to help adults with APD

- Look at the person with APD when you speak to them (many need to lipread). Use their name and get their attention before speaking, and hold conversations somewhere quiet whenever possible. Speak clearly and use short sentences.

- If the adult with APD does not understand or has not processed what you said, ask them if they prefer repetition of what is said or for you to reword it. To aid or avoid verbal communication, some prefer text, email or even handwritten notes, letters or diagrams (particularly useful for those who also have reading difficulties). Sign language might be another option if you or someone in the workplace/college knows it.

- Misinterpretation of the meaning of words can lead to miscommunication. Provide work-related, subject-specific vocabulary lists. For meetings, seminars and training and so on, also provide written material beforehand to aid pre-learning and participation.

- Provide assistive listening technology to improve the volume and clarity of speech and to aid processing (as explained in Chapter 7). Allow recording, if requested, or offer to take notes for the person with APD, or provide a note-taker. Sitting where they can see the speaker will help, too, as they might rely on visual cues like lipreading, facial expressions and body language to aid understanding.

- Keep workplaces free from auditory and visual distractions. Background noise reduces the already diminished ability to process speech. Visual distractions make this worse.

- Be patient if someone with APD speaks more loudly or more quietly than others; this is due to an inability to self-regulate speech volume that they cannot process, cannot help and may be unaware of. This can also affect their tone of voice. People can form assumptions based on the way someone speaks. If an individual with APD speaks loudly, this can be misinterpreted as being brash, over-confident, condescending, or even aggressive. Similarly, someone with APD who speaks quietly may appear shy, withdrawn, anti-social, even lacking in intelligence. It is not their fault and they are usually unaware that they are doing it. A gentle reminder about their volume or tone can be helpful.

- The person with APD who fails to respond quickly or appropriately due to their delayed processing or word retrieval for example might also seem to lack interest in the conversation. By the time they form a response, the topic may well have changed, leaving them confused, embarrassed and less likely to respond. Over time, it may also cause them to avoid social interaction altogether.

- A person with APD might misinterpret the tone of voice of others; humour can also cause difficulty, because they may have processed it incorrectly and missed the 'punch line'. Sarcasm can also be difficult for some people with APD to understand, and sarcastic comments can be interpreted as hurtful. This can lead to miscommunication and arguments. Try to reassure them and explain that they have misunderstood what you meant, that you were not making fun of them, and are not annoyed or being insulting. Idioms can also be hard for some people with APD to understand. Try to use simple language (without being condescending) and short sentences with gaps between them, to allow time to process.

- Adults with APD may have problems with telephones and people with strong accents or rapid speech. This is caused by degradation of sound quality, sound distortion, unfamiliar voices and speech patterns, and so on. Use other forms of communication wherever possible (as described earlier), or speak clearly and slowly, allowing the listener extra time to process what you say. Using the telephone should ideally be avoided, but when it is essential, calls taken in a quiet environment are preferable, especially at work, or supply speech to text software or an answerphone.

- Give written instructions wherever possible (or, if verbally, give them one at a time, allowing time for completion before giving another one). This is to avoid misunderstanding due to poor auditory sequencing.

- Some people with APD might also stutter or stammer at times when trying to reply or express themselves, especially when stressed. These difficulties can be frustrating and embarrassing for someone with APD. Be patient and always allow the person time to process what you say and to find the words that they need to respond to you. If it is apparent, explain discreetly what you feel has been misunderstood.

- In some people, APD can cause problems with reading and/ or spelling. APD is thought to be one of the major causes of Dyslexia. Use of spellcheckers and assistive reading technology such as speech to text software can help here.

- Avoid noisy places for social gatherings. Background noise makes processing harder and can be unpleasant, exhausting and overwhelming, even leading to sensory overload. Crowded venues and those that play music (also loud restaurants and bars with music) should also be avoided.

- People with APD become tired very easily and might not always want to (or be able to) have a conversation, so other methods of communication should be used (as described earlier). Or postpone the conversation until they feel more able to converse, and turn off any music. They will also need frequent breaks from noise. A quiet place should be provided, to prevent exhaustion and sensory overload.

- People with APD need to develop their own unique coping strategies. This isn't because they are selfish or demanding; these are vital to help them to process speech and to communicate effectively. Support their needs as much as possible, but if you find their routines restrictive, talk about this calmly with them, and try to come to a compromise.

Home-working

An ideal place for many people to work is in their own home. However, there are several important factors to consider, especially if they have additional implications for those with APD and other difficulties. Whether you are working for an employer at home, are self-employed, or run your own business, these tips can help you to manage your workspace and working day.

A suitable workspace

- You will need a space/room that you can use as a home office or workshop with enough room for all the furniture, materials, equipment or stock you might need (as appropriate). Some people prefer to work in their living room or a spare room, but I recommend that you keep your bedroom as a work-free zone, or you may not be able to relax there.

Distractions

- Your work space should be quiet enough to work without visual or auditory distractions (such as clutter or noise) or it can be improved by getting rid of unwanted items, donating them to charity or moving them to another room; also use sound-proofing or ear defenders.

- Family can also be distracting, especially if you have young children, so try to work when they are at school/nursery, have someone to look after them, or work when they are taking a nap or after they go to bed at night.

- If your pets are likely to distract you, close the door (or let them in, if they will settle near you or make more noise with the door closed just to get to you).

- It also helps to have a business mobile phone for work calls only, and ask friends and family not to call your personal phone during your chosen working hours, unless it is urgent.

- Some people find it helps to keep regular working hours. It is your choice whether you do that, and it will also depend on your home circumstances.

- It might seem strange, but what you wear can have psychological importance. Some people prefer to dress as if they were going to work, to get into that frame of mind. Others who work from home find that they are more motivated and work better if they dress casually, even remaining in their nightwear. However, I recommend being fully dressed if you are expecting a client or taking part in a video-conferencing call!

As you can see, there are benefits to home-working with APD and other disabilities, in that you are more in control:

- You can manage your surroundings and working environment and set your hours.

- You don't have to speak to people when you're working if you don't want to.

- You don't have to use the telephone (you can ask people to email or text you); but if you do need to do so, you can manage the call on your terms: call them and write a script of what you want to say or make notes beforehand and end the call when you want.

- You can take breaks when you want, so long as the work gets done.

- It is also easier and less stressful to work from home, because there are fewer distractions and people to deal with.

Running your own business also has advantages. You are answerable to no one and you can do things when and how you decide in order to accommodate your APD and other difficulties. But there are drawbacks – mainly that it is expensive to set up a business, extremely hard work, stressful and tiring (and most new businesses fail in the first year). But it is another option nonetheless.

Self-care

As with any job with APD and other difficulties, even if you work from home in a seemingly more suitable and relaxed environment, any job can be stressful, and it is still very important to look after yourself. Those in adult education also need to practise self-care. Take frequent breaks, make sure you are hydrated and eat regularly and healthily. Exercise is important, too – even half an hour out walking in the fresh air can help you to have a healthy lifestyle, clear your thoughts and reduce sensory sensitivity and stress. Make sure to maintain a life/work/study balance; make time to do the things you like and spend time with your loved ones. Accept help, advice and support wherever it is offered.

These are just a few factors about APD and home-working; you can search on the internet for more information. Be flexible if you can: it is less stressful. More importantly, find out what works for you.

Stress

One of the biggest issues for people with APD and other invisible disabilities is stress, which in some people can lead to a range of physical and emotional symptoms including stress migraines, other physical symptoms and mental health problems like anxiety or depression (which are also invisible disabilities in their own right). Dealing with APD is stressful enough on its own. There might be problems at work, difficulty with seeking work, receptive and expressive communication problems, lack of appropriate support and not being able to find a suitable work environment (thus leading to added money worries and difficulty negotiating the benefits system). All of these increase the impact of stress on people with APD.

Also stressful are other people's poor awareness of APD at work and limited knowledge about APD elsewhere, as well as the lack of acceptance of a person's APD by their family and friends, one of the biggest issues they face. Even though they may have developed effective coping strategies in familiar situations, being placed in a new situation (with new people or in a new location) can override these coping mechanisms, causing panic, worsening the effects of APD, and coping strategies then fail, further compounding their stress (and distress). New situations call for new strategies, but they take time, and slow processing hinder their development there and then. There are also unfamiliar voice patterns to get used to when they meet new people. Familiarity is necessary for many people with APD to feel comfortable, and change can be very difficult to deal with. All of this takes time, which may not be possible when starting a new job, course or relationship (especially if the people you interact with know nothing of the APD and other difficulties, the need for this adjustment or the type of support required in order to help you to function efficiently).

Stress makes it harder for people to cope with their APD and symptoms can become worse as a result of reluctance or failure of their coping strategies, due to the brain's diverted focus on the causes of stress. Lack of sleep due to worry is another factor that can cause the coping strategies to falter, creating a vicious circle of worry, stress, tiredness and anxiety. This is not at all helpful to those seeking and maintaining a job, running a family or just living day to day, even without the added factor of coping with APD. People with APD need to find their own individual ways of dealing with stress (see Chapter 11).

Age

APD should not worsen unless there is further injury to the brain, which can happen for various reasons, as mentioned. However, adults often find that their ability to cope gets worse as they get older, making the APD appear worse. It can be worrying and disorienting because coping strategies should improve with age and experience, not worsen; however, they can become less effective simply because vision and hearing deteriorate as we get older. Clarity and volume of hearing make processing easier and the opposite applies if there is hearing loss. Also, vision is the primary sense and it provides many of the coping strategies that people with APD rely on, every day. Adults with APD need to be prepared for this sensory decline as they age and make sure that they have vision and hearing tests as soon as problems develop. Prescribed glasses and/or hearing aids can help to compensate for diminished quality of vision and hearing in order to improve coping strategies once again. Repeat vision and hearing tests should be carried out as recommended by the providers.

There are separate articles on the APD Support UK website[2] with additional information and advice on the topics of:

- Telephone use and video conferencing, suitable for remote teaching or tutorials.

- Finding and maintaining employment.

- Stress.

---

2   https://apdsupportuk.yolasite.com/information.php

11

Anxiety

STRESS AND MENTAL HEALTH

This chapter deals with many already discussed issues, but from a mental health perspective. Living with APD can be very difficult at any age, especially while learning coping strategies and waiting for a diagnosis, as well as when waiting for adequate and appropriate support to be put in place at school. It can also be equally stressful for their loved ones.

> It's stressful at the best of times, but what makes it more stressful are the battles with the school and other professionals to get her the right help and support... (Parent of a child aged 12 with APD)

Children with APD are under constant pressure, and this only increases as they get older and school workload and difficulty increase too. Stress, anxiety (and social anxiety) are common among people with APD, and they can even develop in very young children, as can depression. They can easily become overwhelmed, unable to relax, angry and frustrated. Puberty is also a very challenging time, when hormones make coping with APD worse. Adults with APD are also affected, as are families and partners (see Chapters 9 and 10).

Children and adults with APD may have other unrelated yet coexisting mental health issues too, and these will naturally impact on APD and other difficulties and vice versa, adding to their stress.

There can be other issues that manifest as a result of living and coping with APD and other coexisting difficulties, for adults as well as children.

> I already have anxiety and depression, but I think my depression is affected when someone is being especially intolerant or when I find myself feeling very alone in a crowd. (Adult aged 49 with APD)

APD can become harder to deal with at times when the person is stressed, tired or unwell. One explanation is that the brain becomes exhausted and overloaded; another is that the body is diverting effort and energy to cope with these situations and aiding recovery. Either way, the person with APD can find that at these times their coping strategies can fail, leading to a vicious cycle of misery, at any age.

> I find it's worse when I am stressed and overwhelmed…
> When I feel like I might miss something important, I stress out… I also get a little nervous in meetings or when I know someone is talking too fast. (Adult aged 24 with APD)

Emotional and mental health difficulties

APD is a complex and far-reaching disability that affects all aspects of a person's life, not only in education, but also communication, socialization and employment. It causes difficulties in communicating with family and friends, choice of suitable careers and enjoyment of hobbies. Therefore, the stressors as a child will also affect them as teenagers and adults. Lack of appropriate and adequate support at an early age, at home or at school, can take its toll not only on a child's education, but also on their emotional wellbeing, their confidence and self-esteem. As mentioned previously, diagnosis, validation and acceptance can go a long way to helping with this, at any age.

> He masks when at school, so school don't see any emotional issues. He was referred to [mental health services] for school anxiety. (Parent of a child aged 10 with APD)

Lack of understanding can do untold emotional and psychological damage. A child with APD can feel isolated and helpless due to being in a regular position of failure. Adults who have lived with this all their life have described it to me as always being on the 'back foot' or feeling 'broken' or even 'faulty', 'worthless' or 'useless'. Imagine what that constant pressure does to someone, especially someone as yet undiagnosed, who doesn't understand why this is happening to them and is unable to explain it to others. Knowing that it isn't their fault and that other people understand and accept them can help to ease these feelings.

Vulnerability

As already discussed, the issues that any child with a disability or learning difficulties must deal with every day can be many and will vary from child to child, according to the nature and extent of the difficulties. These difficulties can leave them vulnerable. Children with APD and/or other so-called invisible disabilities are particularly vulnerable, because they have none of the outward signs of disability, like those who have physical disabilities and use a stick or a wheelchair, for example. They will appear to unknowing children and adults as being just the same as all the other children in their class and those they come across outside school. Neurotypical children (and adults) will expect them to behave and respond like the rest of their peers. But their communication difficulties in both receptive and expressive language will leave them disadvantaged; they might often misunderstand the words and intentions of others and be misunderstood in return. They can suffer greatly emotionally as a result, even worrying what is to become of them.

> ...she worries about things that are years away. (Parent of a child aged 12 with APD)

As well as being socially less able, a lot of children with APD can seem to act and respond differently to their peers, and can be immature, no matter how intelligent they may be. These children will therefore appear 'different' to their peers (and they often realize that they come across as different). This can lead children with APD, like those who have other difficulties and disabilities, to also be vulnerable to bullies. Any weakness will be preyed upon, and children who appear different, lacking in self-esteem and confidence, such as those with additional needs, can be prime targets.

Spotting the signs

Often the first indications that there is something wrong in any child (whether because of bullying, self-esteem issues, lack of support at school, social difficulties or other stress factors) are instances of tearful or angry outbursts at home. It is at home that they feel safe, having kept their frustrations in at school during the day for fear of getting into trouble. They may seemingly over-react to insignificant incidents that they would normally ignore. Over time, if not noticed, or if the cause is not found and dealt with, this can spill over at school and might even affect previously enjoyable activities.

> She gets stressed and anxious if someone like the SALT [Speech and Language Therapist] is coming in to see her or she has a dance/gym competition... (Parent of a child aged 8 with APD)

There might be uncharacteristic bad behaviour, attention-seeking and increased sensitivity to criticism. They could become withdrawn, reluctant to go out to play, perhaps losing interest in favourite games or hobbies. There might even be stress-related indicators like aggression, nightmares or bedwetting, stress-related migraines, stuttering or stammering, occasional vocal or physical tics at times of stress (unlike those of Tourette's Syndrome, which are generally present all the time, in varying degrees).

> There is a lot of tension in the house, a lot of angry outbursts, lashing out...arguments with her and avoidance tactics. (Parent of a child aged 12 with APD)

They might take comfort in reverting to toys, books or activities from when they were younger, or thumb-sucking, anything that brought them comfort when they were little, taking them back to a time when they felt safer, more in control. All these things can be symptoms of a bigger problem, which in some cases can even lead to school phobia, and in the worst cases, post-traumatic stress. It can even set the child on a downward spiral to depression and worsening social anxiety. These are all indicators of very unhappy children and should not be ignored. If not helped, this can lead to disaffection at school, or total withdrawal;

at that point the child has effectively given up. If you suspect stress or anxiety, talk to your child.

> The NHS report identified stress and anxiety as a risk. [She] does get very stressed and can be withdrawn... We talk a lot about stress and anxiety and what is normal stress and how to deal with it. (Parent of a teenager aged 14 with APD)

In a child who is not being fully supported at school and who feels that they are failing, if they have problems with friendships inside or outside school or are being bullied, frustration can mount, leading to angry outbursts, self-loathing or self-isolation. A crisis point could arise either at school or at home, and this might be misinterpreted as a behaviour problem without looking for the cause. A child doesn't suddenly change their personality overnight without good reason. Instead of punishing uncharacteristic bad behaviour, parents and teachers should ask why it is happening. Instead of telling the child they are under-achieving, teachers should find out why, and work with the child to help them to achieve. Instead of isolating children with difficulties and allowing other children to reject and exclude them, they should ensure that other children in their class understand why the child behaves as they do, why they cannot communicate in the same way, and help them to find friendship and encourage support from their peers.

> He can be easily stressed by...forgetting a piece of school equipment and [fears] making a mistake in class and the other kids not wanting to play with him...
>
> ...it's upsetting and stressful for him not to be able to comm-unicate... (Parent of a child aged 9 with Spatial Processing Disorder)

In my experience of working with children with emotional and behavioural problems, children do not 'act up' without a reason. Parents and professionals should always ask 'Why?'. They usually do it to gain attention, often to let people know that in some way they are struggling emotionally and need help. I have since realized, from what I have learned over the last 20 years, that many of the children I worked with had undiagnosed learning difficulties. The signs were there, but I was not experienced enough to recognize them at the time. I have come to learn that this sort of behaviour is common in children who have not been properly diagnosed or adequately supported at school, at home, or both, as was the case with many of the children I worked with.

> Sitting exams in different subjects on the same day causes memory issues and great stress... (Parent of a teenager aged 14 with APD)

Major problem

Mental health issues like anxiety and stress are not isolated occurrences among children, but a major problem that so often accompanies APD and those with additional learning difficulties. They should not be ignored or underestimated by parents, teachers or other associated professionals. A child who struggles both in school and out is doubly vulnerable, making the learning issues and often-related social problems so much worse. This is a child who may suffer daily, often in silence, from increasing feelings of self-doubt and inadequacy. This must stop.

Parental stress

As well as being difficult for the child, it can also be awful for a parent to cope with. It is heart-breaking to see your child's happiness slip away with each passing day. One day you are looking on as your happy, lively toddler runs readily into nursery, full of anticipation and eager to learn and make friends. After a few days or weeks, you are helpless as your very unhappy child, maybe angry or friendless, cries himself to sleep at night, hating school and wondering why he is so stupid. It is a living nightmare, holding a double-edged sword of wanting to do what's best for your child and knowing what is causing it, yet feeling powerless to stop it. I know, I have been there.

> The stress and worry have come from trying to get him a referral, diagnosis, and the help he needs...it's very difficult knowing where to turn to get him help and I worry I am failing him... It's isolating as no one gets it and I worry about his future and emotional wellbeing... (Parent of a child aged 9 with Spatial Processing Disorder)

Professional help

If you suspect anxiety, stress, depression or any other mental health problem affecting you or your child, speak to your GP/family doctor as soon as you can. They can refer you or your child on to local mental health services. Explain every aspect of the issues, the impact at home as well at school. They will refer you or your child to an appropriate therapist, usually a counsellor, psychiatrist or psychologist, as needed. It is important that these appointments are kept and any exercises or tasks that the therapist requests carried out.

> I also have depression and anxiety and am attending Cognitive Behavioural Therapy (CBT), while also taking antidepressants and anti-anxiety tablets. (Parent of a child aged 12 with APD)

Mental health support problems

If your child already has a counsellor or therapist and the sessions don't seem to be helping, there may be several reasons for this. (The same reasons can apply to teenagers and adults too.)

- Maybe the therapist hasn't built a rapport with your child, so it might be more beneficial to find another one.

- It can take a person with APD some time to get used to unfamiliar voice patterns; it could be that they simply don't understand the therapist. I would ask them, and if that is the case, switch to a therapist whose voice they can understand. If this is not possible, or not the issue, ask the therapist to use your child's preferred methods of communication (writing, drawing, texting etc.). If they come home after a few sessions and say they still can't understand them, it might be time to find a new therapist.

- It could be the type of therapy or therapist. A psychologist or psychiatrist might be better for your child's needs than a counsellor, or vice versa. Maybe talking therapy is not the best or easiest approach to take with a child with APD. You could try one that uses art or music therapy, or maybe just making sure they take time every evening to de-stress and relax might work better for your child than therapy. In any case, always ask them to use your child's preferred methods of communication.

Therapy may not work for all children (or adults). A child with a disability will already feel different because of their difficulties, and seeing a therapist might emphasize their underlying feelings that there is something wrong with them and reinforce their feeling of failure, which they may naturally want to avoid talking about. Some people prefer to find their own ways of dealing with stress and they can be undertaken in addition to therapy.

> [She is] anxious, stressed about school, definitely worse as getting older now and realizes she's not the same as other children and is treated differently by peers, that is, [as if she has] a lower mental age... [She] has meltdowns at school as [she is] frustrated at not learning and various teachers not being sympathetic to her needs...
>
> ...she has been given self-regulating tips to de-stress herself but she finds it difficult to do them once in full melt-down mode... (Parent of a child aged 12 with APD)

> She will remove herself from a stressful situation. (Parent of a teenager aged 14 with APD)

Some other ways to combat stress

Non-verbal activities give the brain a chance to wind down, a rest from struggling with speech. Alternative methods to combat stress and anxiety include the following:

- Hobbies and interests can help, as a distraction from what is troubling you.

- Yoga focuses on relaxing the body. For those who don't want to take a class, there are videos online, some of which also have subtitles.

- Mindfulness is another method. It is based on the concept of living for the moment, letting go of what happens today and taking each new day as a fresh start. It can be very helpful.

- Simple breathing exercises involve focusing on your breath and not thinking about anything else.

- Listening to music, singing or dancing can also be very therapeutic.

- Alternative/complementary therapies can also be very beneficial in reducing stress.

All of these are distractions, but they are also relaxing, and any form of exercise or relaxation is also good for the body, which can show evidence of stress via tension in the neck, nausea and headaches. They can be used for children as well as adults.

> She gets very down about her APD, about friends, being 'normal'...
> If you feel your child's mental health is affected – seek advice.
> (Parent of a child aged 12 with APD)

Dual approach

For any sort of therapy, distraction or relaxation to help fully, you must also address the cause of the distress and deal with it. Strategies to reduce stress won't work in the long term if the stressors are still there; the child or adult will only become anxious again when placed back in the stressful situation. For a child, making sure that any bullying is dealt with and that your child has adequate support at school for the APD and other difficulties (such as social skills etc.) is essential. The same applies to adults at work.

If the stressors cannot be removed, for the sake of their long-term wellbeing it is best to remove the child from the stress (or the adult from the negative environment in which they work). If adequate and appropriate school support is not forthcoming, or fails to help even after pursuing an EHCP (Education, Health and Care Plan) or SEN (Special Educational Needs) Statement, or if bullying continues despite following the correct process, find a different school more suited to meeting your child's needs and ensuring their safety. Or you could look at removing them from school together to home educate, or think about a more flexible education route (as discussed in Chapter 8). Long-term stress can be damaging to anyone. It is best to consider all options when you need to ensure the mental health, safety and happiness of a person with APD.

> ...secondary school did not see the mental health issues and bullying that increased whilst she was in their care...
>
> It is us as parents and [the] current school that have made her take a step back from school for her mental health. She has taken two overdoses...
>
> We are working on her telling people about her APD and how it affects her, but because of depression and anxiety we are a long way off achieving this. (Parent of a teenager aged 15 with APD)

Sleep and stress

Lack of sleep is a common problem in both children and adults with APD, and it can make daily living very difficult. Difficulties can include the inability to fall asleep, stay asleep, or enjoy restful sleep; stress is one of the factors responsible for this, and lack of sleep can also cause stress itself. A distressed child might wet the bed, and this can add to the wakefulness. Having a regular nightly routine can help, such as a set bedtime, warm bath and not allowing your child to use a telephone, tablet or gaming device the hour before going to bed or having caffeinated drinks then. Reading at bedtime can also be a helpful way to relax and it can help people fall asleep. (If insomnia, bedwetting or anxiety and stress are ongoing problems for your child, I would recommend consulting your GP/family doctor.)

> [She] gets very tired, particularly since starting high school with the increased classes and workload with more responsibility. This can lead to emotional outbursts/high levels of stress at times. (Parent of a teenager aged 14 with APD)

Post-processing

Another factor preventing sleep is that children (and adults) with APD may not process what they have heard until a long time after the event. It is common for a parent to ask a child with APD what happened at school and they say they can't remember; this is because they haven't processed it all yet. The information may just appear in their heads all together, often at bedtime, and they must try to make sense of it all. This act of going over everything in your mind after the event is known as post-processing. For some, they find it helps to 'offload' what happened in their day by talking about it. It isn't that they just become chatty to avoid going to sleep; they are effectively getting it out of their head just so that they *can* sleep.

During the process of post-processing, they might relive conversations that happened in the day and be upset when they realize that they had misunderstood something that they now understand, responded inappropriately, or replied to something unrelated to what was asked. This can cause worry and distress; analysis and self-criticism can follow when they realize that they did something wrong. They might go over it in their heard again and again, thinking about what they wish they had said and blaming themselves for the embarrassing response at the time. Other worrying factors are that it is now too late to correct the error and any negative perception that others might have of them.

> She suffers from anxiety but only with regards to socializing. (Parent of a home-educated teenager aged 14 with APD)

People with APD doubt what they hear and what they have said all the time. This isn't a negative response to a single event; rather it is a way of life because often they do 'get it wrong'. It all adds to the effects of stress, which can also affect self-esteem and self-confidence, and keeps them awake at night.

Some parents might actively stop their child talking at bedtime for fear it will keep them awake longer, but for children who employ this coping strategy, there is a very real need to do this, as their mind is racing with post-processed information and they don't know how to handle it, apart from talking about it, 'getting it out of their head', and then they can relax. Talking about worries and fears raised by self-criticism can help too. Another method might be allowing them to write it down or record it, although this may take longer.

Allowing your child to tell you what is on their mind might be time-consuming, so an earlier bedtime might be necessary, but if it is what they need, they won't sleep until they have completed it. Also, it is best not to interrupt or rush the process, as this might make some children have to start again from the beginning, disrupting their thoughts and distressing them.

If offloading is not a natural coping strategy, it is a skill that can be learned and one that can be very useful: simply encourage your child to discuss whatever is in their head and allow them to get it all out. It might help your child, or it might not, but it is worth trying if it could help them to have a good night's sleep.

During post-processing something that happened at school might be remembered, possibly bullying, an argument with a friend, or being told off over a piece of work. Anything can stick in their minds and feelings of failure are common and hard to shake off, all preventing a child from falling asleep.

Other issues and strategies

Some people with APD also have Hyperacusis (hypersensitive or hyperacute hearing), and this can make it hard to relax and get to sleep. They might regularly hear (and be disturbed by) conversation or sounds from another room, downstairs or even down the street and beyond, depending on their level of sensitivity. Tinnitus (ringing in the ears) is another issue that can accompany APD in some people, which, like Hyperacusis, can be diagnosed by any audiologist who may recommend desensitizing treatments. Some people have both. Bland noise like white, pink or brown noise can help with Tinnitus and to block unwanted noise for those with Hyperacusis. Various bland noise apps and a wide variety of meditation and relaxation apps are free and available online.

> ...he spent three months seeing a psychologist each week to work on school anxiety, stress and how to live in his noisy world. (Parent of a child aged 10 with APD)

Forward-remembering

Some children might need to engage in forward-remembering, making notes so that they won't forget something, or planning something they might want to do and could forget. Fear of forgetting can keep them awake. For those who cannot easily put their thoughts into words, a quick sketch, doodle or symbols can act as a reminder and allow the visual thinker to fall asleep. Writing things down can also help if they wake in the night and their mind is racing. Waking at night is not a restful sleep and it can be as harmful as no sleep.

Why the brain needs rest

Rest is vital to the health of both the mind and body. The brain needs to recover from the strains of the day, to post-process information and store long-term memories. It cannot do this when it is overloaded, so if sensory overload, fatigue and stress prevent this from happening, the cycle of stressful circumstances continues. Some people complete this process only when they are asleep (if they can get to sleep). Stress can affect anyone at any time, but the daily pressures on children with APD are huge, both at home and at school, and often there is little or no escape from it. This cycle needs to be broken, and relaxation methods can help with this process. APD can leave a person exhausted, and lack of sleep only adds to their distress.

Guidance

Parents and educators need to be aware that prolonged exposure to stress can have a huge impact on their child's mental health, physical heath and general wellbeing (and adults are just as much at risk). They should look out for them and be ready to step in to alleviate the stressors (or remove the child from the stressful environment) and help the child regain their self-esteem, with positive reinforcement, praise and encouragement. A thoughtless comment that implies that a child is lazy, slow or has a bad attitude to work can damage a child, and anyone who engages with a child with APD or any disability should think very carefully of the impact that their words might have. Such comments are unacceptable, especially as children who see teachers or even parents behaving in this way will copy such attitudes to perpetuate bullying, both in and out of the classroom, as they think it is appropriate to do so.

A child with APD who is stressed and anxious should be obvious to the people closest to them, both at home and at school. The signs are there if you look. The support and understanding of partners, friends, family and teachers is vital in helping our vulnerable children. You can help them to learn to cope with the emotional distress caused by their difficulties, low self-confidence, poor self-esteem and the accompanying educational and social pressures. They don't have to suffer alone.

> Watch out for the signs of anxiety in your child and get early help. (Parent of a child aged 10 with APD)

Conclusion

As we have now learned, APD should not worsen on its own and it cannot be cured, but with the right strategies and support, life can be improved. We must all encourage others to learn all that they can about APD: hopefully this book will have helped you with that. Anyone with APD deserves acceptance as individuals, from partners, family, friends and colleagues, as well as from employers and any professionals they encounter. It is what others have and take for granted and it is not too much to ask for anyone with a disability. It is what the law is meant to safeguard.

The case studies

The case study quotes included in this book describe a variety of children, teenagers and adults with different APD difficulties and comorbid conditions to deal with.[1] The participants were of varying ages and circumstances. Some of them were not from the UK or were diagnosed outside the UK (although most of them were UK residents and diagnosed there). Two of the case studies were siblings; this showed how differently children with APD can be affected, even in the same family. The participants were neither handpicked nor coached; they simply responded to an appeal for volunteers and answered a questionnaire on the topics that are included in this book, if they were applicable to them.

This randomized sample of individuals who explained how they

---

1 Selected extracts have been included here, but the full case studies can be viewed at https://library.jkp.com/redeem using the voucher code ZYASEZE. Please read them all, to get the full impact of APD on all ages.

(and their loved ones) had been affected by APD were added after the rest of the book was finished, yet I was amazed to find how so many of their responses confirmed the existence of all the problems identified in this book. The case studies reflect well the lack of awareness of APD and the limited understanding, acceptance and support (for all ages) by family friends, medical and education professionals. They also show that there is no consistency in access to referral and support in the UK is often described as a 'postcode lottery'.

The participants describe the various barriers to obtaining reliable testing and lack of knowledge around APD plus understanding, acceptance and support by employers and work colleagues. They confirm the specific problems that exist for teenagers and adults and the potential benefits of alternative education. The impact on the participants and their families includes anxiety, stress and other mental health issues, reduced self-confidence and self-esteem in most cases. Varying levels of self-advocacy skills and willingness to declare their APD were seen. Most have few friends.

The current situation for these families and individuals shows some improvement after diagnosis, where support is provided, but that support is neither consistent nor adequate. This situation must improve, for them and everyone else affected by APD, both in the UK and worldwide.

The road to success

Every child and adult with APD must be properly diagnosed, along with all the conditions and difficulties that affect them. They should develop their own unique coping strategies, be provided with the right sort of accommodations to suit them as individuals (and know how to ask for them). They should expect and receive an appropriate education in a suitable environment and have a job with a supportive place of work.

As frustrating as it can be, neither parents nor adults with APD can expect others to know about APD, provide support or understand the implications if they don't say anything. The same applies to children when they are old enough, and it should start with children. Self-advocacy is so important. If they grow up speaking openly about their APD to anyone who will listen, it will no longer be such an invisible disability, or one of those conditions that affect other people: it will be known and recognized. No one will have to explain APD because everyone will know what it is and support will be automatic at school, at work, everywhere. That level of support and acceptance is key to both their success and their happiness. It is vital that the information passed on about APD is *accurate* APD information. Misinformation can do a lot of damage.

Next steps

Parents should fight for APD testing and support in their area; it will help their child greatly. But that testing will also go on to help other children and families who will never have to go through what our case study participants and too many other people have had to deal with over the years. That level of testing can spread to other areas if you set a precedent and demonstrate a need. Your local health board might not realize just how many children need APD testing; every parental request can make a difference. The same applies to school support in your local authority area, either in mainstream schools, specialist schools or academies. Then your child and others who follow will have a decent chance to succeed in all aspects of their life. The same applies to adults who need to ask for local testing, and support in further education and in the workplace.

Professional support

Parental involvement is essential, but this will work far better and more quickly with the support and participation of medical and education professionals. I hope that knowing the effect that lack of awareness and support can do to people with APD every day will encourage you all to improve the reactions and actions of your colleagues to this debilitating condition.

The aim of this book was not to shame anyone into feeling guilty. I have just related the facts as I see them repeated daily, all over the UK and internationally. I know that the current situation does not arise from either a lack of interest or compassion, and I appreciate that your hands might be tied by budget restrictions. Access to information and the promotion of it (such as sharing a website) is free and acceptance costs nothing. Much of what a person with APD needs by way of reasonable adjustments does not have monetary implications. But the impact on a child's education and working life will be immeasurable, and in the UK,[2] they are legally entitled to receive it.

When the 'A' Plan works

If all the elements are provided, success is more than possible; it is likely. I have seen it work. Without realizing it, I have been advising parents and adults to take this approach for years, only now have I recorded it all in one place.

I have been told by parents in my group of their children's successes. For example, there are children who go to farm schools and learn a trade there, gaining vocational qualifications not available in a mainstream school. Such education options can be just as effective for those for whom academic success via a traditional, formal education is not the correct route. It is also not the only route.

Some of the children whose parents were in my groups went on to college and followed their dreams; others went to university and have a degree and a good job. They received the support needed from their family, their school and at university. They sing, dance and play music or sport at a high level. They are adults now, leading independent lives. They know who they are and they accept it and because of that, others do too. They have gained confidence and self-esteem by doing what they love to do, by being themselves.

Those young people have been naturally following the 'A' Plan all this time, years before I gave it a name. They have been fortunate enough to gain the acceptance and support that they need. Although I take no credit for their success, their actions and those of many others are now recorded together in this book. They are my inspiration. It might not have been easy, but they made it, and so many more children can, too. Each one of us can make it easier for the children and adults who are still struggling to get there. You might be surprised to find that you already know some of them.

Children with APD can grow up to have satisfying, happy, well-rounded lives using the attributes and gifts that they are born with, even

---

2   Please research the education and workplace laws in your country if you are not a UK resident.

without a long list of qualifications. After navigating their childhood and teenage years well-supported, people with APD can go on to succeed and create amazing things. Maybe your child or one you know (or teach) will be one of them; they can follow any route that suits their individual skills. But they might not succeed without the type of help outlined in this book. You can help them to get there.

Success as adults

I have also seen adults with APD diagnosed in later life achieve great things with the right support. They, too, have gained degrees and good jobs, using their coping strategies, reasonable adjustments and workarounds. These are adults who may have never gained a qualification or tasted success until their APD was diagnosed, finally accessing support. Success, however small and at whatever level, can make such a difference to a person's life. For some, experiencing it was the first time that they accepted themselves, finally viewing themselves as capable and worthy.

Similarly, I know adults with late-onset APD who have learned to live and cope with the changes that it brings; they have overcome extraordinary challenges. Some of them have used their experiences to make them stronger and helped others along the way. But first they had to accept that their lives had changed, and they had to adapt to those changes. They understood that this new life with APD would be different, but there was no reason why it had to be worse.

The journey

The journey of a person with APD and those who care for them starts with seeking information, and it should ultimately lead to their success and ability to live independently. There might be many pitfalls and setbacks along the way and, as with any disability, strength and determination are needed for all concerned.

Never give up on your child, yourself or anyone you come across with APD (or any other disabling condition). Be a guide on their journey, not an obstacle. Share what you have read in this book and help them to reach their own personal goals.

If you care about someone with APD in any way, whether they are a child, teenager or adult, accept that they will always have APD and give them your continued support. It is a commitment, not a temporary fix. Learn all you can about APD and the range of possible difficulties and strategies. Reading this book is just the beginning.

Top tips for all

The most important things to take from this book are that each person with APD is unique, and they might not be able to accept themselves until others do so first, so your validation is vital and your support can be life-changing. Be that person.

The people in your life with APD will not have all the difficulties mentioned, or they may prefer different support to that which is listed in this book. Ironically, what someone with APD needs most is that others listen and understand. Whatever your relationship with someone with APD:

- Always ask what causes *them* problems and what *you* can do to make communication easier for them. It might change day to day.

- Explain that your relationship with them (whatever that may be) is more important than the ability to follow a conversation flawlessly.

- Be there for them when they need to vent to or exhibit or express stress or anxiety (and support them to seek appropriate help, and beyond).

- Let them know that you accept and value them, that you want to help and be there for them.

- Provide whatever help they need with communication, social skills, life skills, education, finding and sustaining a job, and so on.

- Encourage them to use their strengths and self-advocate (or advocate for them if they ask you to, while helping them to learn how to do so themselves).

- Try to raise their confidence and self-esteem whenever you can.

- Cherish their uniqueness.

- Always try to share *accurate* information and raise awareness.

Help that person to become the best that they can be and you will gain so much by supporting them. This book is my contribution: the rest is up to you.

Index